SAS

UNDERCOVER OPERATIONS

SAS UNDERCOVER OPERATIONS

MIKE RYAN

amber BOOKS

This Amber edition first published in 2019

First published in 2003 as *Secret Operations of the SAS*

Published by
Amber Books Ltd
United House
North Road
London N7 NDP
United Kingdom
www.amberbooks.co.uk
Instagram: www.instagram.com/amberbooksltd
Facebook: www.facebook.com/amberbooks
Twitter: @amberbooks

ISBN: 978-1-78274-753-6

Printed in the United Kingdom

Picture credits
Aerospace Publishing: 138, 139. Patrick Allen: 160. Amber Books: 119. Australian Department of Defence: 183. Dilip Banerjee: 162, 172. Andrew Chittock: 174. Steve Lewis: 168. PA Photos: 185, 186. Popperfoto: 51, 144, 176. Private Collection: 34, 132, 166, 137, 141. James Rowlands: 165. TRH Pictures: 6, 8, 10, 12, 13, 15, 16, 17, 18, 19, 20, 21, 22, 23, 25, 26, 29, 31, 32, 33, 35, 36, 39, 40, 42, 44, 45, 46, 48, 49, 52, 54, 55, 56, 57, 58, 59, 61, 62, 65, 66, 68, 69, 70, 72, 75, 77, 78, 79, 80, 83, 84, 87, 89, 91, 93, 97, 98, 99, 100, 101, 102, 103, 104, 108, 109, 111, 115, 116, 118, 123, 124, 127, 129, 130, 131, 140, 142, 145, 148, 153, 154, 155, 156, 159, 188. US Department of Defense: 182, 184. US Marine Corps: 181. US Air Force: 178, 180.

Maps and artworks:
Amber Books: 11, 30, 38, 41, 64, 88, 107, 112–113, 128, 146, 170. Aerospace Publishing: 96, 106, 133, 152, 164. De Agostini UK: 24, 28, 50, 53, 71, 76, 90, 92, 114, 117, 136, 141, 147. Mark Franklin: 74, 81, 94–95, 110, 120–121, 134–135, 150, 167, 171, 179. Patrick Mulrey: 49, 122.

CONTENTS

CHAPTER ONE

THE BEGINNING

Although the Special Air Service was not established until the summer of 1941 in Egypt, it is useful to look back a few months before that day to understand the historical context that made the creation of the SAS and various other special forces units possible. Like many other British success stories, it really begins with disaster, blunder and improvisation.

After the defeat of France in May/June 1940, the new Prime Minister, Winston Churchill, inspired his country and its leaders to fight on against Nazi Germany. But as he told General Montgomery when the two first met in July 1940, Churchill had no real idea how Britain could win the war. The only aggressive land warfare operations that Britain could undertake against Germany at that time were raiding and sabotage actions. Following this strategy quickly led to the establishment of regular forces like the Commandos, and irregular organizations like the Special Operations Executive.

Many enterprising and belligerent young soldiers had little liking for the prospect of years of training and defensive duties – all that the army seemed to be able to offer in the summer of 1940 – and they welcomed these developments. Many of the officers who would find their way to the special forces also came from privileged and prosperous backgrounds that, in pre-war days, had given them the money and leisure to follow adventurous interests like mountaineering or desert exploration. Once war broke out, they used their social connections to pull strings, thus avoiding being assigned to what they saw as mundane regimental duties.

Left: Lt Col David Stirling DSO, the founder of the Special Air Service (SAS), pictured shortly before his capture. Note the crudely tailored 'winged dagger' cloth badge loosely attached to the front of his cap.

This rather superior and sometimes irresponsible attitude was balanced, however, by a willingness to accept unpleasant and arduous service in conditions of unusual danger. The new leaders of the special forces and some senior officers also believed that the existing Army organization had proved so inadequate that a fresh approach was needed. However, setting up the new forces was one thing; finding a role for them was another.

The story of the SAS actually begins with a bold infiltration of a guarded headquarters and what might be called a surprise attack on a senior officer. One day in July 1941, the sentry on duty outside the main entrance to the British Army's Middle East Headquarters in Cairo was approached by a Scots Guards lieutenant who wanted to get in, even though, as he claimed, he had forgotten to bring his pass. The sentry quite correctly refused to admit him. The officer was 1.96m (6ft 5in) tall and walking with the help of crutches, so it was hard for him to pretend to be one of the regular visitors or staff. The disappointed officer moved away, but a few moments later, while the guard's attention was momentarily distracted by the arrival of a staff car, the officer spotted a gap in the perimeter wire round the HQ. He dropped his crutches, just managed to squeeze through, and limped off towards the main building. As he disappeared inside, he heard an outcry starting from the sentry post. The sentry had seen the giant figure duck out of sight and had raised the alarm.

The young officer was Lt David Stirling, and his mission was to speak (without an appointment) to the recently appointed Commander-in-Chief, General Sir Claude Auchinleck. He hoped to persuade 'the Auk' to establish a new special forces unit that would assist in taking the fight to the German *Afrika Korps*, now proving all too tough an opponent for the Eighth Army in the desert.

Below: David Stirling, commander of the newly formed SAS Regiment, and Don Steele, commander of A Squadron, at Siwa, in the North African desert. The long supply lines of the *Afrika Korps* were vulnerable to attacks by small units like the SAS.

CHEVROLET WA TRUCK

Above: A Chevrolet truck used by the Long Range Desert Group (LRDG) in the Western Desert. In the early days, the SAS relied on the LRDG to transport them back from their targets. Later in the campaign they used their own vehicles.

Once inside the headquarters building, the lieutenant blundered into various offices, eventually barging into the office of the Deputy Chief of Staff, Major-General Neil Ritchie. Stirling apologized for his unconventional arrival and gave Ritchie a paper he had prepared, telling him that it dealt with matters of great operational importance, even though it was hand-written in pencil. Perhaps Ritchie was impressed by the young man, or perhaps he was amused by his daring approach and looked forward to an interesting interlude in a dull day; in any case, the senior officer did not have Stirling thrown out, but instead invited him to sit down.

Stirling outlined the gist of his plan. He wanted to recruit a small team of hand-picked men who would parachute behind enemy lines before the next Allied offensive and destroy Axis aircraft in the Western Desert while they were still on the ground. General Ritchie listened attentively and with growing interest. The concept seemed sound and the young officer was convinced he could carry it off. Within a couple of days, Ritchie had spoken to Auchinleck and confirmed his initial approval. Stirling was to be promoted to captain and permitted to recruit 6 officers and 60 men for his new command, which was to be known as L Detachment, Special Air Service Brigade. This was a cover name. There was no such brigade, the title being used in attempt to convince enemy intelligence that there was a parachute formation at large in the Middle East.

STIRLING'S BACKGROUND

Stirling was not a professional soldier but had joined up at the beginning of the war. At school, and later at Cambridge University – where he was seemingly more interested in following the form at Newmarket racecourse than in his studies – there was little to distinguish him from many of his contemporaries. After Cambridge his major interest had been climbing: his ambition, to conquer Everest. When war broke out, however, Stirling immediately joined his family's traditional regiment, the Scots Guards.

Left: Blair 'Paddy' Mayne, probably the best SAS soldier ever, and an early recruit. His bravery in battle won him four Distinguished Service Orders. Tragically he lost his life in a car crash in Ireland in 1955.

In the late summer of 1940, when Commando units were first established, Stirling transferred to No 8 (Guards) Commando and, at the beginning of 1941, sailed to the Middle East with a composite Commando unit known as Layforce. Layforce's original objective was the capture of the Italian-held island of Rhodes, but in February 1941, Rommel arrived in North Africa with the *Deutsches Afrika Korps* (DAK) and soon had the British forces on the retreat in the Western Desert. Then in April and May, the Germans overran Yugoslavia, Greece and Crete, transforming the strategic situation in the Eastern Mediterranean. The Rhodes operation was scrapped and parts of Layforce were deployed here and there throughout the theatre. Stirling's only active service was preparation for various raids that were planned for No 8 Commando along the North African coast, but which all came to nothing.

Stirling was so frustrated by this confusion and defeat that he resorted to feigning illness for a time and had himself admitted to a Cairo hospital so that he could slip out nightly to enjoy the city's bars and restaurants. He soon returned to duty, however, and with an 8 Commando friend, J.S. 'Jock' Lewes – an Australian-born former Oxford oarsman, now an officer of the Welsh Guards – managed to lay his hands on some parachutes. They had no instructors and no properly rigged aircraft, but undeterred, Stirling, Lewes and four other Guardsmen decided to give it a go.

Remarkably, even though they had no training, there was only one casualty from their first jump: Stirling himself. Jumping from a biplane Vickers Valentia bomber, which had long since been relegated to mail deliveries, Stirling's chute caught and ripped on the plane's tail assembly. He landed heavily on hard ground, severely damaging his back and suffering temporary paralysis of the legs. He was in hospital for some two months, but used the time well to hatch the plan he presented to Major General Ritchie in July 1941.

STIRLING'S PLAN

Stirling argued that the abortive Commando raids had been wrongly conceived. Landing a Commando of some 200 men placed heavy demands on the Navy, which had plenty of other work to do, and this and other preparations for such a big operation were difficult to keep secret. Instead, Stirling asserted, an independent raiding force, responsible directly to the C-in-C, could react quickly and effectively. At this stage, he proposed that his attack teams should be of five men who, he argued, with the aid of surprise, would be able to do just as much damage to a weakly-defended enemy airfield as a far bigger Commando force. Stirling knew that Auchinleck would have orders from London to prepare a major offensive against the *Afrika Korps* and said that he could have his new raiding force ready in time to neutralize

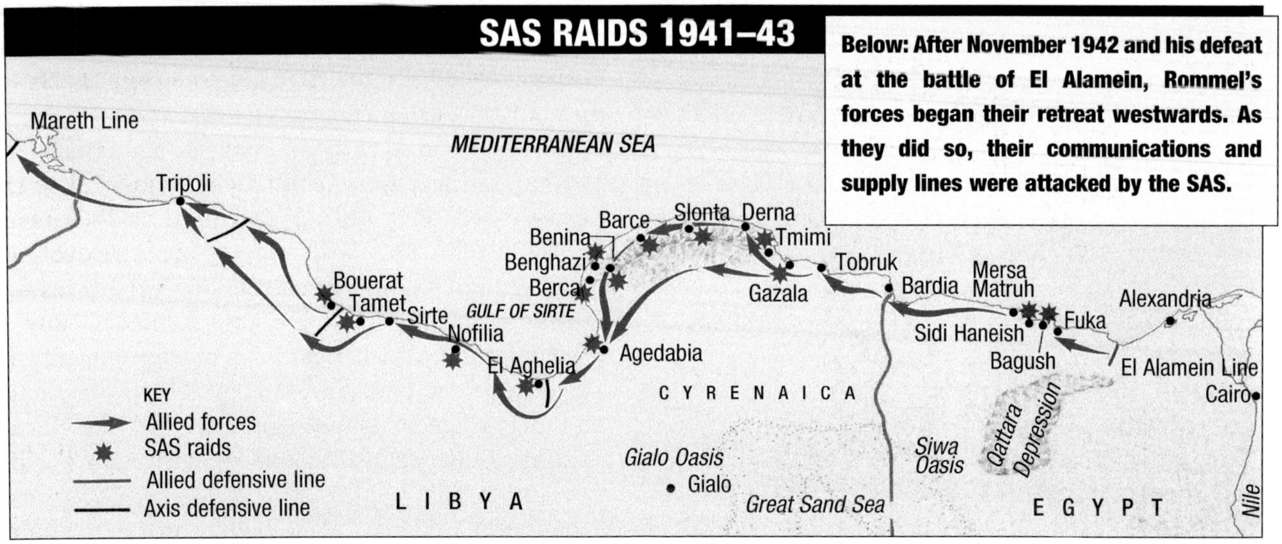

Below: After November 1942 and his defeat at the battle of El Alamein, Rommel's forces began their retreat westwards. As they did so, their communications and supply lines were attacked by the SAS.

vital enemy airfields when that battle started. In this first operation, Stirling intended that his men would parachute in to attack their targets and afterwards be withdrawn by patrols of the intelligence-gathering Long Range Desert Group, the acknowledged experts in clandestine desert travel.

L Detachment, SAS Brigade began life at Kabrit in the Suez Canal Zone with half a dozen tents, a placard proclaiming the new unit's identity, and a 2.95 tonne (3 ton) truck. Stirling had already begun recruiting the 6 officers and 60 men he was allotted, drawing on No 8 Commando and the 2nd Scots Guards, to which some Commandos had been transferred. The first job of the new recruits was reportedly launched against the New Zealand Division, which happened to be based near Kabrit, to steal additional equipment as Stirling had not been able to obtain enough through the proper channels.

From the beginning, L Detachment attracted a high calibre of volunteers, though few had as yet had combat experience. Above all, these were men who welcomed a chance to get to grips with the then rampant enemy. Stirling's most notable early officer recruits were the parachuting Jock Lewes and Blair 'Paddy' Mayne, well-known as a boxer and for his six caps with the Ireland rugby team. Mayne would soon prove to be a magnificent fighting leader, but out of combat he could also be unpredictable, immensely powerful and an aggressive, drunken menace.

HARD TRAINING

Now that he had the cadre of L Detachment, Stirling set about getting it ready to fight. Although many of the men had previously undergone commando training, they found Stirling's regime exceptionally hard. He was not prepared to accept, as other army units had to do, that these were his men and that he should aim towards as high a standard as was possible, while accepting that it might not be achievable. Instead, Stirling set a high level of training as a minimum to be attained. If men failed to reach this level, they would be RTU (Returned to Unit) – still the ultimate sanction in SAS recruiting today.

Stirling himself actually spent comparatively little time supervising the unit's training, often being away in Cairo fighting the Quartermaster and Adjutant General's Departments for what his men needed, and working to plan future operations. Most of the detail of the training programme was devised and put into action by Lewes, but he was at least as tough a taskmaster as Stirling might have wished. Forced marches through the desert at any hour of the day or night were standard; distances of 65km

(40 miles) or more with weights of over 30kg (66lb) were not uncommon. The ability to navigate was vital for all ranks and great emphasis was placed on endurance and willpower. Indeed, the early selection process of L Detachment bore a strong resemblance to that undertaken by prospective SAS members today. The skills and personal characteristics required have changed very little over the years.

Parachute training went hand-in-hand with the toughening-up process. This time it was slightly more sophisticated than Stirling's first jump had been. The candidates practised jumping from scaffolding platforms and exiting from grounded aircraft, just as

Below: SAS troopers carry out an exercise known as 'lifting the log', which was very effective for developing stomach and arm muscles. All of Stirling's recruits were expected to be extremely fit, spending hours each day in training.

they might do today. However, the trick of jumping from moving trucks caused so many broken legs that it had to be abandoned.

L Detachment had the use of a Bristol Bombay aircraft, an improvement on the Vickers Valentia, but despite this advance, two parachutists were killed on the first jump when their chutes failed to open. The problem was traced to the clip that connected the static line to the anchor rail inside the aircraft. In certain conditions, the clip could slip off the rail; without an anchor, the static line could not tauten and open the chute. A different clip was substituted and Stirling was the first to jump the following morning.

THE LEWES BOMB

While training was in progress, Jock Lewes worked on the development of a bomb that was suitable for the type of operation L Detachment would be carrying out. Once they had infiltrated an enemy airfield, the men needed something that was light enough to carry on foot, but powerful enough to destroy an aircraft to which it was attached. With the constraints of size, neither a pure explosive device nor a simple incendiary would do the job. Ordnance experts said the task was impossible, but Lewes set up a rough-and-ready laboratory and eventually came up with an effective solution, known as the Lewes bomb. This weighed less than 500g (1lb) so that a raider could carry 20 or more, each one capable of destroying an enemy aircraft.

General Auchinleck's long-planned Crusader offensive was due to begin on the night of 17/18 November 1941, and Stirling reckoned that his men were ready to play what he hoped would be

VICKERS MK 1

Above: The Vickers machine gun was a veteran of World War I, but was used to good effect by the SAS in World War II, usually mounted on vehicles to provide a heavy suppressive fire on enemy positions.

Left: SAS volunteers undergo parachute training prior to their first operational jump. It was intended that the SAS would use parachute drops to reach their targets, but it was found to be easier and safer to use trucks and jeeps.

a vital part in its success. The plan was to drop L Detachment the night before the offensive began close to the target airfields at Tmimi and Gazala, near the coast some 242km (150 miles) behind the front line. The attackers were to get into position and scout their targets during the next day, then mount their attack the following night. The SAS men were to move in under cover of darkness, plant their Lewes bombs on the aircraft, and then move on foot some 80km (50 miles) inland to rendezvous with the LRDG, who would take them home.

The weather turned the operation into a complete disaster. On the evening of 16 November, 64 officers and men from L Detachment boarded 5 Bombay transport aircraft of 216 Squadron. Stirling knew the weather was bad and would get worse, and should probably have cancelled the operation. However, he did not want to give his enemies on the staff the opportunity to say that the SAS had failed before it had even got started, and he did not want to disrupt the morale of his men, many of whom had experience of Commando operations that had been aborted in similar ways. They had been promised that this would not happen to them with the SAS.

The weather duly deteriorated. Dense cloud obscured the drop zones, and three of the aircraft dropped their parachutists miles off course; the men from the fourth aircraft were never seen again, and the fifth aircraft had to land behind enemy lines with engine trouble. It managed to get airborne again, only to be shot down, with many aboard being killed or captured.

In addition, many of the parachutists were injured after being dragged across the desert by the strong winds. Most of the supply containers were lost; those that were found contained some Lewes bombs but no fuses. The bombs were useless. The attack was called off, and the survivors of the aborted mission made their way to the LRDG rendezvous. Out of the 60 that started out on the raid, only 4 officers and 18 other ranks survived.

One thing was clear from this disastrous start: an alternative way of infiltrating behind enemy lines had to be found. The obvious choice was to turn to the LRDG for more help. Stirling sent his survivors to a new base at Jalo Oasis, deep in the desert behind enemy lines. He managed to avoid having to give too

Right: A Long Range Desert Group (LRDG) truck in soft sand. The LRDG, long-distance raiders operating behind Axis lines, were forerunners of the SAS in a sense, and initially the SAS used the LRDG as a 'taxi service' to reach their objectives.

SAS CHRONOLOGY

Date	1941
Location	North Africa
Operation	SAS is formed and carries out hit-and-run attacks on German and Italian airfields, with great success.
Date	1942
Location	North Africa
Operation	SAS again carries out attacks on German and Italian airfields with great success; however, other raids on Axis shipping in enemy-held ports end in failure, or are aborted.

many explanations of this first débacle when he briefly returned to HQ, but knew that his next mission had to be a success and that there was no point in asking for replacements or reinforcements before then.

NEW MISSIONS

Two operations were planned for 14 December and a third for the 21st. Stirling and Mayne would lead one group against Sirte airfield on the 14th; Lewes would strike at Agheila airfield the same night; and another officer, Bill Fraser, would lead the final attack of the series against Agedabia.

Below: A patrol rest up in the North African desert. Their truck has been camouflaged with a mixture of netting and local scrub. If spotted by an enemy aircraft, the men would be horribly exposed and left without any protective cover.

Stirling and Mayne, together with nine men, set off for Sirte, about 560km (348 miles) away, transported by an all-Rhodesian LRDG patrol. They travelled in seven of the LRDG's usual 30cwt trucks, painted in their surprisingly effective dull-pink camouflage to make them more difficult to spot from the air. The first 480km (298 miles) passed uneventfully, then, on the third day, they were spotted and attacked by Italian aircraft. No damage was done, but Stirling decided that the enemy might be ready for an attack and changed his plan. He would lead one group to the original objective at Sirte, while Mayne took the rest of the men to the airfield at Tamit, about 50km (30 miles) to the west.

Stirling's group were dropped off close to the target by the LRDG. They moved up to the airfield perimeter and blundered into a minefield before they

realized exactly where they were. Unable to carry out the original plan, they instead booby-trapped a few parked vehicles before withdrawing.

Mayne's team was more successful. They walked onto the target airfield without being challenged and simply wandered around in the dark putting bombs into every aircraft they could find, 24 in all. Not content with that, they shot up what seemed to be an aircrew mess and destroyed a fuel dump and other stores. During their withdrawal, Mayne, by now out of bombs, came across another aircraft and pulled the instrument panel out of the cockpit with his bare hands. He and all his men returned to the rendezvous safely.

Lewes and his patrol were not quite so successful. They reached Agheila airfield but found no aircraft using it at the time. Not to be denied, Lewes switched

Above: A Free French patrol operating in the Gabes area in February 1943 talk to a Tunisian Arab who had served in the French Army for ten years. The Free French formed an SAS squadron as early as 1941.

his attention to a nearby vehicle park and its adjacent buildings. The SAS men placed charges on about 30 Italian trucks and had a brief gun battle with the troops nearby before they too all retired to safety.

Fraser's raid on Agedabia on 21 December turned out to be even more successful than Mayne's operation had been. Fraser and his four men set bombs on 37 enemy planes and walked away unscathed, even though some of the bombs had gone off before they had left the airfield and the alerted defenders were busily blazing away into the darkness.

Left: An Special Boat Section (SBS) soldier with a US-made 7.62mm (0.30in) M1 Carbine. Although the SBS were formed as specialists for fighting on and under water, they were equally adept at combat on land.

The whole of L Detachment had no sooner returned to Jalo than they were off on a new series of raids. As before, results were mixed. Stirling's group nearly blundered into a large German tank force and failed to reach their target. Mayne once again had the best luck, destroying 27 aircraft at Tamit airfield. Lewes and his men managed to destroy a few aircraft at Nofilia before being forced to retreat. Unfortunately, after they were picked up by the LRDG, they were caught and strafed by Italian aircraft, and Lewes and others were killed. As for Fraser and his men, they had been sent to attack an airfield near Marble Arch (the Allied nickname for the vast monument built by Mussolini on the border of the Italian province of Cyrenaica). Now they were missing. Even with these losses, though, the SAS had achieved a stunning success in this first series of attacks. In less than a month of operations, 24 men had between them destroyed roughly 100 aircraft, far more than the Desert Air Force in the same time, and in fact more than the whole of RAF Fighter Command on any day of the Battle of Britain.

It also turned out that Fraser and his men had lived to fight another day. Their attack had been a failure: they then missed their RV and found themselves marooned in the desert over 300km (186 miles) from home with about 1 litre (1.75 pints) of water each. They could easily have surrendered, but decided simply to walk back to friendly territory. When they were recovered over a week later, they had raided two enemy trucks, hijacked a German Army car and its crew, and rigged up a do-it-yourself water desalination plant into the bargain. This was just the first of a number of similar feats of determination, endurance and superb desert navigation in which SAS men were rewarded for their daring.

By the end of December 1941, the protracted Crusader battles had finally succeeded in driving back Rommel of Cyrenaica. Tobruk and Benghazi were back in Allied hands, while the Axis forces were re-grouping at Agheila. Stirling now temporarily switched his sights from airfields to ports and presented Auchinleck with a plan for an attack on the harbour at Buerat, halfway between Agheila and Tripoli, which was now likely to become an important supply base for Rommel. Stirling also desperately needed some more men. Auchinleck accepted Stirling's plan, promoted him to major and gave him permission to recruit a further 6 officers and 40 men.

Soon after, the SAS was further reinforced by 50 Free French air commandos. These men would prove to be a brave and aggressive addition to the ranks of the SAS. Wearing British uniforms and badges, they were fully integrated into the unit, so much so that Stirling later described their leader, Commandant Bergé, as a co-founder of the regiment.

'WHO DARES WINS'

No one now is quite sure when the SAS developed its own badges and insignia. Some say that this happened before the first operations, some that it came later, but there is no doubt that by early 1942 the winged dagger with the 'Who Dares Wins' motto had become the unit emblem. The distinctive parachutist badge, comprising a parachute in the centre of the outstretched wings of ancient Egypt's sacred Ibis – supposedly based on a wall painting seen in Cairo's famous Shepheard's Hotel – was also soon being worn. Trained recruits wore these on their left shoulders but were allowed to move them to above their left breast pockets when they had taken part in a number of operations (a custom since discontinued). Initially the SAS men wore white berets when off duty, but these attracted unfavourable comments from other troops and tended to cause brawls, and their very distinctiveness was judged to be a security risk, so they were soon changed to the sand colour that continues to be used, like the two badges, to this day.

It is rather ironic that the parachutist badge (and parachute training) became a constant feature of SAS life from then on, even though parachutes were never used in action in the desert after the first disastrous mission.

The SAS operation against Buerat took place in late January 1942. Two men of the Special Boat Section (SBS) were assigned to support the 16 SAS personnel involved in the raid. The SBS men brought a canoe with them and they were to use it to reach and mine ships at anchor in the harbour. But the operation did not go according to plan. The force was spotted and attacked by Italian planes, losing its radio vehicle, and to make matters worse the canoe was damaged beyond repair when the vehicle carrying it crashed while crossing rough ground. Stirling decided to go ahead and attack secondary targets. He led one group to destroy the petrol storage depot and various vehicles while the SBS men destroyed the port's radio station. When the raiders returned to Jalo, the reason why Buerat had been so quiet became clear. Rommel was counter-attacking and would soon drive the Eighth Army back almost to Tobruk, and Jalo itself was being

THE WINGED DAGGER

The winged dagger is the famous insignia of the SAS Regiment. Although there are many stories about its adoption, Sergeant Bob Tait was its designer, and Stirling himself is credited with the motto, 'Who Dares Wins'. The insignia is worn on a beige beret, reminiscent of the sands of the Western Desert where the unit was born.

Right: A Jeep armed with twin-mounted Vickers 'K' guns leads an SAS column through some desert scrub. The quick-firing Vickers had originally been designed for use on aircraft, and it could lay down a heavy weight of suppressive fire.

evacuated in favour of a new base at Siwa Oasis in Egypt some 500km (310 miles) to the east.

With the changed situation on the main battlefront, there also came considerable debate behind the scenes about the future role of the SAS. Some staff officers at Middle East HQ wanted the unit to be disbanded and its men used to form the cadre of new full-scale paratroop units, while others wanted the SAS to revive its original paratroop skills but to be employed in the vanguard of the army's next major offensive in a tactical role — for example, seizing important locations ahead of advancing ground forces. Stirling fought these proposals tooth and nail. His whole argument was that the SAS should be used against vital strategic objectives, where its highly skilled men could achieve much with limited resources, rather than be lost as tiny cogs in the great grinding wheels of a major battle, where they could do comparatively little.

Below: An SAS Jeep shows off its impressive armament of single and twin Vickers 'K' guns as well as a Browning 12.7mm (0.5in) machine gun. Each Jeep carried at least 20 petrol cans along with enough food and water for a month.

FRESH FIASCO

Unfortunately for Stirling, his arguments were not helped when his next operations, this time against the now Axis-held port of Benghazi, turned out to be even more of a fiasco than the attack on Buerat.

Twice, Stirling and a group of his men drove successfully into the town, even though it was packed with enemy troops, only to find on the first occasion that their canoe was again broken and on the second that their inflatable boats were irreparably punctured and no attack on enemy ships was possible. On the second occasion, the attack party even included Randolph Churchill, the prime minister's son, and Fitzroy Maclean, an MP and recent SAS recruit, who would later become famous as an envoy to Tito's partisans in Yugoslavia. Maclean, Stirling and others wandered vaguely about the harbour, Maclean giving orders to various Italian sentries they bumped into, but finding no worthwhile targets. It was very daring, but hardly a useful military operation, and eventually Stirling decided to withdraw, hoping to be able to return and attack something worthwhile on a future occasion.

By this time it was late May 1942, and the situation on the main battlefront was about to change for the worse once again. On 26 May, Rommel began a series of attacks that in six weeks would push the Eighth Army all the way back into Egypt and a desperate defensive at El Alamein. At least no one could blame the SAS for this catalogue of defeats, for in mid-June Stirling led a successful attack on Benina airfield. However, at the same time two French SAS groups were betrayed and mainly captured. A new departure for the SAS was a mission, again mainly of French personnel, to Crete. This group bombed over 20 aircraft on Heraklion airfield, though several of the attackers were subsequently captured.

Stirling realized that Rommel's rapid advance actually gave the SAS new opportunities, since the Germans' communications and airfield defences

Below: SAS troopers, enjoying a well-deserved break from operations in Cairo, pose for a group photograph. Their scruffy appearance was typical of the unit, and did not endear them to regular army officers.

would be at full stretch; so he planned a change in tactics and equipment to take advantage of this. On a visit to Cairo at the end of June 1942, he managed to lay his hands on an item of equipment that was to change the face of SAS operations in the desert: the US-made Willys Jeep. In SAS hands, these were adapted to become agile, cross-country gun platforms, capable of long-range desert travel. They were usually fitted with two pairs of fast-firing Vickers K 0.303in machine guns, though sometimes one pair was replaced by a Browning 0.5in machine gun. With their Jeeps, and a few 2.95 tonne (3 ton) trucks obtained at the same time, the SAS was now capable of transporting its own supplies and equipment. The new transport allowed the SAS to extend its operations, conducting patrols lasting several weeks, which enabled repeated raids during that time.

Below: Members of the SAS worked as liaison officers with other specialist units, such as the Greek Sacred Squadron. The latter was involved in a number of operations in the Greek islands, notably the Dodecanese in 1943.

NEW TACTIC

The Jeeps were in action at the start of July 1942, when Stirling planned to hit six targets, including the airfields at Daba, Bagush and Sidi Barrani. Mayne led the raid on Bagush, but was furious when only 22 of the 40 Lewes bombs placed by he and his men actually exploded. Mayne's party was now joined by Stirling, and the two led their Jeeps into a new type of attack. They simply drove onto the airfield and roared across it, blasting away at aircraft and any other targets they could see. The new tactic

Above: SAS roadwatchers in the North African desert. The roadwatchers had to remain immobile for the whole day, crawling to and back from their position at night. They took careful note of the type and number of enemy vehicles.

was a complete success. Several more aircraft were destroyed and the men escaped without a scratch.

The next big operation was against the Junkers Ju 52 airfield at Sidi Haneish on the night of 26/27 July. This time, Stirling planned from the start for a new-style Jeep attack. His 18 Jeeps were to adopt a two-column formation and drive all over the airfield, manoeuvring according to flare-pistol signals from Stirling, who would lead the formation.

The attackers thought that they might have been spotted when the runway lights were switched on as they approached, but this was in fact an aircraft coming in to land. Soon things were going much as Stirling had planned, with the scene now illuminated by numerous burning aircraft and stores dumps. Stirling's own vehicle was knocked out by enemy mortar and machine-gun fire, but he transferred to another and led his patrol in a circuit of the airfield, during which his men destroyed further transport aircraft parked on the perimeter before heading off into the desert.

L Detachment had destroyed some 40 aircraft, bringing its total kills in the year since it was formed to around 250, more than that achieved by the Desert Air Force in the same period. L Detachment's achievement was not merely the destruction of enemy aircraft, which in itself contributed handsomely to the Allied effort, but the diversion of Axis troops from the Front to guard the desert airfields.

Auchinleck's faith in the SAS concept had paid off. However, in early August he was sacked and replaced at Middle East HQ by General Alexander, and

General Montgomery was appointed to the Eighth Army. It was these two men who would command the remaining battles in the desert. During August, the SAS was reinforced by men from 1st Special Service Regiment, an ineffective and now moribund unit that was being disbanded. This reinforcement was a mixed blessing, for it was made to help prepare the SAS for a new plan: a large-scale raid on the ports of Benghazi and Tobruk by several hundred men in exactly the sort of operation that Stirling had always maintained the SAS should not touch with a bargepole.

BENGHAZI BOUND

When the SAS men moved in towards Benghazi on 13 September, Stirling's worst fears were confirmed. They were engaged on the approach to the port and had to withdraw after taking casualties and losing many vehicles, with nothing achieved. It was no consolation that the attack on Tobruk, in which the SAS did not participate, was an even worse disaster.

Although careless talk by Stirling himself may have contributed to the loose security that seems to have been a cause of this failure, he was promoted at the end of the month to command what was now to be 1 SAS Regiment, a full regiment of the British Army. For the moment, this included his own desert veterans, the new recruits from the former 1st Special Service Regiment, the Free French, and the SBS, which in turn would shortly also include a Greek detachment known as the Sacred Squadron. Paddy Mayne was to be the principal operational commander at first and through October would lead most of the old L Detachment personnel, now known as A Squadron, in an effective series of attacks on the railway line supplying the Axis front-line forces.

By the time the Battle of El Alamein was won in early November, Stirling was planning for the future.

A member of the Greek Sacred Squadron, part of the SAS Regiment. Note his beige SAS beret, albeit with a Greek badge. He is armed with a US M1 Thompson submachine gun, but the remainder of his clothing and equipment is British.

Above: Corporal Race, a radio operator with the SAS, makes contact with men from the British 6th Armoured Division in Tunisia in early 1943. The 6th Armoured Division had taken part in the Operation Torch landings in North-West Africa.

The SBS and the Greeks went off to Lebanon to train for operations in the Aegean, and A Squadron would soon follow for ski training. By December, David's brother, Bill Stirling, was setting up 2 SAS Regiment in Algeria, following the Operation Torch landings there a few weeks earlier.

STIRLING LOST

David Stirling still insisted in taking part in operations, though it should have been clear to him that he would have served his regiment better by ensuring that it was established on a sound and well-organized footing. Unfortunately, such operations as were possible soon showed that conditions had changed. Eighth Army's long advance had taken the Allied forces into a different type of territory, more densely populated and far more difficult to travel freely in than the great expanses of the Egyptian and Libyan desert. Since SAS missions were now largely being conducted by the less-experienced men of B Squadron, it is no surprise that results were mixed. Even worse, in an operation near Gabes in late January 1943, David Stirling himself was captured by the Germans. He made repeated escape attempts but was soon sent to Colditz, where he saw out the remainder of the war.

With Stirling's capture, the first phase of SAS operations in effect came to an end. Various SAS personnel would be involved in minor raids in the final months of the African campaign, but away from the battlefield more attention was being given to how the SAS might be organized and employed for what was certain to be a very different kind of war when the Allied armies returned to fight on European soil.

CHAPTER TWO

EUROPEAN OPERATIONS

By the final stages of the desert war, the SAS had carved out a conspicuous reputation as a unit. The Germans were delighted when they captured the 'phantom major', as David Stirling had become known, though his removal from the scene obviously did not put a stop to SAS operations. Soon the regiment would be put to the test in mainland Europe.

Some in high places on the Allied side wondered whether the SAS was coming to the end of its usefulness. Born in the desert, and having won its greatest successes by taking advantage of the unique desert conditions, the SAS ought perhaps have been allowed to die in the desert. That was not to happen, but in the remainder of the war the SAS never attained the fame or equalled their achievements of 1941/42.

The Special Air Service had undoubtedly come a long way from its small beginnings at Kabrit. When it was 60-odd men and a few trucks strong, it had been entirely feasible for one man to lead it, plan its operations, and liaise with HQ and the RAF for the support required. As far as HQ was concerned, anything a unit of this size managed to do was a bonus, and if it failed, no great harm was done. By early 1943, 1 and 2 SAS made up a sizeable fighting force, which now required considerable outside resources to support it, as well as significant internal organization to function effectively. Any changes arising from this would need to be combined with the obvious facts that the terrain, the density of population, and the generally smaller areas to manoeuvre in Europe would mean changes in the way the SAS would operate.

Left: SAS troopers undergo ski instruction in the Lebanon during May 1943, after the end of the North African campaign. With the SAS likely to see action on mainland Europe, it was vital for them to gain experience of European-type terrain.

Yet David Stirling had been very poor at the formal aspects of military staff work, preferring to organize matters by exploiting his connections in the 'old boy' network. He also failed to recognize that as the SAS expanded, it could not be run as a private army in the old, rather amateurish way, with its CO disappearing into the desert every now and again to lead a patrol-sized mission. Any clear plans Stirling might have had for the role that the SAS could play in the forthcoming Italian campaign had been stored in his head and had now gone into German captivity with him.

Indeed, as operations closed in North Africa, the SAS had become fragmented: the French SAS Squadron detached itself from the British Army and joined the Free French, laying down the foundations for the future 3 and 4 SAS; the Sacred Squadron returned to Greek control. 1 SAS was seemingly earmarked for disbandment, but was reprieved. A and B Squadrons were renamed the Special Raiding Squadron (SRS), about 250 strong, with Paddy Mayne, Stirling's natural successor, in command. The SRS moved to Palestine for further training. This was also the parting of the ways with the Special Boat teams who had been in D Squadron. These now became the Special Boat Squadron and would operate later in the war in the Aegean and Adriatic, but no longer as part of the SAS.

SICILY INVADED

The next Allied move was the invasion of Sicily in July 1943. Unfortunately, the planners of this operation did not make best use of the particular talents and capabilities of the SAS. Bill Stirling (David's brother) tried to convince his masters that the SAS was best deployed in small parties, probably well behind enemy lines, to hit airfields, lines of communication, and other such targets. However, both the SRS and 2 SAS were instead mainly committed to standard commando-type operations, tackling a number of objectives just in advance of the main force.

In their first action, the SRS captured 3 coastal batteries, killing over 100 enemy and taking a further 600 prisoner, all at a cost of only 1 man dead and 6 wounded. At the same time, a squadron of 2 SAS landed to capture a lighthouse and suspected gun position, only to find the grand total of three Italians waiting to oppose them. Two small groups from 2 SAS were, however, dropped on more traditional SAS missions in the north of the island. They had a range of the mishaps common to such parachute drops: men scattered and unable to find each other; equipment lost or damaged; and difficulty in locating decent targets. Nothing worthwhile was achieved.

When the Allies moved on from Sicily to the Italian mainland in September 1943, the story was much the same. Some parts of the two SAS units were used in the commando or reconnaissance role, fighting bravely and effectively, but arguably not making the best use of their experience and special training; while other, much smaller sections were sent on true SAS missions that, although poorly planned and badly supported, showed just what could have been done.

Despite including the most experienced SAS operatives, the SRS was used only in the regular commando role, deploying each time as a complete squadron. In September the squadron crossed the Straits of Messina with Eighth Army and was landed to capture positions just north of the main beachhead. The naval landing craft kept breaking down and few of the troops' radios worked, but the

MP40

Above: The German MP40 submachine gun was issued to German forces throughout Europe, and SAS troopers on extended operations behind enemy lines found it more convenient to use a gun with a ready supply of ammunition.

Right: A detachment of SAS parade after the capture of Termoli. Their commanding officer, Major Scratchley DSO MC, is in the front row on the left. The man in the right foreground is armed with a captured German MP40 submachine gun.

mission was achieved with modest casualties. A few days later, most of 2 SAS landed by sea at Taranto, along with the paratroops of 1st Airborne Division, who were similarly being misemployed. Some of the SAS men had their Jeeps and used these well to patrol ahead of the main advance and shoot up any German units they happened to encounter.

The second and last SRS operation in Italy was at Termoli as Eighth Army was advancing up the Adriatic coast in early October. The SRS and various commando units landed to capture the town, being joined later by part of 2 SAS, which had advanced from Taranto. The SAS and the commandos then had to fight off a vicious German counterattack to hold their positions. After this, the SRS was withdrawn from the front line and was sent back to Britain at the end of the year to prepare for the coming D-Day campaign.

POW MISSIONS

After Italy had left the war in September, many Allied prisoners who had escaped from camps were still roaming around behind the now German lines. 2 SAS's operations included various attempts to return groups of these men to the Allied side, but these had very mixed results. One 2 SAS group dropped behind German lines also specialized in

2 SAS AND SRS IN ITALY 1943–44

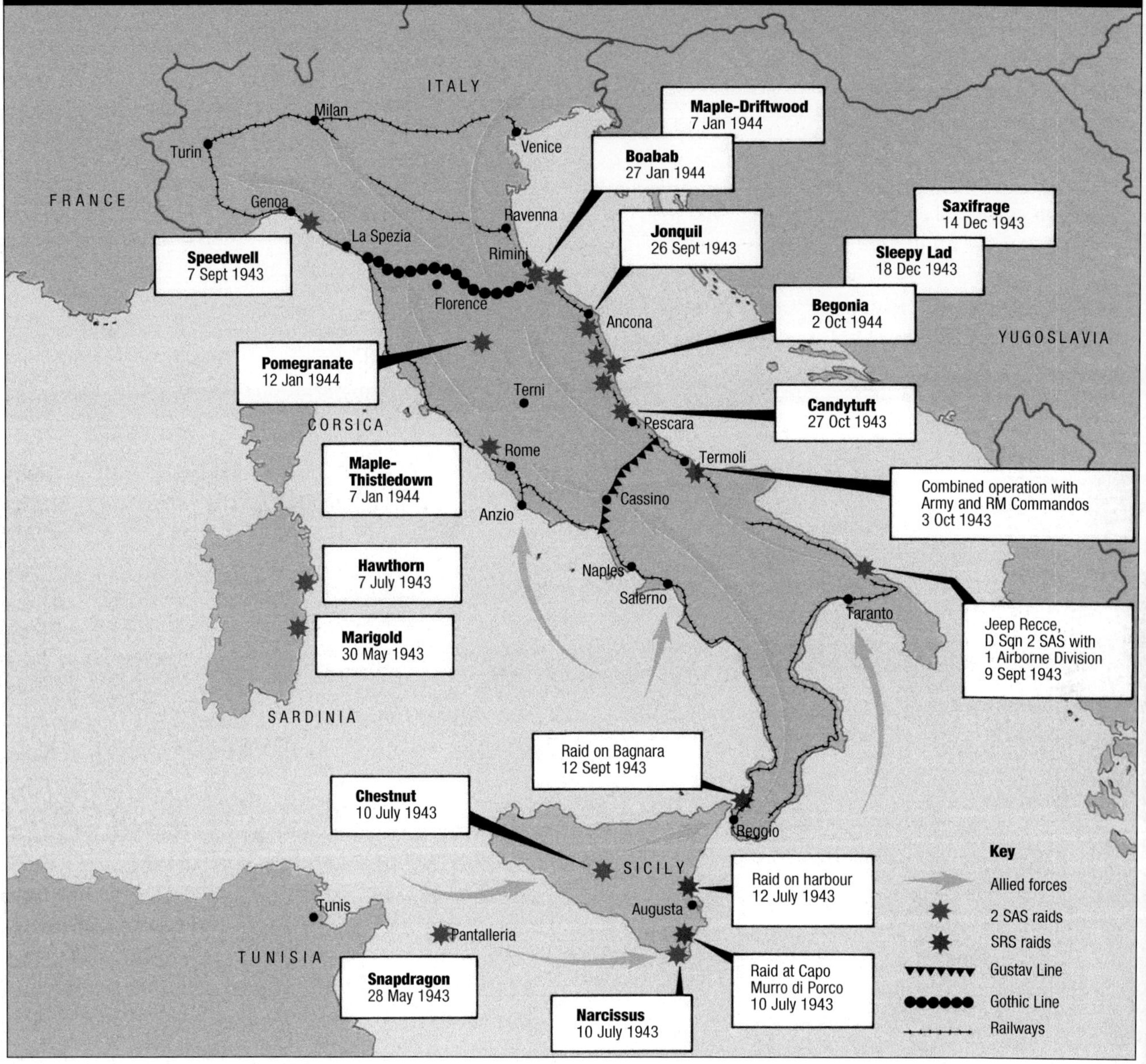

assassinating pro-Nazi Italians who might betray the ex-POWs and their supporters.

The number of more traditional SAS operations was strictly limited. At the start of the campaign, Operation Speedwell was a mission to destroy railway lines between Genoa and La Spezia, Bologna, Pistoia and Prato, and Florence to Arezzo. Two SAS parties, 14 men in all, were parachuted in. One, under the the command of Captain Pinckney, dropped to the south of Bologna; the second, led by Captain Dudgeon, was to destroy the lines between La Spezia and Genoa. The operation began on 7 September 1943 and both patrols had mixed fortunes.

Pinckney himself was never seen again, though reports later suggested that he had met up with some partisans and fought alongside them for a time. His second-in-command split the party into two. They carried out separate attacks, blowing up at least two trains – one inside a tunnel, which completely blocked a major line. One of Dudgeon's teams succeeded in wrecking a further two trains, again inside a tunnel. Dudgeon himself, together with an SAS trooper called Brunt, was captured and shot; two NCOs who went missing are believed to have met the same fate.

The murder of captured SAS men was in accordance with Hitler's so-called Commando Order. In it, he stated that 'captured special forces troops must be handed over at once to the nearest Gestapo unit …these men are very dangerous, and the presence of special forces troops in any area must be immediately reported …they must be ruthlessly exterminated'. The order had never been

Below: Local partisans working with the SAS attend a briefing before carrying out a patrol in the Alba area. The commander of the 2 SAS section in the area was the Canadian Captain MacDonald, who can be seen standing in the car.

implemented by Rommel or the other commanders in North Africa. In Italy, the situation was very different, and SAS officers and men, once caught by the enemy, could expect only torture and death.

Despite the murders, Operation Speedwell was a success: the two SAS patrols had succeeded in hampering the movement of German reinforcements to southern Italy at a vital time. Having used all the explosives they had carried, the survivors had no other option but to set off on the long walk south to Allied lines, with next to no food and winter approaching. One man took seven months, aided by various Italian civilians, to make the journey, and the shortest evasion was almost two months. The achievements of the first few days proved that such SAS operations could be effective, and the long evasions confirmed that SAS men could remain at large for extended periods behind enemy lines, facts that make the failure to support and re-supply these men for more sabotage attacks all the more inexplicable, as many more SAS men than these 14 could have been deployed in similar operations.

There were other small seaborne raids by 2 SAS in October, which were generally successful in a limited sort of way, and another brief flurry of both

Below: SAS troopers enjoy a break during operations in Greece. Local shipping vessels were often used as bases, allowing the SAS and SBS to move between islands without arousing suspicion.

Above: A well armed SAS patrol prepares to move out on operations in North-West Europe. The jeep's driver and front gunner had bulletproof screens to protect them from enemy fire. Note the jeeps are armed with the trusty Vickers 'K's.

parachute and seaborne attacks in January 1944. Successes in these attacks included the destruction of a railway bridge on the Adriatic near Pesaro and an airfield attack near Perugia, in which a number of German reconnaissance aircraft were blown up by Lewes bombs in the best SAS tradition. After this, the regiment was withdrawn from Italy and eventually sent home to the UK in April 1944 as D-Day in Normandy approached.

In January 1944, the SAS Brigade was formed under the command of Brigadier Roderick (later General Sir Roderick) McLeod. It was to comprise the SRS (once again with the title of 1 SAS), 2 SAS, the 2nd and 3rd Free French Parachute Battalions (later designated 3 and 4 SAS), the Belgian Independent Parachute Squadron, later 5 SAS), and F Squadron GHQ Reconnaissance Regiment (Phantom). The brigade had a strength of around 2500, all ranks. HQ SAS troops came under the direction of Lieutenant-General Frederick 'Boy' Browning, commander of I Airborne Corps.

This was not an entirely happy arrangement from an SAS point of view. The SAS commanders did not have direct access to supreme headquarters – as they had had in the first days in the desert – in order to argue for SAS troops to be employed in the ways for which they were best suited. While

Above: Two SAS men pose with a member of the British Special Operations Executive (SOE), who helped coordinate resistance to the German occupying forces. The SAS reconnaissance teams helped disrupt the German war effort.

organizing an invasion on the massive scale of D-Day, Eisenhower, Montgomery and their staffs simply did not have time to devote to a single brigade's operations, and the commanders of the airborne forces also had bigger fish to fry than overseeing patrol- or troop-size missions here and there across France. Indeed, most of the airborne force's staff had no experience of the sort of raiding operations that the SAS was capable of, and little understanding of what was possible in this line. This lack of comprehension made itself clear in minor matters like the order that the SAS soldiers were to wear the red airborne beret, which the planning staff saw as a privilege being granted, and the desert veterans saw as an insult.

There were other rivalries and overlapping responsibilities that also affected how the SAS would operate. The Special Operations Executive (SOE) had been established early in the war to encourage the development of resistance organizations in German-held territory and to carry out sabotage and similar missions. SOE naturally had well-established agents and operational teams in France, and coordinating these with any SAS operations and sorting out a chain of command was obviously going to be difficult. As an organization, SOE was intensely political (in every sense of the word) and had a long-running rivalry with the Secret Service, MI6, with its rather different responsibilities.

Left: A detachment of the SAS in Germany in 1945, with a mixture of equipment and uniform. The men of the SAS drove far in advance of the main Allied forces, causing mayhem in the German rear areas.

There were also many local and national rivalries between resistance organizations in the occupied countries. Resistance groups often had clear political affiliations – communist, liberal, socialist or conservative – and could be as keen on strengthening themselves at the expense of their rivals (with an eye to post-war advantages) as fighting the Germans. The fact that the Allies now definitely seemed to be winning the war naturally made recruitment for all resistance groups much easier, but this could be a mixed blessing. The novice resisters needed training and equipment – and supplying this could hamper SAS operations – and their lack of discipline and security-consciousness could be a positive hindrance.

BILL STIRLING RESIGNS

Arguments about how the SAS should be employed prompted Bill Stirling to resign as commanding officer of 2 SAS. He was replaced by Lieutenant-Colonel Brian Franks, and the role of the SAS in the battle for northwest Europe was eventually decided. The plan was to drop reconnaissance teams into occupied territory; they would then contact local resistance organizations, usually as arranged through SOE, and evaluate the general situation. If an area seemed ripe for exploitation, reinforcements would be brought in and a base established.

Once in position, the SAS patrols advised and, on occasions, trained the local resistance fighters; they also conducted their own guerrilla war against the occupying forces. Bridges were blown, railways destroyed, trains derailed and roads mined. Enemy convoys were attacked and bases targeted for RAF bombing missions.

The RAF (38 Group, 46 Group and the Special Duty Squadron) were responsible for the insertion and re-supply of the SAS operating in France and Belgium. Although the role was a new one for them, they carried it out with great skill, often overcoming difficulties imposed by the lack of effective communications. Besides the normal supplies of arms, ammunition and explosives, the RAF also brought in Jeeps. These vehicles, similar to the ones used in North Africa but without the desert adaptations, were partially fitted with armour plate. They were to prove of great value to the SAS and a real menace to the Germans.

There were more than 40 SAS missions sent to France between D-Day and late October, by which point most of the country was in Allied hands. These were of various sizes, from a handful of men to a full troop 150 strong. Including the French SAS units, total casualties were about 350, a significant number of whom were executed by the Germans after being captured. SAS operations also brought German reprisals, in which resistance fighters and civilians were killed or murdered. SAS reports claimed that the regiment killed or captured over 10,000 Germans, and the long list of physical destruction achieved included 29 locomotives wrecked, 164 railway lines cut and 400 targets passed to the RAF for its attention. This amounted to a massive achievement, and a major contribution to the Allied victory, by a unit that was less than 2500 strong.

The number of operations and the fact that they were spread across roughly two-thirds of rural France means that it is impossible to describe these exhaustively in the space available here. Instead, a few of the more notable missions will be discussed in a little more detail.

THE SAS IN FRANCE

One of the first SAS missions in France was Operation Houndsworth, which was sent to the Saône et Loire department south-west of Dijon. The advance party dropped on the night of 5 June and others arrived later in the month. Eventually most of A Squadron, 1 SAS, took part in Houndsworth, and the operation lasted three months in all. Apart from earmarking targets for the RAF, this group blew up various railway lines a total of 22 times, caused over 200 enemy casualties, and took over 100 prisoners.

A similar operation conducted over a two-month period during the summer of 1944 was Operation Gain. A party of around 60 men, this time of D Squadron, 1 SAS, was tasked with, among other things, disabling the railway system in the area of Rambouillet, Orleans and Chartres. This Jeep-borne squadron, commanded by Major Ian Fenwick, operated with great flair, and nowhere is this better illustrated than in their methods of attacking German supply convoys.

Left: Three members of 2 SAS move out for operations in the Cassino area of Italy, shortly after being parachuted in to provide heavy fire-support for local partisans. The man in the centre carries a Vickers water-cooled machine gun.

Finding that the enemy moved at night with lights on, Fenwick ordered his detachments to do the same, and on occasion SAS vehicles actually travelled unidentified within German convoys. However, one parachute drop was betrayed to the Germans and most of those taking part were either killed on landing or captured and later murdered. Despite this and other losses, including Fenwick being killed in an ambush, Operation Gain, like Houndsworth, made an impact out of all proportion to the size of the force involved and at a very limited price.

OPERATION BULBASKET

One of the least successful missions was Operation Bulbasket. This group was sent to the Poitiers area with the mission of delaying the move of German forces from the south of France to the Normandy battlefield. The most important success achieved by the group was the location of a train of fuel wagons at Châtellerault, which was duly destroyed in an RAF attack. Otherwise, Bulbasket achieved comparatively little. The local resistance groups were insecure and often ineffective and the SAS men seem to have been less enterprising and efficient than elsewhere. In early July, the group's main base was surprised by the Germans; almost 40 SAS men were captured and murdered. The survivors were withdrawn shortly after.

As the invasion progressed and the Allies broke out from the Normandy beaches and began to push inland, the SAS was ordered into northern France. A series of operations was conducted during this phase of the advance, including Operation Loyton, the largest mounted by 2 SAS. This mission was sent to the Vosges area, beginning in mid–August 1944.

The advance party had various difficulties: radios were lost or damaged; the local resistance leaders were at loggerheads and more interested in cornering arms supplies for their own use than helping the SAS; and, as usual, security was a problem. Lieutenant Colonel Franks took personal command of the operation after being dropped with one of a number of groups of reinforcements sent in late August/early September.

CHRONOLOGY

Date	Location	Operation
1943	Europe	SAS is involved in various operations in Italy, Sardinia and Sicily. Missions include attacks on railway lines, communications and airfields, and the rescue of POWs.
1944	Europe	SAS carries out numerous operations in France and Italy, including intelligence-gathering, attacks on road and rail communications, and the harassment of Axis forces.
1945	Europe	SAS carries out attacks and support missions in various countries, including Italy, Germany, Holland and Norway.

With the arrival of Franks and his group, Operation Loyton got underway properly. The SAS commander had only 87 men at his disposal because he preferred to avoid contact with the unreliable local resistance wherever possible. This small force executed a number of successful actions and was responsible for the diversion of two German divisions from the front. Tasked solely with eliminating the SAS, these troops were prevented from joining the battle and were instead forced to roam the countryside hunting an elusive enemy.

However these victories were not achieved without loss. When the survivors of Loyton exfiltrated through to the Allied lines between 9 and 12 October, more than 30 men were missing. Of these, 28 were known to have been captured alive and were subsequently tortured and killed by the Gestapo. The village of Moussey, near which the party was based for a time, had over 200 people taken as hostages by the Germans; most did not return after the war.

By this stage, most surviving SAS personnel were back in Britain, or on their way there, and would spend most of the winter in rest and undergoing further training while their leaders and higher commanders tried to work out how the regiment could contribute to the final defeat of Germany. It was clear that SAS units could not operate deep inside Germany, with its hostile population, and the unliberated parts of Belgium and Holland were far too densely populated and the terrain far too open.

SAS units were therefore prepared for missions close ahead of the main armies' advance when that resumed at full strength in March. Plans were also made for operations in Norway to ensure an orderly transition to Allied control in the event of a German collapse. And, starting in December 1944, 3rd Squadron, 2 SAS, commanded by Major Roy

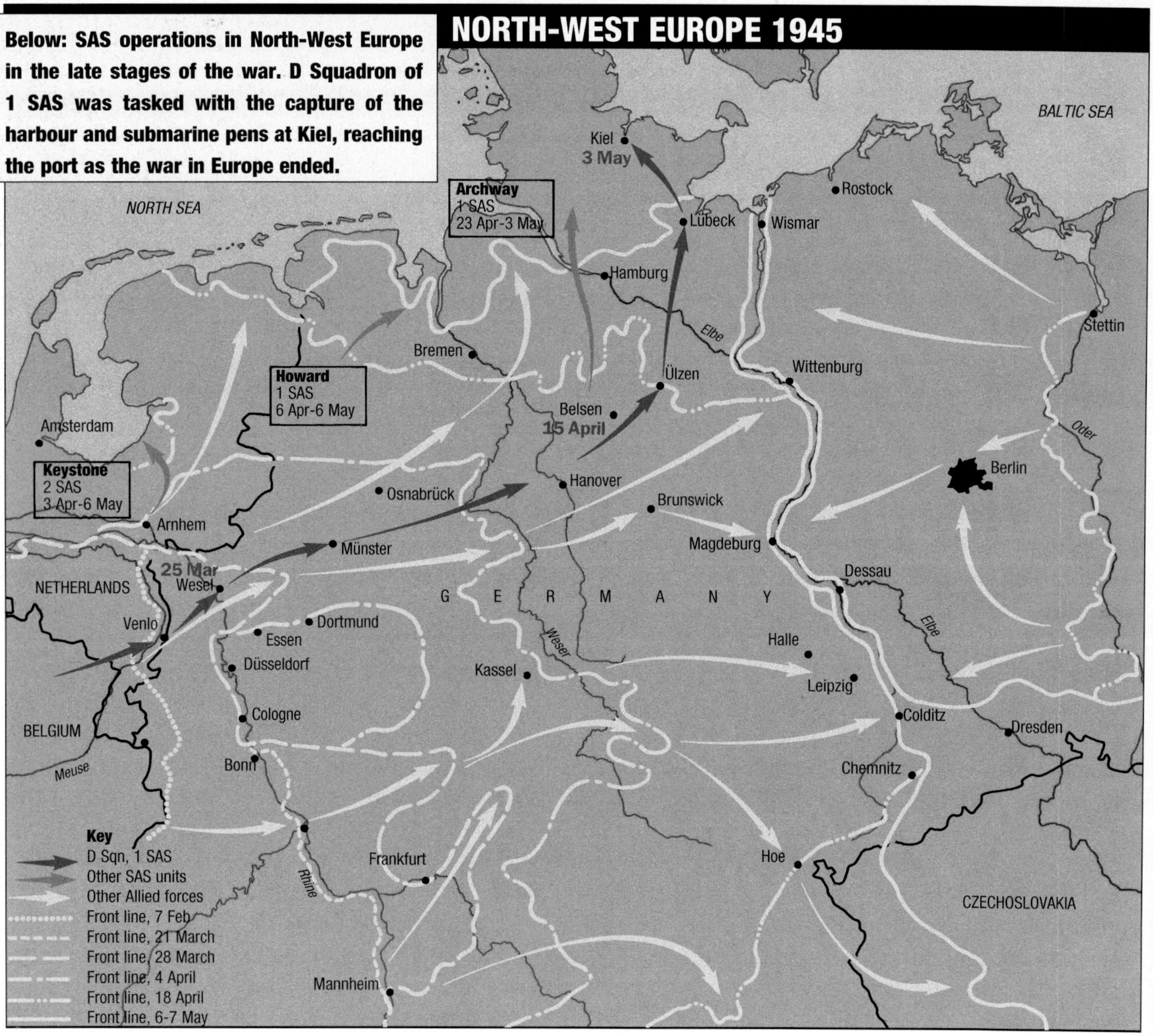

Below: SAS operations in North-West Europe in the late stages of the war. D Squadron of 1 SAS was tasked with the capture of the harbour and submarine pens at Kiel, reaching the port as the war in Europe ended.

Above: To celebrate the end of the war in Italy, an open air mass was held on May 4th in Cuneo near the French border. The main guests of honour were 30 men from 2 SAS (front left) who had parachuted into the area the month before.

Farran, was despatched to Italy to fight alongside the partisans operating behind enemy lines in the final months of the war there.

FINAL OPERATIONS IN ITALY

The squadron's advance guard arrived in Italy in December 1944 and a few men were in action by the end of the month. A number of small operations were carried out between then and March 1945. One party operated near the west coast between Genoa and La Spezia. It succeeded in various sabotage operations and kept a large German force busy hunting for it. Another group, sent to block rail-lines south of the Brenner Pass to Austria, achieved little, and some of its personnel were captured and executed.

The biggest SAS commitment in these months was Operation Tombola, which began in March 1945. Farran had been ordered not to accompany his unit, but he contrived to fall from one of the Dakotas while despatching his men. Tombola was conducted in the area between La Spezia and Bologna. Up until this time, guerrilla operations in the area had been coordinated by SOE under the command of Captain Mike Lees. The guerrillas themselves were a mixed group, comprising Italians of various political persuasions and escaped Russian POWs.

On his arrival, Farran inspected these men, some of whom were still in their early teens, and decided that something drastic would need to be done to turn them into a fighting force. He immediately submitted a long list of supplies, which included a 75mm (2.95in) howitzer; interpreters in Italian, Russian and German; khaki berets with coloured hackles; and a Scottish piper. The last two were morale raisers, intended to inspire the Italians. These supplies, plus arms and ammunition, were dropped in shortly afterwards and training began. Within a fortnight, Farran's guerrilla battalion, including some 50 SAS, was ready for its first operation.

Towards the end of March, Farran decided to attack a major German headquarters situated in two large villas at Albinea. Unfortunately, on the night of the attack, the German corps commander was away, but a number of his staff were killed and the headquarters buildings destroyed; three SAS were killed and other attackers wounded. Under cover

Left: Brigadier Mike Calvert, the final commander of the wartime SAS, inspects members of the French 3 and 4 SAS during a ceremony in October 1945. The French played a large part in the success of the SAS in France in 1944–45.

of Bren-gun fire, the partisans set fire to the house and made good their escape, heading in the opposite direction to the way they had come and away from their hide-out in the mountains to a rendezvous with the remainder of the Tombola base group.

The partisans' first action had been a considerable success, despite the fact that a signal had been sent by 15th Army Group to prevent it going ahead. Farran, aware of the adverse effect that a last-minute cancellation would have on morale, conveniently managed to have left before the message arrived. Estimated enemy casualties of the operation were around 60, including a large number of German officers.

There followed a number of actions around the River Secchia, while the Germans made repeated attempts to track the guerrillas down. The SAS sent out fighting patrols, usually half-British and half-partisan in make-up, and a number of pitched battles took place in which the Anglo–Italian force usually emerged the victors, despite the enemy's numerical superiority.

The fortunes of war were rapidly turning against the Germans, leaving them dispirited. The advancing American 1st Armored Division began to push the remaining three German divisions back across the River Secchia. All the time, they were constantly harassed by the combined SAS and partisan force. By the time Farran received orders to exfiltrate his squadron, the war in Italy had only a fortnight to run.

A NEW COMMANDER

While all this was going on, Brigadier McLeod was replaced in command of the SAS Brigade by Brigadier Mike Calvert, who had made his name fighting with the Chindits behind Japanese lines in Burma. He would be the overall commander of the SAS for the remainder of the war.

In the last weeks of fighting in northern Europe, SAS parties were active in Holland and, following the Rhine crossings, took part in the drive into Germany itself. There were no deep penetrations into enemy territory. Instead, Jeep patrols operated fairly close in front of the Allied advance, capturing bridges, ambushing German units, and seizing suspected war criminals and other prominent Nazis. Although the war was now clearly all but over, some of these actions were bitterly contested, and in one of them, Paddy Mayne won an astonishing third bar to his DSO for rescuing some of his men who had themselves been ambushed.

THE VICTORIA CROSS

Right: Incredibly, no member of the SAS has ever received the highest military decoration in the British Army, the Victoria Cross. A Danish-born SBS Major, Anders Lassen, received it for his valour in Italy in 1945. It is widely thought that Corporal Labalaba deserved one for his actions in Oman in 1972. Recently, there has been talk of an RSM being awarded a VC for his actions in Afghanistan.

In May, after the German surrender, both SAS regiments were sent to Norway for three months, helping to re-establish the legitimate Norwegian Government. Behind the scenes, Calvert and ex-POW David Stirling were arguing for the SAS to be sent to join in the final battles against Japan, but nothing had come of this before the atom-bomb attacks on Hiroshima and Nagasaki brought the war to a final conclusion.

Peace naturally meant a slimming-down of the Army, and the authorities quickly decided that, for all its achievements during the war, they had no further use for the SAS. In October 1945, the regiment was officially disbanded.

CHAPTER THREE

REBIRTH IN THE FAR EAST

There is an old English proverb that says, 'If there is one thing worse then having to fight a war, it is that of not having to fight a war', and for the Special Air Service, this was especially true, because after the end of World War II, the SAS found itself out of a job. However, a communist insurrection in Malaya prompted the unit to be resuscitated by a former SAS veteran.

As with many other unconventional units, Whitehall saw no need for such a force in the new post-war England, feeling that such a war would never be fought again. There were many who argued that the SAS should be represented in some capacity, even if only as a reserve force. These friends in high places valued the SAS and its unique capabilities and were determined to see the regiment survive in some form or other. After intense lobbying to the War Office to reinstate the SAS in the regular army, a compromise was agreed. In 1947, the War Office stated that there would be no SAS Regiment in the regular army; however, a territorial one would be created out of the long-established London-based Territorial Army Regiment, the Artists Rifles.

The unit was to be known as 21 SAS Regiment (Artists Rifles) and initially wore a maroon beret with the old Mars and Minerva cap badge; however, after further lobbying, the men were allowed to revert to their traditional insignia. All the unit needed now was a war to bring about the reformation of a regular SAS Regiment. In 1948 it got one, a different type of war to that fought in North Africa and Europe, but one that would nonetheless test the skills and capabilities of the regiment to the limit.

The background to this conflict dated back to World War II, when Japan occupied Malaya. In an effort to dislodge the enemy, Britain had armed and trained the Malayan People's Anti-Japanese Army (MPAJA). The MPAJA were the military wing of the mainly Chinese Malayan Communist Party and, although they had worked closely with the British during the war, they now viewed these westerners as their enemy. What really irritated the British was the fact that, in many cases, the MPAJA were using British-supplied weapons against British citizens.

In fact, the MPAJA were not alone in their hostility; most of the educated population of Malaya wanted independence from Britain. However, the other two main ethnic groups had different ideas about the country's future. Over half the population was of Malay stock, and favoured the Malaysian

Left: An SAS patrol cross a river in Malaya while searching for Communist rebels. The trooper in the foreground carries a shotgun, a weapon whose short effective range was not a drawback in the close-quarter battles of the dense jungle.

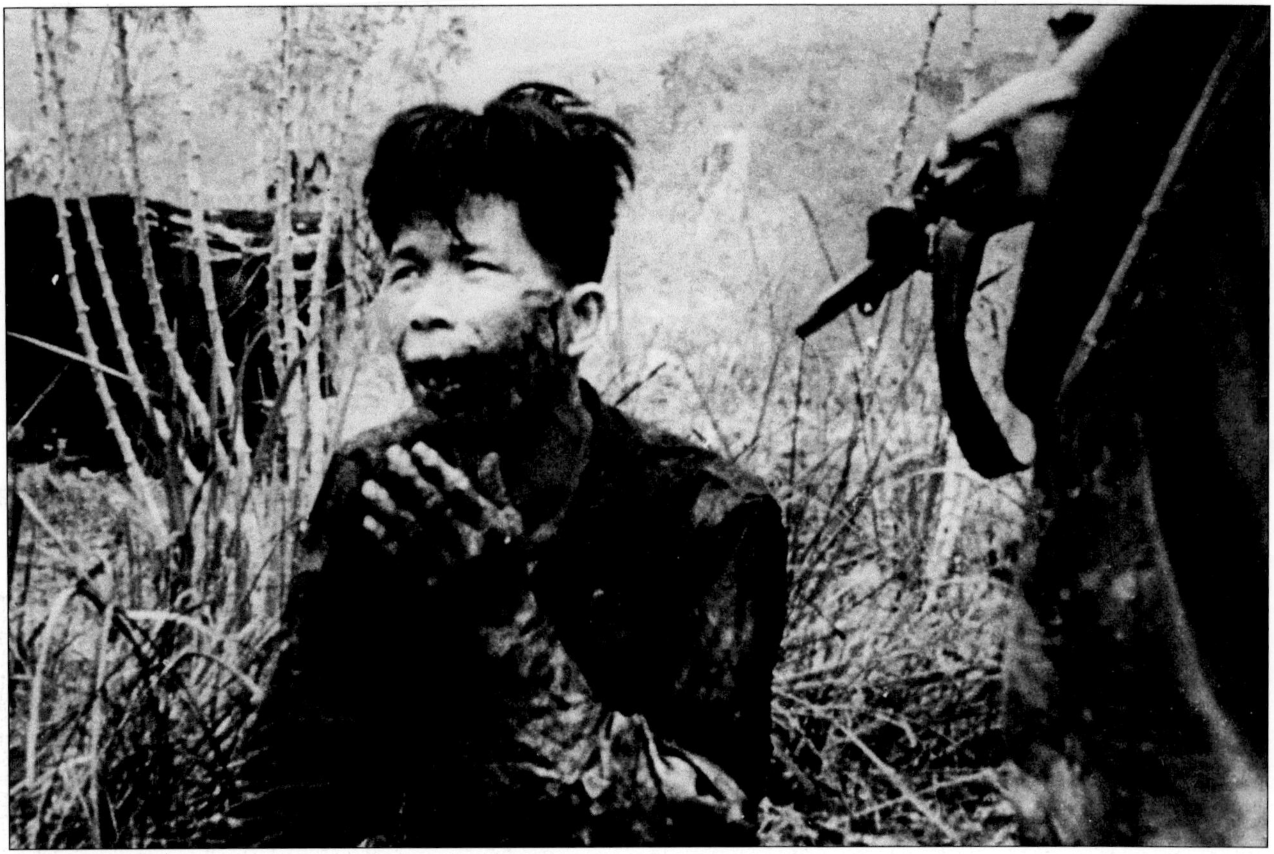

Above: A wounded terrorist is taken prisoner following a successful operation in Malaya in 1950. By winning over the local population and restricting the areas in which the terrorists could operate, the SAS turned the tide in Malaya.

Federation of States idea, which had been proposed by Britain in 1948 and was also supported by the minority Indian community. However, the rest of the population was mainly Chinese and remained totally opposed to the idea of a Federation, fearing that the Malays would dominate with their preferred ideology, that of the Chinese Communists.

Accordingly, in June 1948 a campaign of violence got underway, directed against British rubber planters and their families, many of whom lived and worked in isolated rural areas. The group responsible for these attacks, the Malayan Races Liberation Army (MRLA), was in effect the post-war military wing of the Malayan Communist Party (MCP).

On 16 June 1948, the first deaths of the MRLA's campaign occurred when three rubber estate managers were murdered in the Sungei Siput area of the northern Perak province, close to the border with Siam (now Thailand). Within hours of the murders, a state of emergency was declared in the district, only to be later reviewed and extended to cover the entire country. At the time nobody believed that the situation would continue for long, but in all it would last 12 years, and was referred to as the 'Malayan Emergency'.

The Communist terrorists were led by a man called Chin Peng, who used all of his British training to great effect. He knew when and where to hide, and set up a number of bases within the dense jungle that covered most of the Malayan peninsula, from where he launched attacks against British rubber planters and their Malayan workers, causing great fear and intimidation. To add further insult to injury, Britain had awarded him an OBE for the part he played in defeating Japan during World War II. Now he was repaying them with a terror campaign and causing a crisis amongst his fellow countrymen.

The terrorists, or CTs (Communist Terrorists) as they were called, operated with relative impunity at the start of the Emergency, causing widespread chaos amongst the Malayan population. They numbered around 8000 men at the peak of their campaign, but were impossible to find. This was partly because Chinese squatters, displaced by the Japanese during the war, provided food, shelter and recruits to the CTs. For this, they were hated by the majority of the Malayan people.

As the Emergency continued, it became obvious to the British that all was generally not going well. The Malayan police force and British Army had indeed killed and captured many CTs, but suffered heavy casualties in the process. It was clear that conventional forces simply could not win this guerilla war, unless they had the help of an unorthodox force operating along the same lines as the terrorists.

There was, however, one man who possessed the knowledge and skills necessary to find a solution, and that was Mike Calvert, the former wartime

Below: Following operations in the Fort Kemar area in Malaya, SAS troopers cross a river using a makeshift rope bridge. Note the trooper in the foreground, covering the men crossing the river with his Sten submachine gun.

SAS Brigadier. Calvert had been asked to analyze the war and, from his findings, devise tactics that could bring about a victory. With his previous operational experience in Burma, he was clearly the man for the job. Known as 'Mad Mike' Calvert, he immediately set about producing a report, taking several months to compile it, and undertaking extensive research both in the jungle and with forces on the ground. Calvert had served with Orde Wingate's Chindits in Burma, and had considerable experience fighting behind enemy lines, much of this time being spent in the jungle.

CALVERT'S RECOMMENDATIONS

His report was submitted to the Commander-in-Chief Far East Land Forces, General Sir John Harding, and recommended two courses of action. Firstly, that all vulnerable Malayan natives should be moved into protected villages so that the CTs could not steal their food or force them to provide shelter. Secondly, that it was a priority to form a specialist force that could fight in an unconventional manner, and which had the ability to take the war right to the enemy.

After considering Calvert's report, the general staff accepted his recommendations and tasked him with raising a specialist jungle unit that would operate as part of 'Brigg's Plan', devised by Lieutenant General Sir Harold Brigg. Calvert's unit was to be known as the Malayan Scouts, and initially cherry-picked suitable recruits from existing army units that were serving in the Far East. His priority was to choose men with jungle warfare experience, especially those who had fought against the Japanese in Burma and Malaya.

He recruited a number of former SAS soldiers along with members of 21 SAS based in and around the London area. The Rhodesians also provided a company and, as they were excellent soldiers, were welcomed with open arms. The key members of the Malayan Scouts, however, were the former members of Force 136 and Ferret Force. Force 136 had been responsible for the training of the MPAJA during World War II, and obviously understood the tactics and fighting techniques of their former allies. Ferret Force, however, understood the new CT's operations, as they comprised British soldiers, Gurkhas and Malayan Forces who scouted for regular infantry battalions operating against the CTs. All of these men had good knowledge of jungle warfare and formed the basis for an excellent unit.

Left: SAS troopers carry out a river patrol in the Temenggor area of north Malaya in 1953, with some of their local scouts, who served with great distinction as trackers and guides throughout what was known as the 'Malayan Emergency'.

The men of the Malayan Scouts set about their jungle-warfare training with great zeal, and although their numbers were small, their skill levels were very high, making them extremely effective in combat. Initial training was carried out at the jungle warfare school in Johore with only 100 men, and after a short period, they were deployed on their first mission: to act as forward air controllers for RAF bombing raids on CT positions in the Perak province. They were also tasked with setting up ambushes around known CT bases, in a bid to hit any guerillas who had escaped the bombing raids.

PROBLEMS

Although this mission was a complete success and proved that Calvert's concept was sound, a number of problems were identified relating to the discipline and training of some of the men. A review was carried out in response, and this recommended the return to unit (RTU) of some of the men, who had been found to be unsuitable for long-range jungle operations.

Calvert had been pleased with the results of the Malayan Scouts' first mission, and decided to carry out more ambitious operations as soon as possible. He also set up a number of bases deep within the jungle, to be used for harbouring Malayan Scouts, local police and Chinese-speaking liaison officers. From these communications bases, four-man patrols were sent out on close target recces, and the results of their intelligence-gathering were used for preparing ambushes against CT camps and their supply routes.

Above: SAS troopers on 'Speakmans Hill' in Malaya. The first two troopers are armed with Lee Enfield Mk V carbines, a shortened version of the famous Mk IV rifle, while the third trooper carries a trusty Bren light machine gun.

Critical to the winning of this war was the befriending of local tribespeople, many of whom had never seen a European face before. This process, known as 'winning hearts and minds', involved slowly getting to know the native people and gaining their trust. This was done in a number of ways, the most effective being the provision of medical care. Large numbers of the tribespeople suffered from minor but irritating ailments that were easily cured by the administration of penicillin. Such small gestures were to go a long way with the natives, who reciprocated by teaching the Malayan Scouts how to track the CTs in the jungle using their tried and tested techniques.

As the Malayan Scouts became more successful, a second unit was formed, using members of the TA, 21 SAS Regiment, as the prime recruiting source. Since the original Malayan Scouts were known as A Squadron, this second unit was to be known as B Squadron. It is worth noting that B Squadron was very different to A Squadron in its make-up, and at times almost a different unit, due to the fact that many of B Squadron's members had trained and worked together during World War II, and also had more time at the training camp in Johore to work up.

A NEW SQUADRON

In 1951, a third squadron was formed, primarily made up of volunteers from Rhodesia (now Zimbabwe). These men were nearly all new to soldiering, but what they lacked in knowledge, they more than made up for in enthusiasm. By late 1951, the Malayan Scouts were being informally

Above: SAS troopers parachute into the Malayan jungle in 1953 to form part of a cordon during a search operation. The practice known as 'tree-jumping' – parachuting onto treetops – was later abandoned due to excessive fatalities.

TREE-JUMPING

Below: Tree-jumping was invented by the SAS as a means of inserting a patrol into the jungle at short notice. The trooper's parachute would snag on the thick jungle canopy, and the trooper would lower himself to the ground by rope.

referred to as the Malayan Scouts (SAS); slowly, but surely, their recognition was coming, with three full squadrons in service, plus a battalion headquarters, tasked with patrolling deep into the jungle and performing protection duties around the native villages.

But even with three full squadrons, there was never enough manpower available. Malaria and dysentery soon took its toll. Operating in the jungle for any length of time was hard on the men, as they very rarely saw direct sunlight, and looked pale and drawn when they emerged. With constant dampness and no chance of drying out, clothing would rot and fall away, the material literally dropping off the men's backs. Another major problem was weight loss. For every day a man spent in the jungle, he would lose 500g (1lb) in body weight. Because of this, soldiers were encouraged to put on extra weight before going out on patrol by eating high-calorie foods such as peanuts.

Patrolling in the jungle was extremely demanding. It meant living under the constant threat of guerilla fighters who were hiding only a few feet away. To aid quick recognition in the jungle, each patrol would have a unique feature, such as a coloured bandana. One patrol might wear a yellow one, while the other wore red. This simple, yet effective, idea saved many lives during the conflict and illustrates how much thought went into every aspect of jungle warfare. The tactics developed by the Malayan

LEE ENFIELD NO.5

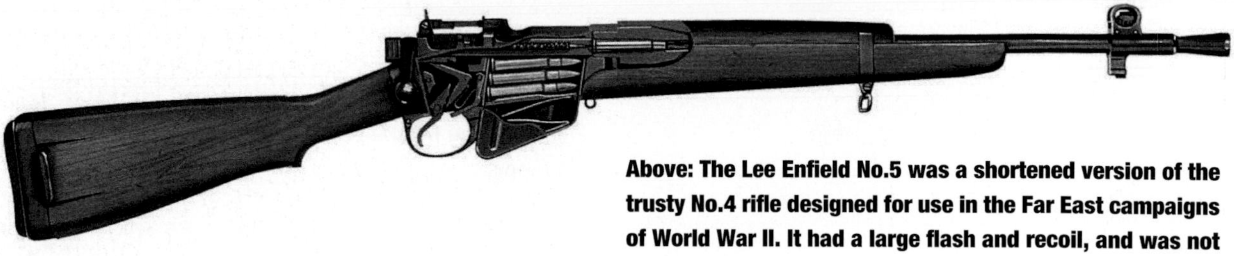

Above: The Lee Enfield No.5 was a shortened version of the trusty No.4 rifle designed for use in the Far East campaigns of World War II. It had a large flash and recoil, and was not a popular weapon.

Scouts were so successful that they were later used by the SAS in Borneo; many of these skills are still taught to the current SAS Regiment.

In late 1951, the Malayan Scouts suffered a slight setback when their founder, Mike Calvert, had to be invalided back to the UK after picking up malaria and dysentery. He was soon replaced by Lieutenant Colonel John Sloane, an infantry officer who had served in Korea but who had no special forces background. However, Sloane was considered an excellent tactician and he wasted no time in making his mark.

RETRAINING

Sloane felt that standards amongst the men had slipped and set about retraining them, even replacing some. Morale had slipped slightly, since the soldiers had been operating for long periods without adequate rest and recreation and had lost focus, resulting in a lower operational efficiency. On one occasion, a patrol spent a staggering 103 days operating in deep jungle, whereas the optimum time for a patrol in the jungle was 14 days: any less, and the men wouldn't have fully adjusted to the conditions; any more, and they would start switching off. By the end of 1951, the Malayan Scouts' name had been officially dropped and replaced by the title 22 Regiment, Special Air Service, generally shortened to 22 SAS. The Regiment also decided to move to Sungei Besi, which was more centrally located.

In February 1952, the SAS launched a major attack against the CTs in the Belum Valley, near the Thai border, involving both an airborne assault and a ground action. With about 100 men in the area, the CTs had forced themselves on the local Malay tribesmen, taking their food and shelter. The first stage of the operation was a parachute jump into a small clearing, using a squadron of 60 men. These men were to cut off the CTs' escape route and provide the tribesmen with protection until the ground force arrived. However, only four men made it onto the clearing; the rest landed in nearby trees almost 30m (100ft) high. Amazingly, nobody got hurt. Although not intentionally done, they had created a new method of insertion, later to be perfected by using ropes to abseil down from the tree canopy.

As the SAS began their insertion, a combined force of two SAS squadrons, Royal Marines, Gurkhas and Malayan police cut their way through the vegetation towards the valley. With the CTs now cornered, a firefight broke out, killing some of the guerillas and injuring others; however, a number did escape, much to the disappointment of the SAS. Although the body count for this operation was low, a number of valuable lessons had been learned, which would be used to great effect in future missions. The tree insertion idea was further developed, each man being issued with 50m (164ft) of rope for

Right: Where possible, SAS teams would be inserted by helicopter rather than parachute. Here a Sikorsky 55 helicopter hovers close to the ground as it deposits an SAS team in a Malayan jungle clearing.

CHRONOLOGY

Date 1950–1960
Location Malaya
Operation The SAS is re-formed to fight Communist Terrorists (CTs) in Malaya following the murder of British citizens and their employees. Known as the 'Malayan Emergency', this period leads to the SAS becoming highly skilled in jungle warfare.

Date 1963–66
Location Borneo
Operation The SAS finds itself back in the jungle fighting Indonesian forces and rebel guerillas who are opposed to the formation of the Federation of Malaysia.

Above: (from left to right) Corporal Lyle, Lieutenant Bruce Murray and Trooper Downing pictured at their base shortly after returning from a marathon patrol in the Malayan jungle, which lasted 122 days.

descending after landing. But every good idea comes with its problems and, on a number of occasions, men suffered broken bones and head injuries during the heavy landings in the tree-tops.

Although the SAS primarily carried out offensive operations against the CTs, a significant amount of time was spent protecting the local tribespeople from the influence and intimidation of the Chinese guerillas. Once the SAS had secured their safety, it would hand over responsibility to either regular Army units or local Malayan police.

In early 1953, the SAS started to use helicopters for their operations. These were flown by 848 Naval Air Squadron, which was at the time operating 10 Sikorsky S51s in support of troop movements and re-supply missions. The introduction of helicopters allowed the SAS to insert small teams of men deep into the jungle at short notice to perform snap or pre-planned ambushes against the CTs, and made extraction much easier.

Another benefit of helicopter operations was the ability to link up with the native Sakai and Semam tribes that lived deep within the jungle. By winning over these tribes, the SAS would reduce the CTs' ability to operate in these areas; it would also be freed up to concentrate its forces in other trouble spots. To increase its effectiveness, the SAS started to deploy four-man teams on three-month tours of duty within the tribes' villages. This was no mean feat; some of them had been cannibals prior to the Emergency, which certainly helped focus the soldiers' minds on keeping the right side of them. To create a bond of trust between the SAS and the natives, each team had a medic that could help treat minor ailments; anything more serious and they could be flown out to a hospital for treatment.

The SAS operations continued against the CTs, and the Rhodesians of C Squadron were recalled home following two years of good service to the SAS, to be replaced by new recruits or elements of the support company already deployed. But this group did not use the C Squadron designation. Placed in suspended animation, it was never used again by the SAS, and to this day, C Squadron has never been re-activated. Nonetheless, it appears on the SAS Regiment's Order of Battle (ORBAT) as a mark of respect for the Rhodesian soldiers.

In October 1953, an SAS unit led by Johnny Cooper embarked on a 122-day operational patrol deep within virgin jungle, tasked with clearing an area alongside the Sungei Brok River for the construction of a helicopter landing zone and a fortified position. From this base, named Fort Brooke, offensive patrols were mounted against the CTs, and in one of them tragedy struck.

An SAS patrol was moving carefully through the jungle when they were suddenly ambushed. Corporal Bancroft and Trooper Wilkins were killed instantly, but the other members of the patrol counterattacked and drove off their attackers. In these confrontations, the man who could fire first, won, very much like the gunslingers of the 'Wild West'. One favoured weapon of the SAS was the shotgun, found to be very effective in close-range combat. Other weapons included rifles and machine guns, which were cleaned and wiped down every night with oil, as the humid conditions could cause rust damage in a very short time.

EXTREME FATIGUE

When Cooper's unit eventually emerged from the jungle, it was down to half strength; diseases – malaria and leptospirosis – and in some cases extreme fatigue had taken their toll. The men had done a great job but were now in need of replacements, since the regiment was under strength. Filling the gap left by the Rhodesians would take some doing, but help was at hand from the New Zealand SAS (NZSAS).

Although formed only in 1954, the New Zealand SAS were highly professional soldiers with much to offer. In 1955, a small company-sized

Right: This soldier from the Malayan conflict is wearing canvas and leather boots with an olive drab uniform, and carries a bare minimum of equipment. He is armed with the Australian Owen submachine gun.

independent squadron was formed, specifically for service in Malaya. Upon arrival in Malaya, the NZSAS Squadron embarked on a six-month training programme, before being deployed to the border provinces of Perak and Kelantan. The Kiwis worked well with the British, and over a period of time a deep mutual respect developed for each other's skills. The Maoris attached to the NZ Squadron proved to be excellent trackers and very valuable in the struggle against the CTs. Not initially appreciated was the Maoris' ability to quickly build relationships with the Malayan natives; they were well liked and trusted by the locals, helping to turn the tide against the CTs.

The NZ Squadron had been trained and equipped to fight deep within the jungle on long-range patrols, requiring them to carry out hit-and-run missions without outside support. They were highly successful in this role, and on one particular mission they killed or captured over 30 Chinese guerillas. After the NZSAS went home, another British squadron was formed from members of the Parachute Regiment, bringing the total strength of 22 SAS Regiment up to around 600 officers and men.

The situation in Malaya was beginning to revert to something resembling normality. Much of the population, including the Chinese squatters, were now in favour of the British desire for Malayan independence. Even so, some of the CTs continued their campaign of violence, even after independence was granted on 31 August 1957. The SAS, however, stayed on in Malaya for a few years, until the State of Emergency ended on 31 July 1960, by which

Below: With weapons at the ready, an SAS patrol slowly makes its way along a shallow river in Borneo. The trooper in front carries a Sterling submachine gun, while the trooper following is armed with an FN FAL automatic rifle.

time the vast majority of the squadrons had returned back to the UK and the situation was well within the control of both the conventional Army and the Malayan Police.

For the SAS, the Malayan Emergency had brought the regiment back to life with a vengeance. At the start of the conflict, the SAS had struggled to put a unit together, but by its end, it had become one of the world's finest fighting forces. Much of the SAS Regiment's tactics and techniques developed in Malaya were employed in the Vietnam War from 1965 to 1975. In some cases, its members fought against the Vietnamese in the service of the Americans and Australians, offering invaluable knowledge and experience.

BORNEO 1963–1966

After the Malayan Emergency and the Jebel Akhdar campaign, the SAS once again found itself out of work, but still assured of a future. 22 SAS Regiment, now officially part of the British Army Order of Battle, was tasked with supporting NATO in Germany. Then came the Sandys Report of 1957. Although good news for the regiment – in that it was now guaranteed a role – the report also recommended that the regiment be reduced from four Sabre Squadrons to two, plus an HQ element that operated out of Merebrook Camp in Malvern for a short period, before moving to Bradbury Lines in Hereford, where they would remain for over 30 years.

During this quiet period, the SAS decided that it needed to develop operating skills in the African Bush, and sent D Squadron over to Kenya for a three-month training exercise. Kenya proved to be an excellent training area for practising tracking and patrolling skills, all of which the SAS would put to great use in forthcoming conflicts. Around this time, the SAS realized that if it was to have a long-term future, it must think out of the box, and be proactive, rather than reactive, in its operating methods. The unit developed a 'killing house' for learning and practising room-clearance skills, which were always useful to have, and which would enable the regiment to carry out hostage-rescue operations anywhere in the world and at a moment's notice. The following year, the SAS further refined itself by creating four specialist troops within each Sabre Squadron. These were named Air Troop, Boat Troop, Mobility Troop and Mountain Troop. The regiment was now well balanced in its capabilities.

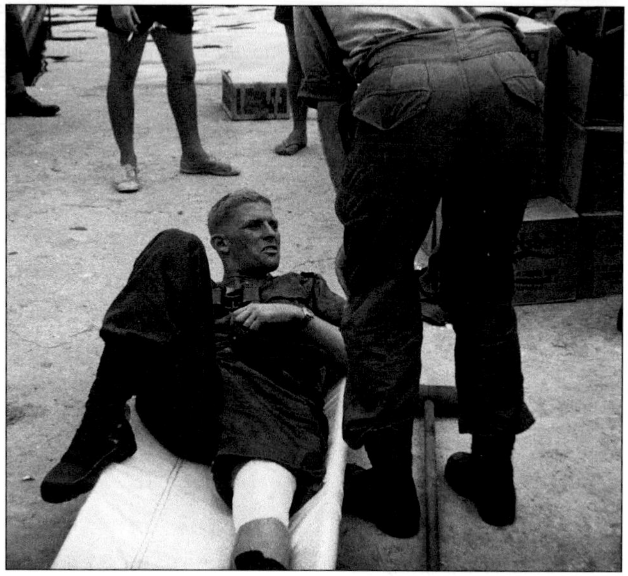

Above: A British Royal Marine officer awaits evacuation from Brunei jetty, his left thigh and knee swathed in bandages, after an early clash with Indonesian forces. The SAS were called in as a result of its success in Malaya.

Around this time, another potential conflict was starting to develop in the Far East, and this aroused the interest of the SAS. President Sukarno of Indonesia had started to express the desire to create a united South-East Asia, regardless of his neighbours' views. He naturally saw himself as its leader, and was also quite prepared to use military force to make this dream a reality.

In 1962, however, the idea of a Federation of Malaysia was proposed. Incorporating Sarawak, Sabah, Malaya, Singapore and Brunei in Borneo, this was a potential threat to his territorial ambitions, so President Sukarno vowed to destroy it. At first, he encouraged internal subversion through what

Above: SAS troopers look on as a helicopter prepares to land in an area of Borneo jungle that has been cleared for helicopter re-supply missions. Helicopters were equally important for rapidly evacuating any casualties for treatment.

was called the Clandestine Communist Organization (CCO). Next he embarked on a propaganda campaign within the region, demanding the closure of British bases and creating an atmosphere of fear in order to destabilize the population. To Sukarno, it seemed that the Sultan of Brunei was the weakest link, and although a member of the British Commonwealth, the Sultan preferred Brunei to be independent, rather than part of the Federation.

In December 1962, a revolt broke out in Brunei and it soon became clear that it was sponsored by Sukarno. Here was the opportunity the SAS had been waiting for, because it could now justify being deployed to the region. The group behind the revolt was the North Kalimantan National Army (NKNA), trained and equipped by Indonesia, which, at the time, of course, denied all involvement.

THE SULTAN'S REQUEST

Well aware that Britain had a large force of soldiers stationed in Singapore, the Sultan of Brunei requested British help in putting down the rebellion. Within a week of their arrival, it was mostly over, although a small number of rebels managed to evade capture for a further six months. Sukarno didn't give up on his plans that easily, however, and decided that the best way forward was to accuse the Federation of supporting British imperialists who were pursuing a hostile policy against Indonesia. The Indonesian Foreign Minister formally announced a state of confrontation with Malaya on 20 January 1963.

The Indonesians had by then already infiltrated Sabah, Sarawak and Brunei, and were now preparing attacks on police facilities near the border, which they saw as soft targets. The first attack took place on 12 April 1963 in the town of Tebedu, when a force of around 35 rebels hit the small police post. There were only a few officers on duty at the time, and although they fought back, they had little chance against such a large force. One officer was killed and two others wounded and the rebels then looted the local market and fled over the border before the Royal Marines arrived at the scene.

Prior to leaving the town, the rebels had scattered propaganda leaflets, claiming that this attack had been carried out by the NKNA. However, at the time, British forces felt that regular Indonesian soldiers were responsible. At this point, an SAS Squadron was in the region, but it had not been deployed operationally against the NKNA. The Squadron was, however, deployed after the Brunei rebellion had been put down, under the command of Lieutenant-Colonel John Woodhouse, a man who clearly saw the potential of the SAS in this conflict. Woodhouse wasted no time in talking to Major-General Walter Walker, commander of British Forces Borneo Territories (BFBT) about the skills of the SAS and exactly how they could benefit his operations.

Walker had previously commanded the Gurkhas in Malaya, where he had developed great respect for the SAS and its exploits during the Malayan Emergency. As a result, he welcomed with open arms its help in fighting this new jungle war and authorized the deployment of A Squadron. The terrain in which the men would operate was very dense jungle, with no roads and very few tracks. In theory, Brunei was shielded from attack by Sarawak.

GOOD CONCEALMENT

The reality, however, was very different. The dense jungle terrain between Sarawak and Brunei gave good cover to the Indonesians and was virtually impossible to police effectively, given the limited resources available. The other problem was the length of the border dividing Indonesian Kalimantan in the south and the Malay provinces of Sabah and Sarawak in the north: it was nearly 1500km (930 miles) long. The SAS had only around 100 men available – including HQ and logistical support – and so decided that the best way to deploy their men would be in four-man teams working closely with local tribesmen who knew the area. They would in effect act as a human trip-wire and cover the known tracks that ran through the jungle.

With experience of jungle warfare in Malaya, the SAS knew that the chances of coming face to face with an Indonesian patrol would be remote; however, all the men were looking for was a trail to follow. Once the SAS and their trackers had picked up signs of recent Indonesian activity, they used their Morse transceivers to contact HQ Squadron, who in turn planned an ambush further down the trail against the insurgents. This proved to be a very good tactic. Movement in the jungle was tediously slow for everyone, including the local tribespeople, but the SAS had one great asset in their arsenal: the helicopter.

Although the SAS had employed helicopters in Malaya, their use had been limited to troop rotations and supply missions, rather than direct combat operations. But here in Borneo they could insert and extract SAS teams on a regular basis, making the task of deploying forces more efficient and effective.

One key objective for the SAS was to win over the local tribespeople using the 'hearts and minds' policy that had been instigated to such great effect in Malaya. It wasted no time in introducing it in Borneo. Here the local tribespeople were generally friendly, although on a few occasions a little wary as they had never seen a white face before. The SAS men were very careful not to

Below: An SAS medic checks over a young child as part of the highly successful 'hearts and minds' campaign that won over the local tribespeople and helped bring about the defeat of the communist terrorists.

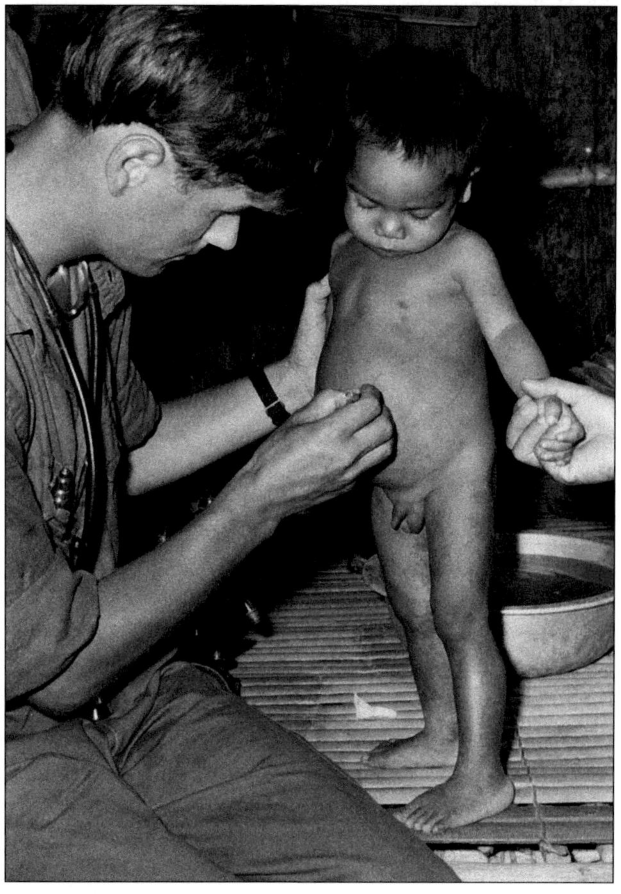

Above: Iban tribesmen waving a Union Jack bring in captured rebels for interrogation by the British. A close partnership with the local tribespeople gave the SAS vital information about the enemy's movements.

impose themselves onto the local tribespeople too rapidly. It was simply a case of slowly building up trust with them, and then asking for their help in fighting the Indonesians.

In the first instance, the SAS men would set up a hide near a village, or Kampong, as it was called by the locals. They would then observe the villagers for a few days to ensure that no Indonesians were present. Once satisfied that all was well, they would introduce themselves to the headman, or elder. For the first few days, they would keep their distance, only moving closer in when they had been invited to set up camp in the village. This was a very important protocol, as they did not want to give the impression that they were taking over. They were extremely careful not to cause offence, doing their utmost to respect any known customs. Again, this was a crucial element in developing a relationship, as the SAS would be living amongst these people for many months and had to be careful not to outstay their welcome.

Once the SAS had established a relationship with the villagers, it would then begin intelligence-gathering operations rather than combat ones. The men were usually assigned an area of responsibility near the border, where they would use all of the local Kampongs as their eyes and ears. This was a simple yet highly effective tactic, which was to pay dividends throughout the conflict. The more the SAS teams worked with the local tribespeople, the harder it was for the Indonesians – or 'Indos', as they were called by the British forces – to infiltrate Brunei without being detected.

Every now and again, the SAS would come across Kampongs where the people needed a little more convincing than the usual pep talk, and for this, they would put on a show that would never cease to impress. Their tactic was to ask the tribespeople to cut down several trees to form a landing area. They would then summon a number of helicopters, and these would land in the new clearing with a large number of Gurkhas. It was an excellent party piece that always worked wonders for the doubters.

D SQUADRON IN ACTION

In May 1963, D Squadron replaced A Squadron to give the men a well-deserved break from operations. Effectively D Squadron did the same job, but continued to expand the 'hearts and minds' campaign further afield. The SAS, however, could not hope to create fortified villages in Borneo as they had done in Malaya, simply due to the fact that there were many more Kampongs then they had troops for.

To surmount this problem, they set up the Border Scouts. This was, in essence, a self-defence force made up of tribespeople from each Kampong. Each force received weapons from the SAS, along with training and support from the Gurkhas, whom they greatly admired and respected. Although they had great enthusiasm

Below: Gurkhas armed with a General Purpose Machine Gun (GPMG) and Bren machine gun man a defensive position near Balai Ringgin, Sarawak. The Gurkhas worked well with the SAS in Borneo, each having great respect for the other.

and were excellent trackers, they were, however, no match for regular Indonesian soldiers.

On 28 September 1963, the British forces suffered a major setback. A group of Gurkhas and Border Scouts had set up a post within the village of Long Jawi in Sarawak. Without warning, they were attacked by a large force of some 200 Indonesian soldiers. Their total strength was only 30 men. With little chance of defending themselves, only three survived: two Gurkhas and one Border Scout. The survivors tried to radio for help, but were unable to do so because of poor atmospheric conditions. Having bravely found a way out through the jungle, they raised the alarm. The British then dispatched a large force of Gurkhas by helicopter to ambush points along the Indonesians' anticipated escape routes. As the Indonesians fled towards Kalimantan, they were caught in an ambush in which many were killed or wounded before they could reach the safety of theborder. With the situation now escalating, the SAS needed more troops if it was to make any impact against the large Indonesian forces deployed near their border areas.

Throughout the year, further raids took place, forcing the SAS to re-form B Squadron in anticipation of a new offensive. In December 1963, the Indonesians launched an attack against the village of Kalabakan in Sabah, killing 8 and wounding 19 members of the Royal Malay Regiment. As the Indonesians withdrew from the attack, they were ambushed by the Gurkhas, who then managed to kill a considerable number of them in revenge for their unprovoked attack on the garrison. That attack had been the final straw for the British, who up till then had been fighting with one hand behind their backs. Now that the gloves were off, they would take the fight to the Indonesians' backyard.

BORDER FIREFIGHT

In January 1964, a patrol of British soldiers discovered an Indonesian force camped on the Sabah–Sarawak border. It was now the turn of the British to attack without warning, and in the short firefight seven Indonesians were killed before the others broke and fled over the border. Examining documentation discovered at the scene of the attack, the British soldiers found irrefutable proof of Indonesian Army involvement in the recent attacks, something which President Sukarno had naturally always denied. When confronted by the evidence, Sukarno called a ceasefire and asked for negotiations to end the hostilities.

Right: Even an SAS man stops to brew up a cup of tea now and again, although his AR-15 rifle is always within reach, even when he sleeps. After his rest, all trace of his presence would be carefully removed to prevent trackers following his trail.

But the ceasefire lasted only a few weeks before the Indonesians walked out of the talks and recommenced military action against the British forces and their supporters. This time they made no attempt to hide the fact that their regular army was involved, rather than an Indonesian guerilla force.

The first open moves against British forces by the regular Indonesian Army took place on 7 March 1964 near the the border of south-west Sarawak. The Indonesians were good fighters, using hit-and-run tactics whenever possible. Knowing that the British were forbidden to pursue them over the border, they made sure that they attacked small, vulnerable garrisons that would be no match for a large force. Feeling extra confident, the Indonesians hit the Gurkhas a few days later.

This time, however, the Gurkhas were well prepared, and beat off the Indonesians with artillery and air support, provided on this occasion by helicopter. After this, the SAS determined to put an end to these attacks and started covert patrolling operations within Indonesian territory, also setting up mutual support fire bases along the border to ensure that the Indonesians would be hit extremely hard hit if they made a move against them again.

For the four-man patrols who carried them out, the SAS infiltrations into Kalimantan were fraught with danger. If compromised by the Indonesians, they knew that they would be on their own. No British forces would be allowed to come to their rescue, because technically the SAS was not there. The soldiers wore regular British Army

Above: An SAS team use a native wooden boat to keep their weapons and equipment dry as they move upstream somewhere in Borneo. Movement along rivers and streams was faster than struggling through dense jungle.

uniforms and carried standard-issue 7.62mm (0.3in) Self-Loading Rifles (SLR) to protect the British Government from any embarrassment, should the soldiers be killed or captured. In that event, the Government would insist these British men were conventional forces who had become disorientated in the jungle and strayed across the border by accident.

The SAS patrols gathered intelligence on the Indonesians and their movements within the border area. They created detailed maps of the territory for their own use and for the conventional British forces who would later become involved in over-the-border operations. The SAS tried to limit the patrols to a maximum of three weeks, as anything more would be too exhausting for the soldiers and their trackers. After completing a number of missions, the soldiers were rotated back to Hereford for recuperation, which was greatly welcomed by everyone.

As the operations intensified, the SAS began to use more unconventional weapons, such as the American 5.56mm (0.22in) Armalite Rifle and hunting shotguns, which were highly effective for jungle warfare. Although other British forces in Borneo used the 7.62mm (0.3in) General Purpose Machine Gun (GPMG) for heavy fire support, the SAS chose not to operate it, as it was too heavy for long-range patrols. Instead, the World War II vintage Bren Light Machine Gun (LMG) was used.

ADAPTING TO BORNEO

Initially the SAS found the conditions in Borneo extremely difficult. But eventually, with their growing knowledge and understanding of jungle warfare, the men saw the jungle as a friend rather than an enemy. Although it hosted numerous poisonous plants, snakes and other hazards, meaning that each soldier had to be on his guard against his surroundings and operational environment, the SAS and their trackers soon became adept at finding good ambush sites for future covert operations against the Indonesians. Their opponents were no walkover and the SAS had to be constantly proactive to ensure survival.

What really frustrated the SAS during their over-the-border operations was the restrictions placed on the types of attacks it could carry out. The men were forbidden to mount any heavy attacks on the Indonesian forces, for fear of taking casualties. Initial orders limited confrontations to 'shoot-and-scoot' engagements only, where usually the first to fire won the firefight.

Within a few months of the over-the-border operations, the Indonesians found themselves under increasing pressure. No longer comfortable in their border base camps, they started to move further within Kalimantan for protection. At this time, both the SAS and the Gurkhas were restricted to infiltrations of only 5km (3 miles), but eventually these increased to 20km (12 miles). The SAS were rapidly gaining respect from the Indonesians for their legendary jungle skills, and within British forces they were known as the 'Tip Toe Boys' because of their ability to sneak up on the enemy without ever being heard.

CLARET OPERATIONS

In September 1964, the Indonesians attacked Johore province in an airborne assault, supported by a further attack on the west coast by a smaller force. From the Indonesians' point of view, the attack ended in failure, and they resumed operations in Borneo. Meanwhile, the British forces started to mount large-scale over-the-border incursions, which were known as Claret Operations. Officially these did not exist, and they were deemed top secret, as, technically, Indonesia was not at war with Britain.

The SAS had one particular weapon that the Indonesians greatly feared — the American 'Claymore' anti-personnel mine. Each mine contained several hundred metal ball-bearings mounted in a horseshoe-shaped casing. Once detonated, these devices were lethal to any soldiers caught within their range. Depending on the tactical situation, the mines could either be electronically fired or set off by a pressure sensor. In effect, they were sleeping soldiers and they instilled great fear into the Indonesian patrols as they moved through the jungle. Inevitably, the SAS had to be very careful to note the location of their Claymores in order not to inflict casualties on their own forces. Indeed, to ensure that there were no blue-on-blue contacts, only one British force at a time was allowed to operate across the Kalimantan border.

Although the Indonesians were being hit hard, they still fought back against the British forces at every opportunity. In one particular mission, the SAS carried out a close target recce (CTR) against an enemy base, from where they noticed most of the soldiers were missing. Little did they know that as they were busily observing the Indonesian camp, its occupiers had infiltrated into Sarawak to carry out

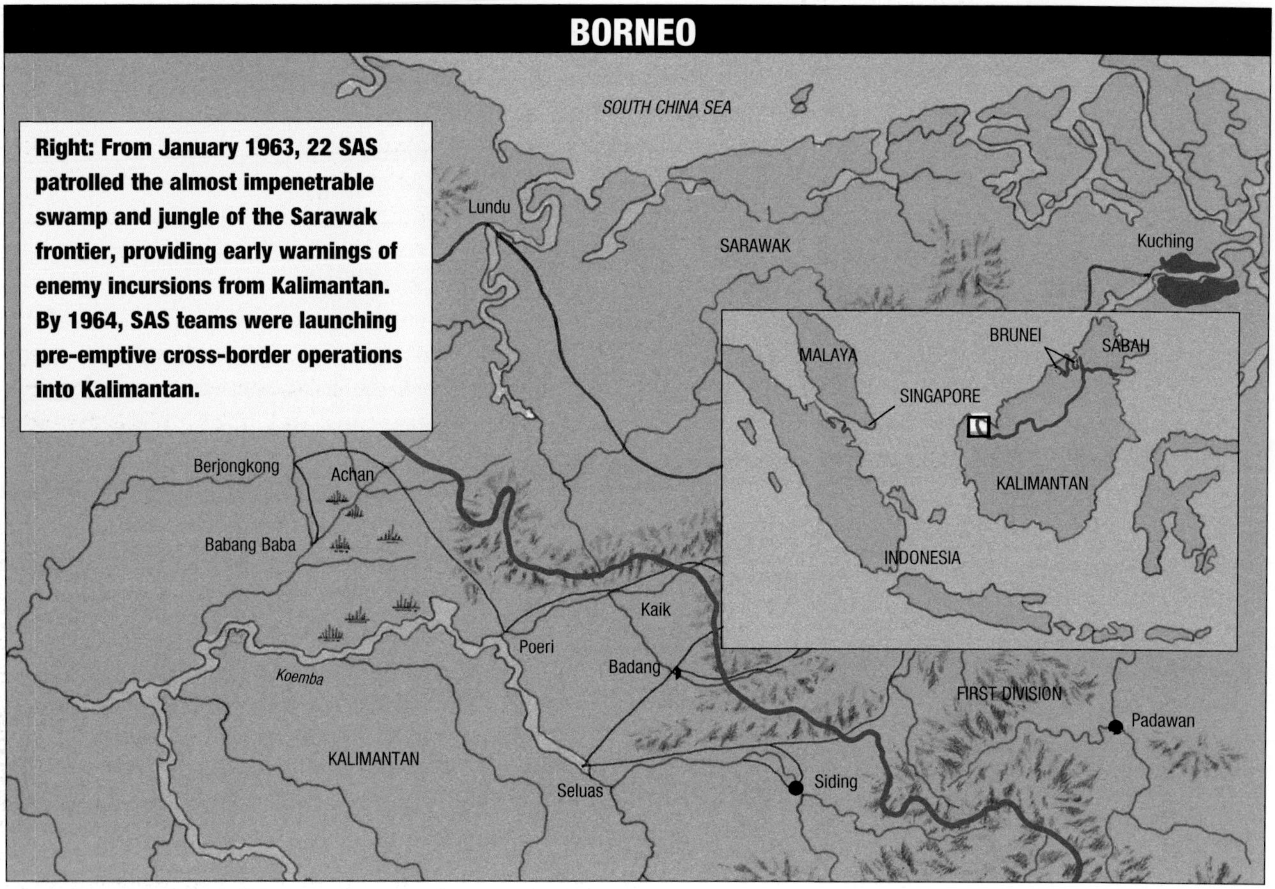

Right: From January 1963, 22 SAS patrolled the almost impenetrable swamp and jungle of the Sarawak frontier, providing early warnings of enemy incursions from Kalimantan. By 1964, SAS teams were launching pre-emptive cross-border operations into Kalimantan.

a large-scale attack on 2 Para, which was based in the village of Plaman Mapu. The Paras at this point had very few men on the base, as they were already deployed on a Claret Operation.

The Indonesians attacked with heavy machine guns and mortars, and the Paras' outer defence collapsed. They came very close to being overrun by sheer weight of numbers. The Paras, however, put up a valiant fight and eventually drove the Indonesians off. For the British, this was the final straw and after this, their forces operated in Kalimantan in a very overt way. The Indonesians were now taking heavy casualties, and it was becoming clear that the tide had turned against them.

In March 1966, the Indonesians mounted an attack against the British in Brunei, but this resulted in complete failure. Out of a force of 50 men who left Kalimantan, only 13 survived the attack. For President Sukarno, this was the final nail in the coffin of his political ambitions. Realizing that it could not defeat the British, the Indonesian General Staff signed a peace treaty with Malaya on 11 August 1966. For the SAS, this had been a long, arduous campaign, in which all of the lessons learned by the Regimentduring the Malayan Emergency were put to use, with highly successful and impressive results.

KEY ROLE FOR THE SAS

Bearing in mind the fact that the Indonesians were expert jungle fighters, and that the SAS and Gurkhas do not normally operate in such an environment, it is an indication of their remarkable professionalism and military skill that they were able to adapt so quickly to an alien terrain and defeat a powerful enemy force in its own backyard. There is no doubt that the SAS played a key role in the defeat of the Indonesians. Their ability to win over the tribes-people with their 'hearts and minds' campaign was a great example of how the troopers of the regiment were willing to live in extreme hardship for months on end for the benefit of others, and, without the eyes and ears of the tribespeople, both the SAS and the conventional British forces operating in Borneo would have had great difficulty in intercepting the Indonesian insurgents.

What is quite remarkable about this campaign is the low level of casualties the SAS incurred while operating in Kalimantan. A small number were killed while on deep recce missions, including one trooper who was captured by the Indonesians and tortured to death.

Yet again, the SAS had served its country well, and many of the hard lessons learned by the regiment in the jungles of Borneo would be used to great effect by the Australian SAS in Vietnam later that decade.

Below: An SAS patrol examines its equipment in a jungle outpost in preparation for forthcoming operations in Sarawak. Note the lack of heavy equipment, with bush hats instead of helmets. The trooper on the left is loading rifle magazines.

CHAPTER FOUR

THE JEBEL AKHDAR AND ADEN

In November 1958, D Squadron, SAS found itself being re-deployed from the humid jungles of Malaya to the dry, rugged terrain of Jebel Akhdar in northern Oman in an operation that would show just how adaptable the SAS Regiment can be when the pressure is on. In Aden, meanwhile, the regiment was required to continue in its role of pacifying the remnants of the British Empire.

Britain's ties with Oman dated back many years. They began officially in 1789, when Britain signed a treaty of friendship with the Sultan of Muscat, giving the British East India Company commercial rights in Oman in exchange for the protection of the Royal Navy. Oman was a trading nation and had suffered constant problems with pirates: that is, until the Royal Navy helped them, and eradicated the pirate threat once and for all. After this point, the British developed a close relationship with the Omanis, one that was to continue under the influence of numerous leaders up until the 1950s. And then, suddenly, maintaining a good relationship became absolutely critical, not just to Britain, but the West.

The reason was oil. Oman had discovered vast amounts of oil under the Arabian sands, making it a very rich, yet at the same time extremely vulnerable, country. Crucially Oman was also in a key strategic position, as it overlooked the straits of Hormuz, through which passed a substantial amount of the West's oil traffic. As a result of these two factors, the British realized that their relationship with Oman was more important than ever. The British Government and its ambassadors now needed to make sure that any new Omani rulers were well disposed towards their western allies.

Left: The barren terrain of the Jebel Akhdar in Oman, with the Tanuf Slab visible top right. In such topography, typical of the campaign, small numbers of men could pin down a much larger force with ease.

However, in 1952 Britain found itself in a fragile position. Saudi Arabia had invaded parts of Abu Dhabi and Muscat and was now on the brink of threatening Oman. The last thing Britain wanted was a confrontation with the Saudis. Although it tried hard to encourage negotiations as a peaceful resolution to the conflict, it was gradually becoming clear that remaining on friendly terms with the Omanis meant honouring the treaty of friendship and providing them with military assistance.

Initially, the British sent in officers to help advise the Omani forces on tactics that could be used to expel the Saudis. Generally, this was only partially successful. The Sultan then took the matter into his own hands, deploying his small army around the towns as a deterrent force. However, in 1957 an open rebellion developed and grew to such a pitch that his soldiers were unable to suppress it. This rebellion was mounted by the Imam Ghalib bin Ali of Oman, and his brother Talib, supported by Sheikh Suleiman bin Hamyar from the Jebel Akhdar region. The rebels, being very well armed, practically wiped out the Sultan's forces. The Sultan, fearing the worst, immediately requested urgent military assistance from Britain.

The British wasted no time in sending forces from nearby Aden and Bahrain, including infantry and light armour. These forces were joined by the Sultan's Trucial Oman Scouts, and together they launched a combined attack on the rebels. Air support was provided by the RAF, using neighbouring states as take-off bases. Within a short period of time, the allies had seen off the rebels.

However, the problem did not disappear. The rebels fled to the Jebel Akhdar ('Green Mountain'), a giant granite outcrop rising to a height of several thousand metres and forming a large plateau 350km sq (135 sq miles) plateau. It was virtually inaccessible in most places and its narrow passes and high mountain peaks made it perfect for setting ambushes. Many of the rebels originated from the region and they possessed an intimate knowledge of the geography of this natural fortress.

There were no roads leading to the top of the Jebel Akhdar, apart from a few donkey paths that wound their way up through the dry valleys. Nor was there any way up it, for the sides of the plateau were virtually sheer cliffs. To use the donkey paths to conduct an assault would have been suicidal: a small force could have held up a whole army just by planting a few mines and a number of machine guns in well sited positions. Helicopters were also out of the question, as the hot and high conditions made their use impossible. Several times, British and Omani forces attempted to patrol the base of the plateau, but on every occasion they came under fire from well-placed snipers high up on the plateau and took casualties. Another major factor was the temperature: at night it was intensely cold, but during the day the scorching heat was unbearable, and many men went down with heat stroke.

Below: Members of 22 SAS receive a briefing on Christmas Day 1958 prior to their assault on the Jebel. The SAS used false information and a diversionary attack to distract and confuse the enemy before their assault.

CONTAINMENT POLICY

At this point, the British decided that since the rebels were up on the plateau, they posed little, or even no, threat to the Sultan. Surely a small force of Omani and British soldiers was adequate to keep them contained within the Jebel Akhdar? As a result, most of the British forces were withdrawn from Oman, and for a while, this tactic of containment seemed to be working.

But in 1958 the situation changed. After laying land mines in their path in a well planned ambush, the rebels attacked and destroyed a number of British armoured cars. To make matters worse, the rebels were now using RAF aircraft flying over the Jebel Akhdar as target practice. The situation could no longer be tolerated and, as the Sultan's forces were unable to take action against the rebels, it was up to the British to do something. Mindful of the fact that it had just been involved in the embarrassing Suez fiasco and was reluctant to be seen carrying

Above: 'Tanky' Smith of 22 SAS gives supporting fire from a 7.62mm (0.3in) Browning machine gun as the SAS attack a cave on the Jebel Akhdar. 'Smokey' Scrivens lies on the right of the picture, next to a pair of SLR rifles.

out large-scale military operations at this politically sensitive time, the British Government searched for a low-key solution to the problem.

The higher powers in the British Government decided that the SAS should be sent in to resolve matters as soon as possible. In November 1958, D Squadron was re-deployed from Malaya to Oman, its mission to clear the Jebel Akhdar of rebel forces. This was going to be no mean feat. The rebels had over 200 well-trained men on their side, as well as the support of some 500 hill tribesmen. They were well armed with modern weapons – machine guns, rifles and mortars – and had more than enough ammunition. They were excellent marksmen, knew the ground, and were used to the region's climate: all in all, they made a daunting adversary.

D Squadron comprised four troops, 16, 17, 18 and 19, plus a small HQ element. Each troop should have had a fighting strength of 16 men; however, the squadron was under strength on deployment, and this had been reduced to an average of 10 men. Compared to the rebels, they had little in the way of heavy-support weapons, such as mortars, and carried only Belgian 7.62mm (0.303in) FN rifles, plus a few light machine guns for fire support.

RAPID ACCLIMATIZATION

For D Squadron, the change in operational conditions from jungle to desert couldn't have been more extreme, each one requiring a different set of skills and operating methods. It takes an average human body 14 days to adjust to a new environment, and D Squadron were only given a very short time to acclimatize. The adjustment period was particularly important for soldiers who had gone from a conflict

Above: Lt Col Tony Deane Drummond MC, commander of the SAS in Oman, seen after the final assault on the Jebel Akhdar plateau. A number of captured rebel weapons are on display in the foreground.

in a low-lying country to one where they were fighting at high altitude. Without acclimatization, an average soldier's marksmanship deteriorates by as much as 50 per cent.

After fighting in the jungle for so long, the SAS soldiers had to adapt their way of thinking rapidly to ensure their survival in the barren, desolate desert of Oman. Everything they needed from food to water had to be carried with their kit, since virtually nothing grew on the Jebel Akhdar. Even the way they moved had to be re-examined: the hard granite underfoot made silent movement very difficult. So, once permission was granted, the standard British Army hobnailed boots were switched to more appropriate footwear.

The SAS also found it had to re-think its weapons training. In the jungle, most engagements were at short range; however, in Oman, the men would find themselves engaging targets at great distances, which meant that each soldier needed excellent marksmanship skills.

CALL TO ACTION

Just as the the SAS soldiers were busily training and acclimatizing, they were told that their services were needed sooner then expected. Their mission was to scale the Jebel Akhdar and occupy a position barely 4km (2.5 miles) from the rebel stronghold of Aquabat al Dhafar. D Squadron was very short of manpower, so some forward planning was necessary to make sure that the men could attack the rebel forces without taking heavy casualties. It was decided to split the squadron into two units: from the north, 16 and 17 Troops would approach the rear of the rebels' position, while 18 and 19 Troops would advance from the south.

As D Squadron slowly advanced, a joint patrol from 18 and 19 Troops had its first contact with the rebels, and Corporal Duke Swindells was killed by a sniper.

The rest of the patrol returned fire, killing one of the rebels before withdrawing. Patrolling in daylight was obviously going to be extremely difficult, so from then on the SAS decided there were more rewards to be reaped from operating in darkness.

On the north side, the men of 16 and 17 Troops scaled the plateau unopposed, using an ancient path known as the Persian Steps. During their ascent, they had discovered a number of unmanned rebel sangars, indicating that the rebels did not feel threatened by the presence of British forces. This gave the SAS the confidence it needed to mount a surprise attack on the stronghold, where the rebels were clearly expecting nothing.

The SAS Troops had made good progress during their ascent and decided to consolidate their position on top of the plateau. Some of the men rested, while the others went back down the Persian Steps to bring up their kit. Although they had to descend a distance of only 2000m (6566ft), it took them the best part of the day because the path was so treacherous. On one occasion, as the SAS men were resting, a sentry heard a noise in the distance and was surprised to discover a number of local villagers with their donkeys advancing towards their position. Luckily for them, the sentry issued a challenge before firing and, in gratitude, the villagers showed him the trail they had used, even offering him their donkeys to carry his supplies.

Now that the SAS was firmly established on the Jebel Akhdar, the men mounted more patrols to gather intelligence and to learn the geography in greater detail. They carefully avoided contact with the rebels, wanting to hide the fact that their numbers were so perilously low. The SAS were particularly worried that if a serious firefight developed, the plateau's inaccessibility would make bringing in reinforcements impossible.

Right: A trooper from 22 SAS deployed in Oman in 1959 on the Jebel Akhdar. He is dressed in a paratrooper's smock and carries a Bren Gun L4, a 7.62mm (0.3in) version of the famous World War II weapon.

Above: Captain 'Abdul' Walker (standing) with other SAS troopers on Sabrina after the end of a cave clearance operation. The cave they successfully assaulted is marked with a circle on the right of the photograph.

To prevent surprise attacks, the SAS set up a forward observation post some 2000m (6566ft) ahead of their main concentration. This would effectively serve as a trip-wire and give the main body of men time to react to any rebel attack. On the very first day of its operation, it was put to the test by an attack force of some 40 rebels. A serious firefight broke out and, during the course of the action, five rebels were killed and a further four fatally wounded. Eventually the rebels withdrew under cover of darkness. Although the SAS had anticipated an attack on their position, the men had not expected one on their first day. They later discovered the reason why it had come so soon: the rebels and the locals could easily spot any rocks that were out of place. From then on, they took care to occupy abandoned rebel positions.

The SAS soldiers quickly learned to respect their enemy. The rebels were good shots and always ready for a fight. On one occasion, the SAS sneaked up on a group that were hiding in a cave. After waiting until they were sure that all the rebels were inside, they opened fire with a number of Carl Gustav rounds. However, as they poured fire into the cave, the SAS suddenly found themselves under attack from a larger rebel force equipped with mortars and heavy machine guns. In anticipation of a counter-attack, the SAS soldiers had fortunately set up a 12.7mm (0.3in) Browning, and this proved highly effective in keeping the rebels pinned down while the SAS withdrew.

CASSINO POSITION

Realizing that using small sangars against the rebels was futile, the SAS set up a well-defended position on a high piece of ground. The rebels were aware of this position – called Cassino by the SAS – and, knowing that it was heavily defended, would not attack it directly; instead, they took to sniping and the odd mortar attack as a means of harassment. For extra support, the SAS was joined by signallers, medics and lifeguards, who brought up machine guns from their damaged armoured cars, and this back-up meant that the SAS could mount more patrols against the rebels on the Jebel Akhdar.

Despite the increasing success of the SAS, the rebels still held several key positions, which would surely have to be overcome to break the rebel control of the region. One of them, set upon a high cliff, had a wide entrance in between two peaks; the SAS called it Sabrina after a well-known TV presenter. It was their key objective, but it was well defended and had a complex, intricate cave system inside.

Regardless of the difficulty, the SAS formulated a daring plan of attack. It launched a diversionary flanking attack, carried out by 17 Troop, while 16 Troop attacked from the rear of the position by scaling the cliffs. As the attack began, the lifeguards fired on the position with their machine guns, while regular Omani forces provided mortar support. Under covering fire, the SAS stormed the caves within the rebels' position and a fierce battle developed. In the hand-to-hand fighting, many rebels were killed or wounded, but no casualties were sustained by the SAS. It was now becoming clear that more men were needed and that one under-strength squadron was insufficient.

In January 1959, A Squadron was deployed from Malaya to Oman to provide additional support. The squadron's commander, Major Johnny Cooper, wasted no time in getting his men acclimatized for the difficult operations that lay ahead. Within two weeks of his arrival, he used both squadrons to launch a major attack on the rebel forces. It was meticulously planned, and designed to ensure that the rebels' hold on the Jebel Akhdar would be broken once and for all. Before the attack started, the RAF was to fly over key rebel strongholds and take reconnaissance photos of the surrounding terrain, thus enabling the SAS squadrons to familiarize themselves with all the paths, tracks or wadis that led into the rebel positions, including some less obvious ones.

To sow confusion amongst the rebels before the attack, the SAS set up a number of well planned diversionary attacks in an attempt to draw them down from the highest peaks. They also summoned their local donkey-handlers and fed them false information about an attack that was apparently to come from Tanuf in the south-west. The rebels, after receiving this information from the donkey-handlers, diverted their forces to the area in anticipation of this attack. Meanwhile, A Squadron ascended the Persian Steps towards the SAS sangars of Cassino, while D Squadron set about mounting small operations near Tanuf to imply that this was indeed the main target area.

HEAVY LOADS

Everything was going to plan, but for the SAS soldiers, it was heavy going. Each man was carrying extra ammunition for both his personal weapon and the Troop support weapons; in some cases, the soldiers' loads weighed as much as 55kg (120lb), excluding rifles. Moving this amount of kit on flat ground would have been hard enough, but these men were climbing steep paths in burning-hot temperatures at high altitude.

However, the attack on the rebels was launched as planned with a diversionary action against Sabrina

CHRONOLOGY

Date	1958–59
Location	Jebel Akhdar, Oman
Operation	Two SAS Squadrons are deployed to Oman to put down a rebellion on the formidable natural fortress of Jebel Akhdar.
Date	1964–67
Location	Aden
Operation	SAS operations are mounted in the Radfan area against tribesmen and guerillas. These are known as 'Keeni-Meeni' operations.

TAKING THE JEBEL AKHDAR

Key

1 A Squadron captures Sabrina in the early hours of 26 January.
2 A Squadron joins D Squadron in Tanuf. One D Squadron troop launches a diversionary attack.
3 A and D Squadrons move to Kamah by truck in the evening of 26 January.
4 A Squadron takes Vincent. D Squadron takes Pyramid and Beercan. The RAF resupply the SAS by parachute.
5 The rebel leaders make their escape from the Jebel. Mopping up begins on the morning of 27 January.

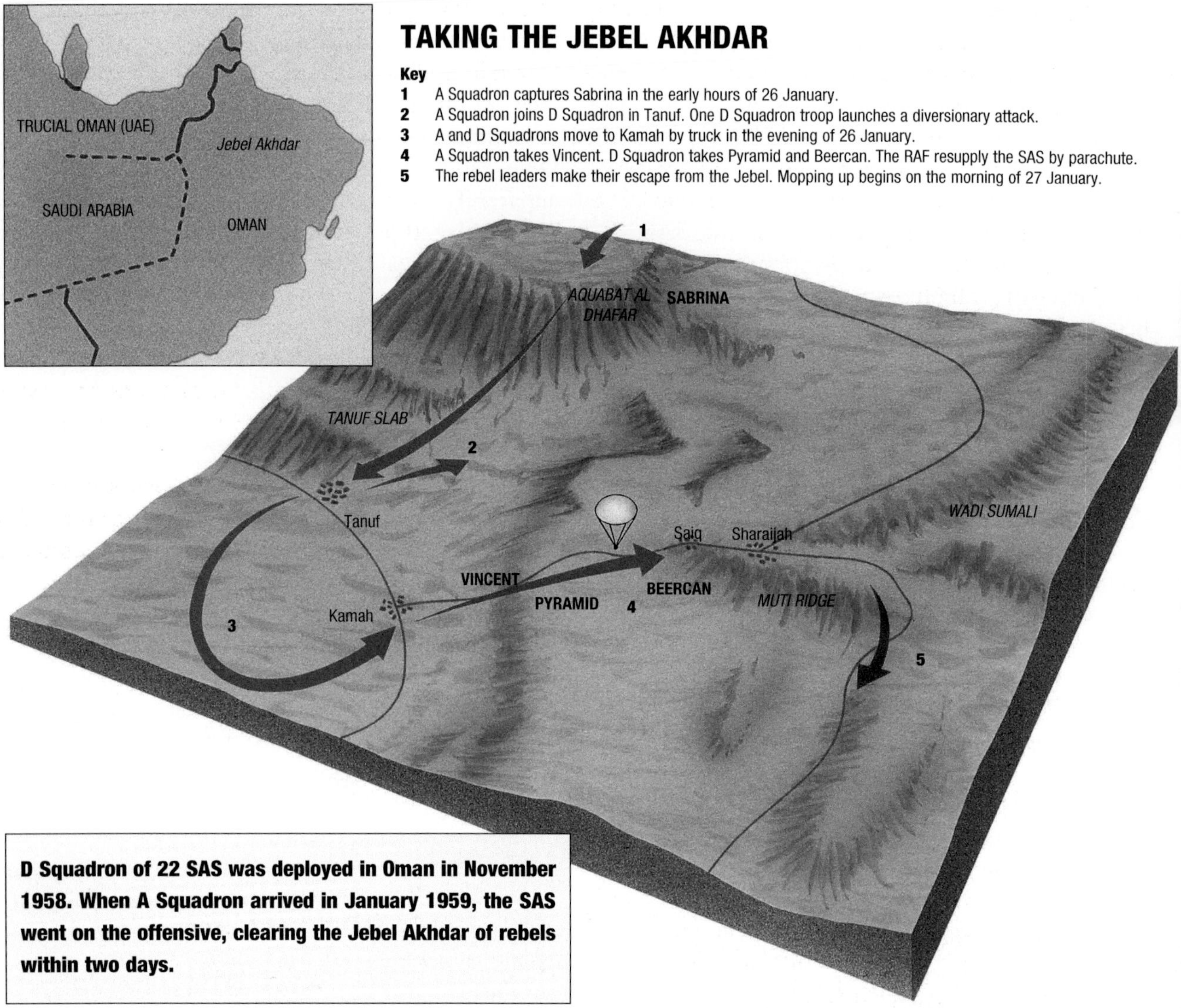

D Squadron of 22 SAS was deployed in Oman in November 1958. When A Squadron arrived in January 1959, the SAS went on the offensive, clearing the Jebel Akhdar of rebels within two days.

by A Squadron. Although it was involved in a fierce firefight, only one soldier was injured.

This part of the operation now complete, 4 Troop was left behind on Sabrina, while the rest moved back down to lower ground to meet up with the trucks that would take them to Tanuf.

At the same time, D Squadron made a number of diversionary attacks and then left one Troop behind, while the others joined up with A Squadron. They then moved to the village of Kamah to prepare for their main attack. So far, the rebels had fallen for the deception, but the worst was yet to come. At the forming-up point, D Squadron decided to advance first up the 2500m (8200ft) cliff, a journey that would take them some nine hours. The RAF photos helped them to negotiate the steep paths; the men at least knew that these paths led to a rebel position, and not a dead end. To avoid being ambushed on the way up, they made the climb mainly at night, with small scouting teams leading the way.

On their arduous journey up the steep slopes, two members of 16 Troop came across a machine-gun post. Fortunately for them, the rebels were sleeping. As for the rebels, their luck had just run out, and the SAS silenced them for good. D Squadron continued on its way up the plateau but, just as it reached the top, came under enemy fire from several different directions. Once D Squadron had summoned up air support, however, the rebels fled their positions, having failed to inflict any casualties.

For A Squadron, though, things went badly. As they were climbing up the slopes, dawn was breaking, and in the early morning light several soldiers were left exposed against the skyline. Taking aim, a rebel sniper fired a single shot, and his round managed to penetrate a soldier's backpack, causing a grenade inside it to explode. As a result, two soldiers were killed – troopers W. Carter and A. Bembridge – and another wounded.

Despite this setback, the remaining soldiers continued up the slope and joined up with D Squadron. As they dug in for an expected counterattack, the RAF flew overhead and dropped a number of supply containers by parachute near to their positions. The rebels assumed that an airborne assault was underway and, terrified, immediately fled their positions. The SAS was surprised at the rebels' hasty withdrawal, as it had always met stiff resistance on previous occasions. In the wake of the rebels' retreat, the men found documentation, maps and many heavy weapons, thus providing excellent intelligence for the Omani forces.

The SAS now only had one remaining pocket of resistance to take care of, and that was the rebels' main base at Saiq. As the men advanced across the

Below: Troopers take a break after establishing a forward operations base during Radfan operations. Like the Jebel Akhdar, the Radfan was inhospitable and all rations and ammunition had to be carried or supplied by the RAF.

SLR

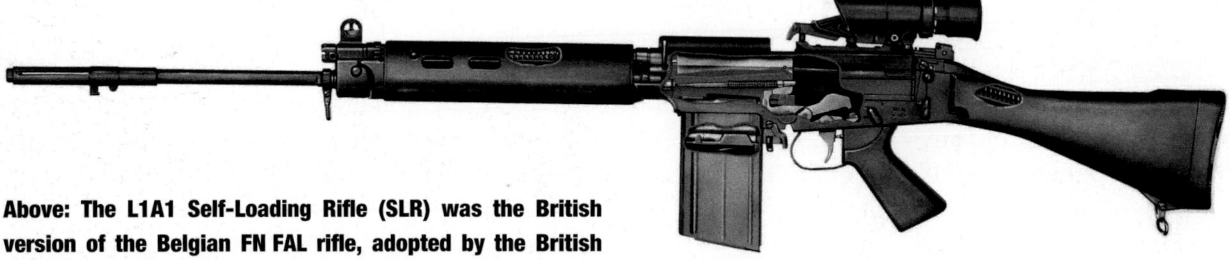

Above: The L1A1 Self-Loading Rifle (SLR) was the British version of the Belgian FN FAL rifle, adopted by the British Army in 1954. Its accuracy over ranges of more than 800m (2600ft) saw its use by some SAS troopers in the Gulf War.

plateau towards it, the RAF executed another airdrop near to the rebel position. Again it was only containers that were being dropped, but the rebels panicked just as their comrades had done, thinking it the start of a full-scale airborne assault. The Imam and some of his closest followers jumped on camels and fled towards Saudi Arabia, abandoning the rest of the rebels to their fates. Outnumbered and with no clear leader, these men naturally decided that enough was enough and gave up the rebellion, surrendering to the SAS.

For the SAS, the Jebel Akhdar campaign had been a remarkable success; it had completely crushed the rebellion within 10 weeks, in one of the world's most remote places, with the loss of only 3 men. The campaign made the SAS Regiment very popular with the British Government of the day, as it guaranteed a closer relationship with Oman, and the regiment's status grew in consequence.

The Jebel Akhdar had secured the survival of the SAS and proved that it had the ability to deploy at a moment's notice anywhere in the world, and perform in an effective and exemplary manner.

ADEN AND THE RADFAN 1964–67

In the early 1960s, Britain made a decision that was to have huge repercussions in the Middle East. The British Government would withdraw from her colonial responsibilities in Aden (now Yemen), which was at that time divided between the independent North Yemen, and a British Protectorate in the south. As they made preparations to leave, the British realized that their withdrawal would create a political powder-keg. They therefore proposed the creation of a federation that would comprise the region's various tribes. This idea was well intentioned, but it failed to reach fruition: Aden's political make-up was just too complicated. Some elements were pro-Soviet, while others were in favour of the British. Either way, it was inevitable that Britain's withdrawal would not be a peaceful affair.

The British understood that the problems in the region were of their own making and, indeed, they had done little to encourage loyalty to the Crown. In British hands since 1839, Aden had been coveted because it provided a good strategic position at the entrance to the Red Sea – hence the establishment of a large Royal Navy base there. The British had always been good at spotting countries that were rich in minerals or had geographic significance for the Empire, and they often furthered their own interests by following a foreign policy of 'divide and rule'. A common feature of the once-powerful

Right: Under heavy enemy fire, a patrol from the Parachute Regiment cautiously moves forward to a new position for better cover in the Radfan area. The SAS was called in to help the regular British Army units pacify the Radfan.

British Empire, this left a lasting legacy of division in Aden.

COLLAPSE OF ORDER

The final catalyst for trouble was the British decision to renege on an understanding with the leaders of the various states within the protectorate. These states had agreed to form the Federation of South Arabia (FSA) under the auspices of the British Government, but only on the understanding that the British would remain in Aden until after full independence. The provisional date scheduled for independence was 1968; however, once it was clear that the British were pulling out, all hell broke loose.

For years, the British had kept the lid on potential trouble by paying off the various factions' leaders with weapons and money. But as these pay-offs ended, so too did the loyalty to their Crown paymasters. The die had now been cast. As the British distanced themselves from the local warlords, Egypt provided aid for a coup in North Yemen and assisted the Yemenis in their bid to destabilize Aden. By now, Communist ideologies were circulating amongst the various tribespeople, and federal troops were regularly coming under fire from the Queteibi hill tribesmen. These tribespeople populated the Radfan area of Dhala to the north of Aden, and had a reputation for being violent and unpredictable.

By 1963, the situation had deteriorated to such an extent that the British were forced to take action, supporting the Federal Regular Army (FRA) with ground-attack aircraft and helicopters. For a while, the rebellion appeared to have been suppressed, but when the FRA were re-deployed to another region, things hotted up all over again, and the British forces were sent back to the Radfan for further operations against the rebels.

It was now becoming obvious that half-hearted operations were not the answer. What the British needed was a sustained campaign of action that would suppress the rebels and prevent any further escalation in the war. At this point, however, they had few military assets to use for such a campaign, so a Joint Reaction Force was set up. Known as Radforce, it comprised Royal Marines, members of the local FRA, the East Anglian Regiment, one company from 3rd Parachute Brigade, plus support assets such as an armoured car squadron and a battery of pack howitzers from the Royal Horse Artillery. Air support was provided by two squadrons of RAF Hunter ground-attack aircraft, plus a number of transport aircraft and helicopters.

As the situation deteriorated even further, A Squadron, SAS was recuperating back at Hereford after a second five-month jungle tour in Borneo. These men had been due to go to Aden for desert warfare training before the troubles started, and already had a small team based there carrying out a pre-deployment recce.

YEMENI OPERATIONS

The SAS had been involved in North Yemen since June 1963, when both Britain and France had become alarmed at the spread of Arab nationalism,

Left: An RAF Belvedere carries out a resupply mission to a gun position in Radfan in 1964. The air support from the RAF's ground attack aircraft and resupply helicopters was a vital factor in the success of the SAS.

Above: A Squadron, 22 SAS provide aid to locals as part of the 'hearts and minds' strategy near Falij in the Radfan. The trooper on the left is armed with a 7.62mm (0.3in) L1A1 SLR (Self-Loading Rifle).

which threatened the stability of the Gulf region. This upsurge of violence began in September 1962, when North Yemen's ruler, Imam Mohammed al-Badr, was toppled by a coup led by Colonel Abdullah Sallal. Sallal changed the country's name to the Yemen Arab Republic, and for this he received support from the Egyptians. In the aftermath, a task was assigned to the four-man SAS team: to link up with Royalist forces near Sana and train them with British-supplied weapons. This three-year operation was commanded by SAS veteran Johnny Cooper.

MOVE TO THE RADFAN

The main body of the SAS arrived in Aden during April 1964, and immediately began acclimatization training. It was decided that the men should move up to the Radfan Mountains as soon as was possible in preparation for future operations. A Squadron was based in a small desert town called Thumier less than 50km (30 miles) from the North Yemeni border. The plan was that its men would scale the highest peaks in the area overlooking the rebels' supply route from North Yemen. Once established, they would be able to report on rebel movements and call in air attacks if necessary. Both the Paras and Marines had been given objectives within the area, but for the Paras there was a major problem: they had no pathfinder unit available in theatre to designate a drop zone (DZ).

Here the SAS stepped in and offered to do the job, confirming that it had suitably qualified personnel available. On 29 April, 3 Troop, A Squadron despatched a nine-man patrol from Thumier to the proposed DZ to ensure its safety and to secure it for a drop the following night. The patrol, led by Captain Robin Edwards – who was relatively new to the SAS, having served in an infantry regiment

Above: An SAS soldier talks to villagers about possible rebel hideouts nearby. Valuable intelligence about the enemy's activities could be gained from such interactions and the SAS was careful to tap any potential source of information.

before joining A Squadron – was divided into two four-man teams with an experienced sergeant leading each one. Also within each team was a corporal and two troopers, most of whom had already seen action in Borneo.

As the patrol slowly made its way through the Radfan Mountains, one of the soldiers, Trooper Warburton, started to feel extremely ill. The SAS was now faced with a problem: the area was crawling with rebels, and a helicopter casevac was out of the question, given that the SAS was operating at night in hostile and difficult terrain. With only a few hours of darkness left, the men were forced to take drastic action. They removed Trooper Warburton's kit and evenly distributed it amongst the patrol. To ensure that he was looked after, they positioned him in the centre of the patrol and moved at his pace. After a short time, however, it became clear to Edwards that his men had no chance of making it to their objective before sunrise, and that an alternative lay-up point would have to be found.

By sheer luck, just above them was a group of rock sangars. These would provide useful cover during the day and allow them to observe the DZ and the surrounding area; accordingly, the patrol moved into the sangars and took up defensive positions against an attack. But all was not well. As day broke, the SAS spotted a small group of rebels moving up the mountain side, and to make matters worse, just below them was a hamlet complete with children and animals. This was an SAS soldier's nightmare scenario.

ENCOUNTER WITH A GOATHERD

For the first few hours, the SAS soldiers' luck held, until a goatherd and his goats started to make their way through a wadi just below the SAS position.

Edwards hoped that the goatherd would overlook them, but this was wishful thinking. Very soon after, the inevitable happened and a shot rang out around the mountains. From that point onwards, everything went rapidly downhill. Hearing the shot, the villagers spilled out of their houses and ran up towards the SAS position. As they approached the sangar, a short burst of gunfire took out a number of the rebels, and the rest of them hit the dirt. Some tried to outflank the SAS team, but they were quickly cut down.

The rebels took stock of the situation and evidently decided it would be best to move to a ridge overlooking the sangars. From there, they could snipe at the SAS team, knowing full well that if the troopers tried to break out, they could be easily picked off. Unfortunately for them, Edwards, however, had anticipated their move and called in air support. As the rebels took up their positions on the ridge line, a pair of RAF Hunters appeared overhead and strafed them with their cannon.

Taken completely by surprise, a number of the rebels were killed in the initial attack. The rest, however, took cover, knowing that all they need do was to wait until the aircraft were forced to return to base for refuelling. And even with this air support, the SAS team were still pinned down. Their only hope of escaping from this nightmare was to wait for the cover of darkness.

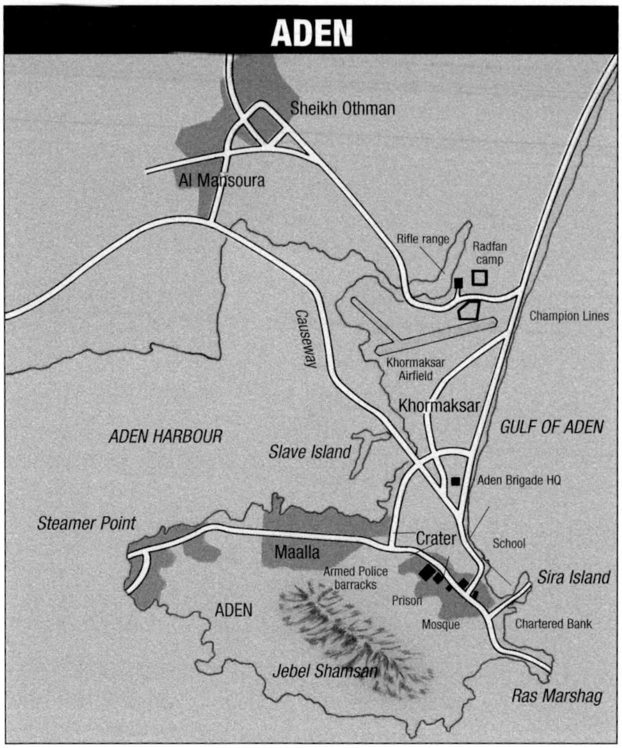

REBEL ONSLAUGHT

Shortly before sunset, the RAF Hunters were called in again to rake the ground above the sangars, and this they did with deadly effect. After the aircraft had flown back to base, however, the rebels resumed their sniping at the SAS team and hit two of the troopers. Fortunately, their wounds were minor and they went on fighting. As the sun finally set, the rebels rushed the sangars, but were cut to pieces by the deadly accurate SAS fire.

As soon as it was dark, the SAS began to move out of the sangars, each team providing mutual support to cover the withdrawal. Before smashing the radio to ensure that no rebels could monitor the British forces channels, they used it to call in a delayed artillery barrage on the sangars. This would, they presumed, take care of any rebels still loitering around after they had withdrawn. At this point, Trooper Warburton's body was discovered. He had been killed in the last firefight, and it was with great reluctance that his comrades were forced to leave his body behind.

However, as the SAS teams moved out of the sangars, Captain Edwards was hit by several rounds and fell to the ground. Other members of his team tried in vain to pull him into cover, but it was too late: he, too, was dead. The rebels had zeroed in on him, making it impossible for the others to attempt a rescue. As the team slowly vacated the sangars with the wounded, and made their way forwards, two of the troopers soon realized that they were being trailed by rebels and set up a snap ambush to catch them off guard. Springing their ambush with deadly effect, they killed all of the rebels who had been on their trail since leaving the sangars.

Some time later, the very same thing happened: more rebels trailed them as they made their way towards Thumier, and again the same two troopers set an identical ambush and were just as successful. The SAS soldiers eventually reached the Dhala Road and flagged down a passing armoured car, which took care of the wounded troopers, while the remaining members of the patrol walked back to their base and safety. After the conflict was over, one of the corporals involved in ambushing the rebels received the Military Medal for outstanding bravery.

LOW-INTENSITY CONFLICT

For the British, Aden was a political disaster on a grand scale, yet for the military, it was initially deemed a low-intensity conflict. As time went on, it became clear that the British knew little or nothing about the Radfan rebels, and this dearth of intelligence was surely the reason why 9 Troop had encountered so many problems on its patrol. Nonetheless, under pressing circumstances, they had successfully fought their way out of an area that was crawling with rebels.

The SAS was not alone in meeting problems on its first operation within Aden. The East Anglians and 4 RTR also ran into stiff rebel opposition while carrying out a diversionary attack on Wadi Rabwa. This had been set up as a means of drawing the rebels away from the DZ so that the Paras would have an unopposed landing. To the Paras' credit, they were still willing to make a jump at the proposed DZ, but their mission was cancelled. Ultimately, it took the entire Radforce a month to finally clear the Radfan Mountains of rebels.

For the SAS, operations continued within Aden, but they were now conducted on a smaller and less risky scale. The men were tasked with deep recce patrols and manning desert observation hides that monitored the movement of rebels from North Yemen and other areas within Aden. As the campaign wore on, the SAS was also tasked with intelligence-gathering within the urban areas of Aden, something it would do in Northern Ireland a few years later. From now on, the main area of conflict centred around the port area of Aden, and was mainly linked to terrorist-related violence.

Many political organizations within Aden jockeyed for position prior to the British declaration of independence. Some were pro-British, while others were Soviet-controlled, such as the National Liberation Front (NLF). The other organization heavily involved in terrorism was the Egyptian-backed Front for the Liberation of South Yemen (FLOSY). Once the British Government formally announced its decision to withdraw from Aden in 1966, the power struggle between the NLF and FLOSY intensified to such a degree that local people started to attack British servicemen's families stationed there. Soon the situation was rapidly spiralling out of control.

The SAS was tasked with anti-terrorist operations within the Crater and Sheikh Othman district of Aden, an area notorious for its narrow alleys and streets, which made it perfect for ambushing British forces. The key problem for the British was the lack of intelligence on terrorist movements. Consequently an operation was mounted within Aden, which required members of the SAS to dress up and pass themselves off as Arabs.

'KEENI MEENI' JOBS

A 20-man team was put together for this highly sensitive role and operated out of Ballycastle House, essentially a block of flats within the Kormaksar military district of the port. These operations were known as 'Keeni Meeni' jobs, taken from the Swahili phrase describing the undulating movement of a snake in long grass. At the time, there was considerable doubts over the SAS soldiers' ability to fool the locals into thinking that they really were Arabs.

However, far from making a mess of this operation, the SAS soldiers were superb at passing themselves off as Arabs, for several reasons: some of the SAS soldiers were Fijian, with dark skin very similar to the locals'; and many of the troopers had beards and spoke perfect Arabic.

By December 1967, the protectorates were abandoned and power fell to the NLF, who created the pro-Soviet People's Democratic Republic of Yemen. After the British left Aden, this new régime wasted no time in trying to destabilize its neighbour Oman, meaning that British forces would again see action in the region — all this the result of the short-sighted policies of the British Government.

For the SAS, Aden had been a useful campaign, honing the regiment's desert fighting skills. During their involvement in the campaign, three of the regiment's squadrons had seen action. It was also a worthwhile experience in preparing the SAS for future anti-terrorist operations around the world.

However, there was one particular incident that marred the regiment's deployment in Aden, and this was the way in which the deaths of Edwards and Warburton were handled by the media and the regiment. The SAS later learned that the heads of their fallen comrades had been cut off by the rebels and mounted on poles for all to see in the Yemeni capital of Taiz. Obviously, for these soldiers' families, it was extremely distressing to learn the truth of what really happened in Aden from the media, rather than from the SAS Regiment itself. For Operational Security (OPSEC) reasons, they had been under the impression that their loved ones were training in relative safety on Salisbury Plain, England.

Aden will always be seen by many as a campaign that could have been avoided if only politicians had thought through their actions. Their failure to do so meant that there many unnecessary British – and local – deaths.

Below: A Radfan tribesman surrenders to members of the 3rd Battalion of the Parachute Regiment in Wadi Taym. Lacking a white flag, the tribesman has improvised with a multi-coloured piece of material instead.

CHAPTER FIVE

OMAN 1970–76

For the SAS, the end of the Aden fiasco brought a well-earned period of rest and recuperation from what had been a long, and at times, harsh campaign. By now, the SAS had well and truly established itself as a key unit in the British Army, but there was no way of predicting where the regiment would be required to fight next.

Around this time, the SAS was tasked with few varied operational deployments around the world, apart from routine training exercises in Germany in support of the British Army of the Rhine (BAOR). For this reason, the SAS contacted the Sultan, Said bin Taimur of Oman, asking for his permission to deploy in Oman for training purposes. The Sultan readily agreed, and the SAS was inserted there a short time later.

There was, of course, a hidden agenda – on both sides. For the SAS, war is work. Its men had seen potential trouble brewing in the Omani region after the British withdrawal from Aden, and their deployment in Oman meant that they would be in a position to react quickly to any emergency. The Sultan too was worried about the deterioration in the region's stability, and knew that an SAS presence could be hugely valuable to him in case anything should develop there.

Left: In the background of the photograph is the Gendarmerie Fort at Mirbat, prior to the rebels' attack. Note the SAS mortar pit in the foreground, which played a key part in the defence of the BATT (British Army Training Team) house.

Oman held a key strategic position in the Persian Gulf, through which most of the region's oil exports passed. As a co-owner of the Musandum Peninsula, along with the United Arab Emirates, Oman could easily threaten Iraq's oil trade, and to counter this threat Iraq had set about befriending the independent hill tribesmen of the Musandum, providing them with effective weapons and military training. All this covert assistance was carried out by Iraqi forces who had illegally entered the country, and were now openly encouraging insurrection against the Sultan and his forces.

EVICTING THE IRAQIS

The Iraqi infiltration of Musandum was discovered, and a request via the British-officered Sultan's Armed Forces was made to the SAS to help evict the invaders. The SAS wasted no time in deploying a reinforced Boat Troop to Musandum by inflatables: its men meant business. Simultaneously, to ensure that no Iraqis could escape inland, Air Troop made a parachute jump behind their known positions to act as a cut-off group. Ultimately, they were not needed, as the Iraqis were quickly rounded up and taken prisoner by Boat Troop. Sadly there was one SAS casualty during the operation, a soldier from Air Troop who died when his parachute failed to open after performing a HALO (High Altitude Low Opening) jump.

For a while, it seemed as if this action had stemmed the impending revolt, However, the SAS men were aware that all was not well within Oman, and that serious trouble was on the horizon for the Sultan, and for them. For the average Omani, life had dealt a bad hand: the Sultan denied them education, medical care and any hint of democracy, and although Oman was an immensely wealthy country, the Sultan believed its wealth belonged to him personally, and gave next to nothing back to his people.

THE SULTAN'S UNPOPULARITY

Consequently, Oman was a fertile country in which to cultivate hate and loathing for its ruler. The Sultan's enemies saw him as an excellent recruiting sergeant for their own cause, and thus made no attempts at assassination. For those who did openly show contempt, justice was swift and unmerciful. Serious crimes were answered by execution, and the offender's family was punished by having its water supply turned off. Needless to say, the British Government knew it would have to find a bloodless way to remove him. Although Oman had always been a good friend to Britain, the Sultan had now become a hindrance.

As the situation in Oman continued to deteriorate, the Sultan's son and the Wali of Dhofar contacted the British Government with the information that they were about to mount a peaceful coup against the Sultan. The British Government gave its support, and on 23 July 1970, the Wali confronted him in his apartment. A short struggle took place in which both men were injured. However the outcome was positive for the Omani people, as the Sultan abdicated in favour of his son, Prince Qaboos. As part of the deal, the former Sultan was exiled to London for the rest of his life, while the SAS provided bodyguards for Qaboos.

For the British, Sultan Qaboos was a different proposition from his father. Educated in England, he had attended Sandhurst Military Academy, where he had learned much about the British military. While Qaboos set about reforming his country and introducing basic human rights for his people, the SAS was employed in devising a strategy for his country, loosely based on the 'hearts and minds' campaign that had been conducted in Malaya and Borneo.

The new strategy, devised by Lieutenant-Colonel Johnny Watts, was based on the following principles:

1. The establishment of an intelligence cell that would monitor Radio Aden and its propaganda machine, and then counter it.
2. Founding and running an information cell that provided reliable and accurate information about the Omani Government's civil aid programme.
3. The establishment of a medical officer supported by SAS medics.
4. The establishment of a veterinary officer to treat animals owned by the local Omani people.
5. The raising of Dhofari units to fight for Sultan Qaboos.

The strategy became known as the 'Five Fronts' Campaign, and it effectively called for the SAS initially to train the Omanis, with the aim that they would eventually take over and be self-sufficient. In support of the campaign, the SAS carried out leaflet drops over the rebels' positions, informing them that changes in Oman were for the best, and that they should switch sides. For those rebels who joined up with the Sultan's Dhofari units, an amnesty was granted, guaranteeing them protection from prosecution.

ADOO REBELS

The rebels were known in Oman as the 'adoo' (Arabic for enemy) and were made up of the Dhofar Liberation Front (DLF) and the People's Front for the Liberation of the Occupied Arabian Gulf (PFLOAG). These two groups were different in their make-up. The DLF were essentially traditional Dhofaris, while the PFLOAG was a Communist group based in Yemen. Eventually the two amalgamated, but this caused problems for their Muslim members, many of whom felt ostracized from the group, and they took advantage of the amnesty to defect.

The first success for the SAS and the Sultan came when a large group of guerillas under the command of Salim Mubarak turned themselves in. Mubarak revealed that he had become disenchanted with the PFLOAG's attitudes, and so he and his men had fought their way off the Jebel Dhofar to reach the Sultan's forces. The SAS and Army intelligence were quick to debrief Mubarak and were amazed at the level of valuable intelligence he possessed. Only too keen to help the British, he advocated the formation of an anti-rebel 'firqat' (Arabic for company) made up of disenchanted guerillas.

The SAS set about retraining some of the ex-rebels in British tactics and operational doctrine. The firqats' AK-47 assault rifles were replaced by 7.62mm (0.3in) FN self-loading rifles. One problem was the language barrier; normally one trooper in each four-man SAS team was a linguistic specialist, but here this ratio was insufficient. Eventually every

Below: Sultan Qaboos (left) greets members of his armed forces. The Sultan had been educated at the Royal Military Academy Sandhurst, in England, and requested British military help in Oman.

SAS trooper needed a working knowledge of Arabic in order to train the firqats. However, on an official level, the British forces were in Oman for training purposes only, and hence were referred to as British Army Training Teams, or BATTs. Back in the UK, the Oman operation was a low-key affair. Very few people were even aware that British forces were fighting in this part of the world. The situation in Northern Ireland was so critical at the time that all eyes were fixed on the streets there.

HEARTS AND MINDS

While engaged in the firqat training, the SAS was heavily involved in the 'hearts and minds' programme, helping the locals by providing medical treatment for basic ailments and, where possible, building new water wells. Their efforts were, of course, greatly appreciated, and within six months of the campaign more than 200 rebels changed sides. Some had previously served in the Sultan's Armed Forces (SAF) under Qaboos' father, but had become disillusioned. After seeing the country change for the better under Qaboos, they re-enlisted.

These men were so valuable to the SAS that, wherever possible, they were assigned to their local villages as protection. By 1971, both B and G Squadrons were deployed in Oman, and the time seemed right to go on the offensive against the adoo. By now, the firqats were well established along the Salalah coastal plain in camps south of the desert highlands, known as the Jebel Massif. However, this area was heavily occupied by rebels, and so a plan was devised to shift them out gradually by moving British and Omani forces into a set area for a short period. Once the rebels had been ousted from their positions, landing strips, helipads and water wells were built, giving the firqats a solid base from which to launch future operations.

On 24 February 1971, the SAS and a firqat mounted a joint operation against the coastal town of Sudh. From their point of view, it was a complete success, helping strengthen confidence between both forces. After this, the SAS were quick to realize that the firqats' strengths lay in small, recce-type operations rather than large-scale infantry assaults. Each firqat was made up of between 30 and 40 men, and by the end of the campaign the number of former rebels serving in these units totalled almost 2000.

In March 1971, Lt Col Johnny Watts mounted an attack on the Jebel Dhofar, using the SAS and the firqats in a short, probing operation. Despite being limited in scope, the combined operation was successful and Watts decided that a bigger operation should be mounted on the Jebel Dhofar to clear the adoos away, thus establishing a foothold on this strategic position.

Codenamed 'Jaguar', the operation would involve both SAS squadrons, the firqats, two companies of the Sultan's Armed Forces, and a platoon of the Askari tribesmen; in all, a combined force of over 800 men, many of whom were highly experienced in desert warfare. The only potential problem was the timing of Operation 'Jaguar', as it coincided with Ramadan, which began that year on 20 October. Acutely aware of the significance of this date, Watts was careful to obtain a dispensation from the religious leaders so that his Omani soldiers and the firqats could fight during Ramadan.

OPERATION JAGUAR

Operation 'Jaguar' was launched on 2 October 1971 with an attack against the adoo, who were now occupying an old government airstrip to the east of Jibjat on the Jebel Dhofar. The attack force had been split into two groups for the first stage of 'Jaguar'. The first group consisted of B Squadron, two firqats and the Askaris, who were to advance from the lower foothills towards the airstrip under cover of darkness. Advancing on foot – it was impossible for vehicles to operate in this rough terrain – meant that each man had to carry a large amount of kit in very hot, uncomfortable conditions. To the south, the second group, a small contingent from

Right: Captain Roe of the Sultan of Muscat and Oman Armed Forces, translates on behalf of 22 SAS' Regimental Quartermaster Sergeant Amor during a bartering session with local traders.

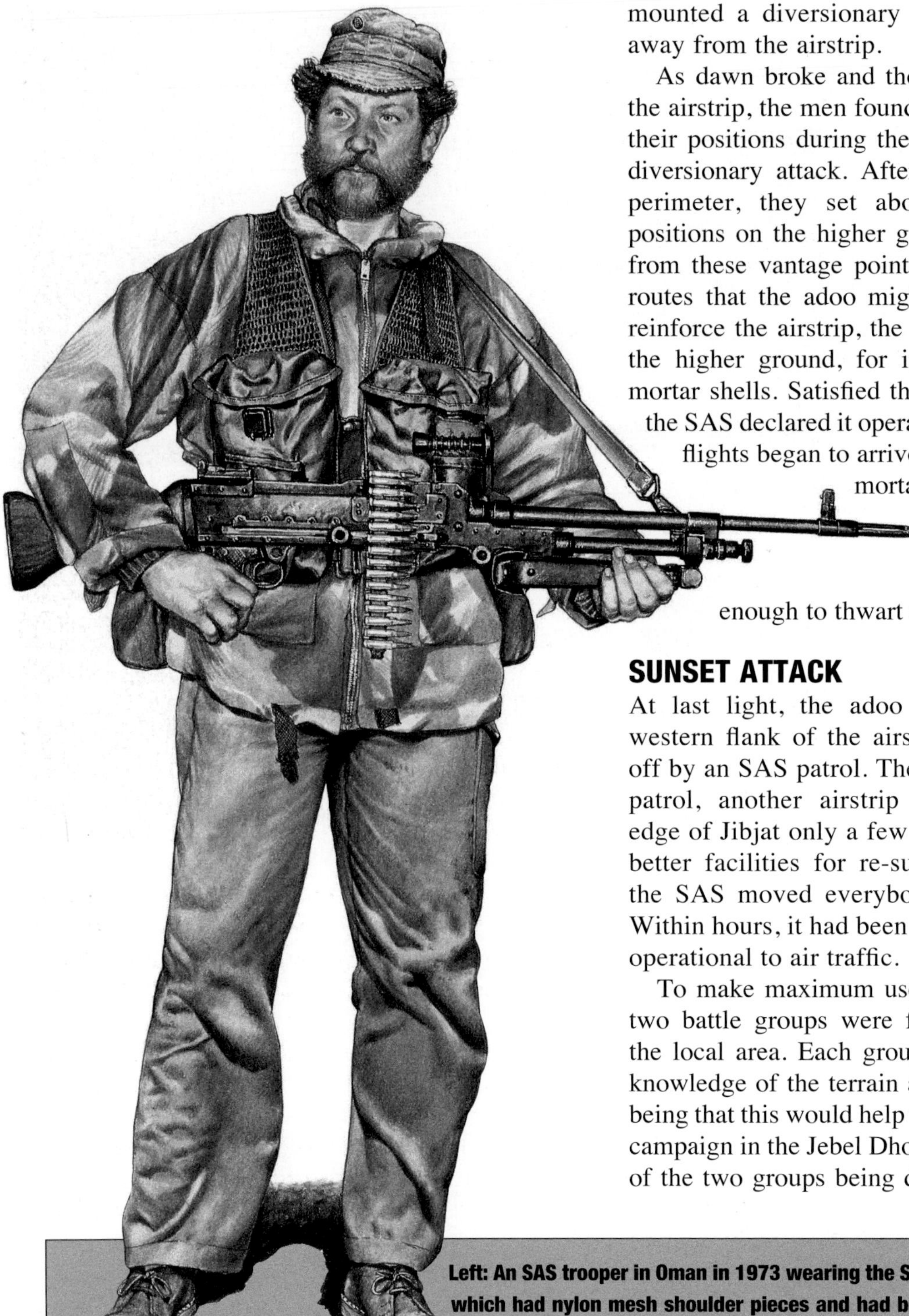

mounted a diversionary attack to draw the adoo away from the airstrip.

As dawn broke and the SAS proceeded towards the airstrip, the men found that all the adoo had fled their positions during the night, warned off by the diversionary attack. After securing the immediate perimeter, they set about occupying defensive positions on the higher ground around the airstrip; from these vantage points, they could observe the routes that the adoo might use to attack. To help reinforce the airstrip, the SAS built sangars around the higher ground, for improved protection from mortar shells. Satisfied that the airstrip was secure, the SAS declared it operational, and the first supply flights began to arrive, bringing in extra troops, mortars, artillery and supplies. By mid–afternoon, over 800 men were in position, more than enough to thwart an enemy counterattack.

SUNSET ATTACK

At last light, the adoo made an attack on the western flank of the airstrip, but this was beaten off by an SAS patrol. The next day, during a recce patrol, another airstrip was discovered on the edge of Jibjat only a few miles away. This offered better facilities for re-supply, and the day after, the SAS moved everybody to this new location. Within hours, it had been secured and was declared operational to air traffic.

To make maximum use of the combined forces, two battle groups were formed in order to probe the local area. Each group had its own firqat with knowledge of the terrain and the people, the theory being that this would help win the 'hearts and minds' campaign in the Jebel Dhofar. However, within days of the two groups being deployed, one came under

Left: An SAS trooper in Oman in 1973 wearing the SAS Lightweight Combat Pack, which had nylon mesh shoulder pieces and had been first tested by the SAS in Borneo. Typically he wears civilian suede shoes for comfort.

sustained attack from a strong rebel force, which was both well armed and trained. During the firefight, an SAS Sergeant was killed before the rebels were driven back. Several days later, the other group found itself under attack, after coming across an important rebel water hole that was well defended by a large rebel force. The SAS decided to mount an assault. It took just a few days for the men and their support force to evict the rebels successfully, incurring only light casualties.

Around this time, thy were forced to deal with a crisis that defies belief. Here they were, right in the middle of the rebels' backyard, fighting for their lives, and the firqats suddenly decided to stop fighting and observe Ramadan. Absolutely furious, Lt Col Watts threatened to withdraw SAS support for the firqats. The setback in his plans was so serious that he was forced to abandon positions his men had just taken and withdraw to a place known as 'White City'.

After holding a quickly convened meeting, the firqats decided better of their actions and resumed fighting alongside the SAS. An even more determined Watts now mounted a maximum strike against the adoo in an effort to break their hold on the Jebel Dhofar, and by 12 October, the SAS and the Sultan's forces had succeeded in advancing 25km (15 miles) into rebel-held territory and had set up a forward operations base only 8km (5 miles) from the adoos' main stronghold.

Above: A photograph of Danny Elliott of 22 SAS in Oman, on whom the artwork opposite is based. He is armed with a 7.62mm (0.3in) General Purpose Machine Gun (GPMG), a Belgian design still occassionally used by the British Army.

DAILY BATTLES

By now, the SAS and the adoos were engaging each other on an almost daily basis. The adoo would often employ their mortars against the British base in a desperate attempt to drive them away, but this was far from effective, since clearly the SAS, with the Sultan's forces and firqats, now had the upper hand. Over the next few months, the adoo were forced out of the Jebel Dhofar's key strategic locations. Frustrated at their lack of success against the superior British operational tactics, they decided that they needed a major victory over the Sultan's forces to prove that they still presented a threat. They mounted the odd token attack against both British and firqat patrols, but these operations did little to raise their morale.

The adoo also had another difficulty concerning recruitment; the SAS 'hearts and minds' campaign was functioning so efficiently that nobody wanted to join them. Retaining men was now also starting to become a problem, since the Sultan's amnesty deal and his promises of aid were far more attractive then living in abject fear on a bleak, barren hill. For the adoo, the only hope of survival lay in carrying out

such a spectacular attack against Sultan Qaboos and his supporters that their credibility with the people of Oman would be restored.

The place chosen for this attack was the coastal hamlet of Mirbat, which lay 65km (40 miles) east of Salalah. For the adoo, Mirbat seemed to be very vulnerable to attack. It was at the end of the Salalah road, meaning that after an attack, reinforcements would take some time to arrive there. It was also attractive as a target because of its proximity to the foothills of Jebel Dhofar. The adoo could easily come down from their strongholds, hit Mirbat, and effortlessly melt away in dozens of directions. Looking at all their options, the rebel leaders agreed that nothing on the table was as attractive a target as Mirbat. Their men would go in at first light on 19 July 1972.

MIRBAT

From a military point of view, the hamlet was merely a small garrison, containing a firqat and a nine-man SAS training team billeted in an old house. Also present was the local police station for the Dhofar Gendarmerie, which was located on the northern outskirts of the hamlet. The weather on the day of the assault was perfect from an attacker's point of view: it was raining and visibility was poor, which meant that the Sultan of Oman's Air Force (SOAF) could not provide air support once the shooting started. The attack had been meticulously planned, right down to the adoo using the low cloud base on the hills to cover the movement of their forces prior to the first assault. They were extremely well armed with AK-47 assault rifles, 12.7mm (0.5in) heavy machine guns, mortars, rocket-propelled grenades and one 75mm (2.95in) gun; in addition, they were also excellent marksmen.

Left: An adoo guerrilla seen in 1973. He is armed with a 7.62mm (0.3in) AKM Soviet-built assault rifle, and wears a camouflage smock over his traditional local dress. Despite his lack of boots, he could move quickly across broken terrain.

Above: Sometimes there are places where even a four-wheel-drive vehicle is useless. This SAS trooper is making good use of a local mule for a resupply mission. In Oman, it was impossible for the SAS to live off the land.

LACK OF ACTIVITY

Prior to the attack, the adoo had deliberately wound down activity in the area to give the impression that they were a spent force and had little fight left. This tactic worked to a point, and the occupants of Mirbat started to switch off and become a little too relaxed. The SAS team based in the BATT house was also guilty of winding down, knowing that its tour was almost over. A few days before the main attack, however, the first hint came that something was in the air, after a small group of rebels mounted a limited action near Mirbat as a diversion. However, apart from sending out a firqat of around 60 men to search for these rebels, little else was done to reinforce security.

The first adoo attack came at first light. It was launched against a small force of gendarmes who were mounting a picket about 1000m (3280ft) from the wire compound north of their fort. Most of the gendarmes were quickly silenced with knives, although one of them managed to fire a warning shot before being killed. With the element of surprise now gone, the adoo opened fire on the fort with their mortars from a position just north of it, known as the Jebel Ali.

By this time, the men from 8 Troop, B Squadron were awake and following orders from their commanding officer, 23-year-old Captain Mike Kealy. Everyone had a set defensive position to assume during an attack; it was a well-rehearsed and frequently practised movement. Most of the SAS team went to the top of the BATT house and, from the roof, manned the 7.62mm (0.3in) General Purpose Machine Gun (GPMG), 12.7mm (0.5in) Browning heavy machine gun, and 81mm (3.2in) mortar from their sandbagged positions. Meanwhile, as the team prepared for the imminent attack due to come from the north side, one of the SAS troopers, Fijian Corporal Labalaba, sprinted from the BATT house over to the old Gendarmerie fort to man an 25-pounder field gun that was emplaced near to the fort's front door.

MORTAR ATTACKS

As the SAS waited in the BATT house for the main attack to come, the men realized that the adoo mortars were being used to break down the barbed wire surrounding the fort. At this stage, though, there was little they could do about it. Their mortar was busily engaging the 200-plus adoo now attacking both them and the gendarmes in the fort. One of the SAS troopers radioed for reinforcements from Salalah, explaining that they were in dire straits and needed help fast. By a stroke of good fortune, B Squadron's replacements, G Squadron, were already preparing to move out of their base camp for a day's range practice, and had nine GPMGs available for only 23 troopers – an amazing amount of firepower for such a small team to wield. For their besieged colleagues at Mirbat, their arrival could not come quick enough.

Right: The battle for Mirbat should have been a resounding victory for the adoo, but the resilience and fighting spirit of the SAS and local forces inflicted a major defeat, from which they were unable to recover.

ATTACK ON MIRBAT 19 JULY 1972

Key

1 A Dhofar Gendarmerie picket on Jebel Ali is disturbed by the adoo, raising the alarm
2 The Gendarmarie fort is targeted by the adoo, whose first attacks are repulsed.
3 The SAS lay down supporting fire from their mortar and the roof of the BATT House.
4 Kealy and Tobin head for the fort from the BATT House.
5 Labalaba and Tobin are mortally wounded.
6 Omani Strikemaster jets arrive, strafing the adoo and driving them back.
7 SAS reinforcements arrive by helicopter. The adoo retreat.

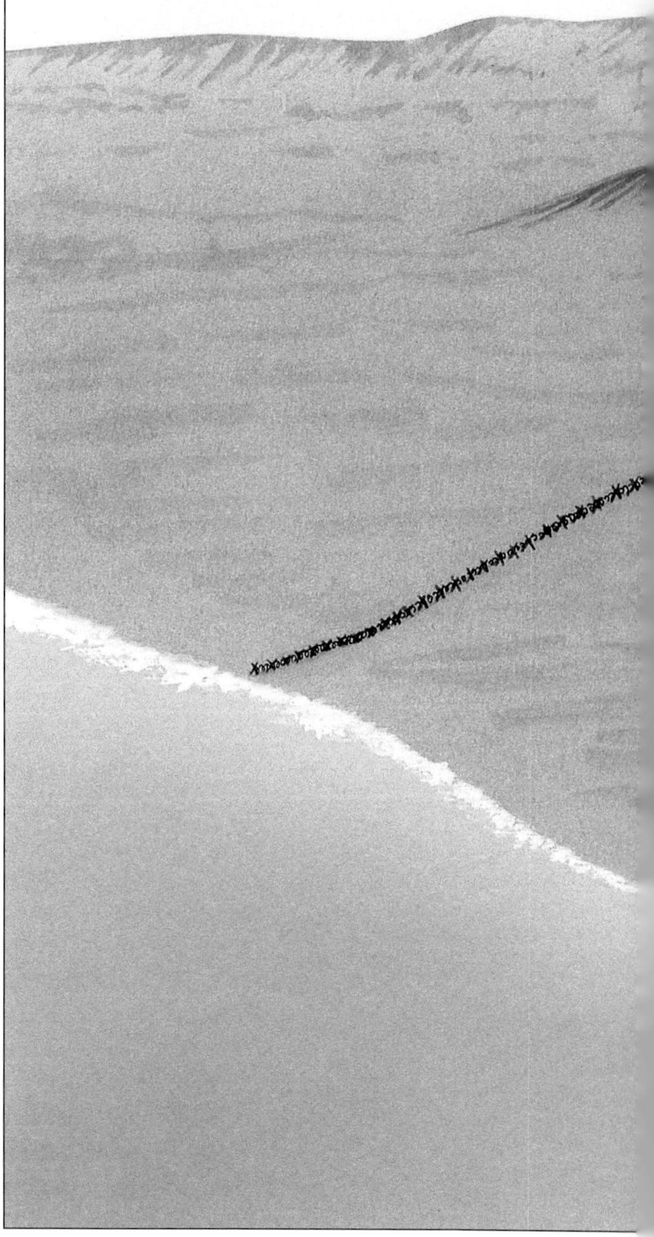

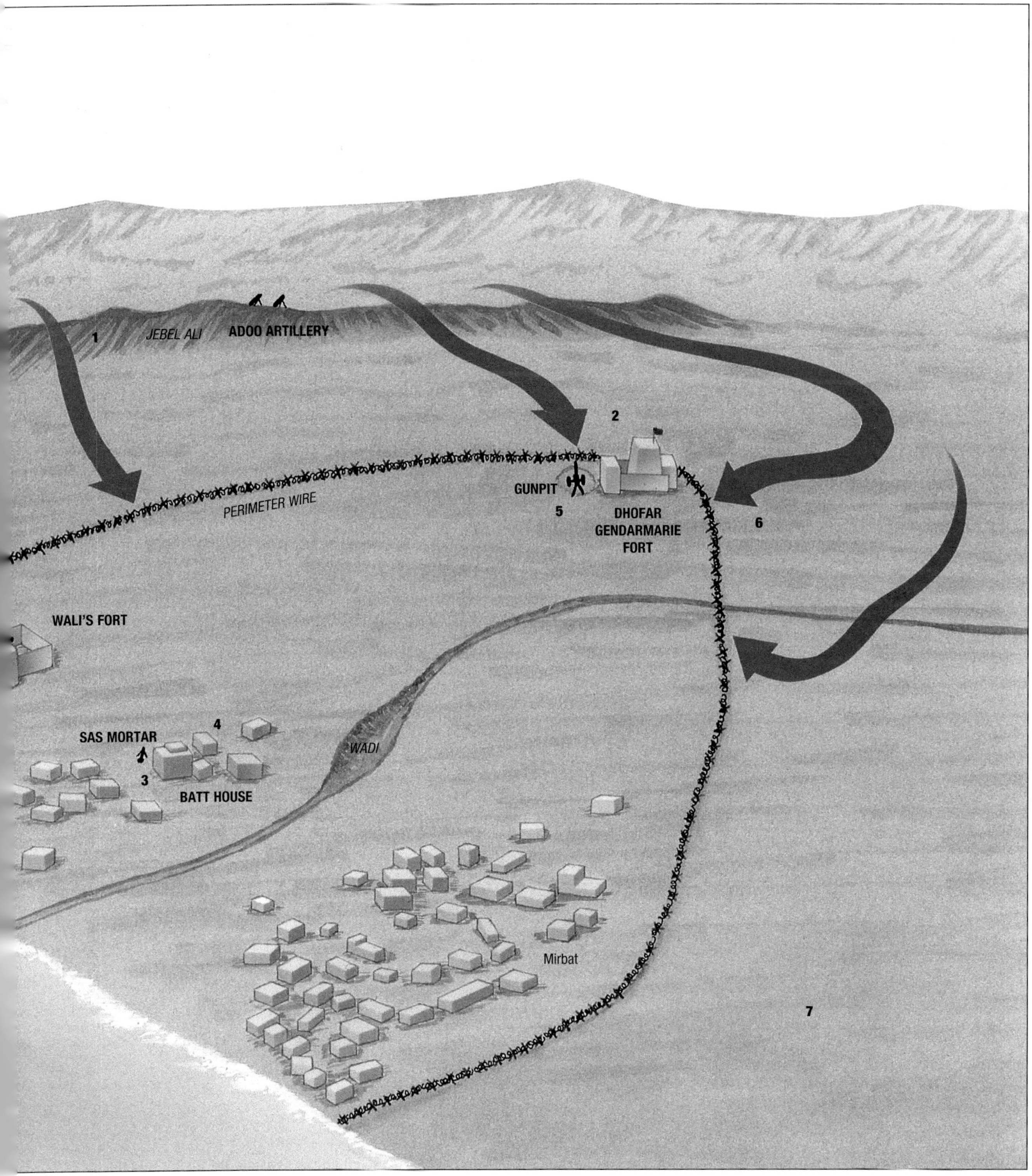
1
JEBEL ALI
ADOO ARTILLERY
2
GUNPIT
5
PERIMETER WIRE
DHOFAR
GENDARMARIE
FORT
6
WALI'S FORT
4
SAS MORTAR
3
BATT HOUSE
WADI
Mirbat
7

25-POUNDER

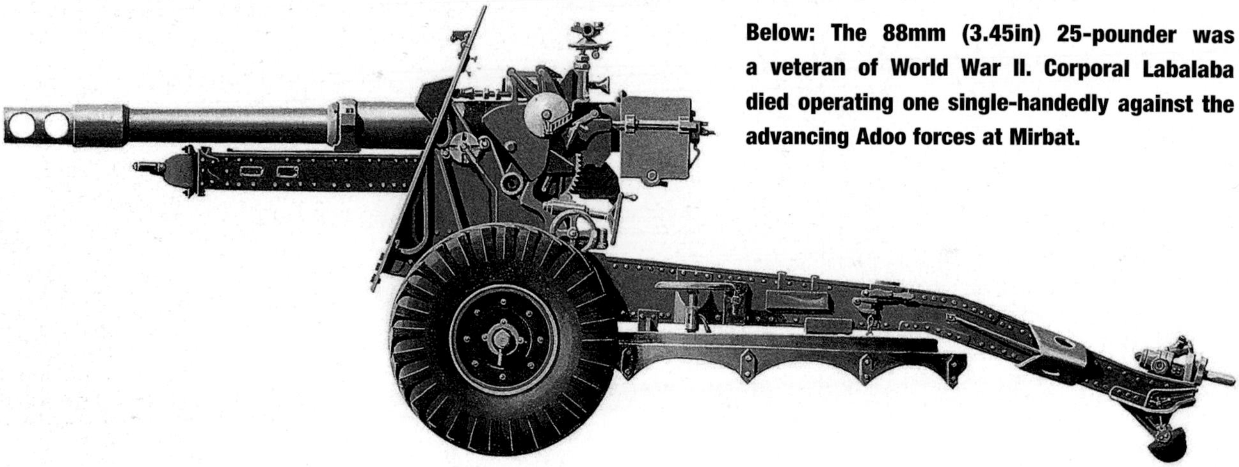

Below: The 88mm (3.45in) 25-pounder was a veteran of World War II. Corporal Labalaba died operating one single-handedly against the advancing Adoo forces at Mirbat.

As the SAS poured heavy fire onto the attacking adoo, it became obvious that the rebels' priority targets were the Gendarmes fort and the BATT house. The situation was now increasingly desperate for the defenders of Mirbat, and Kealy knew it. He realized that his men would have to pull out all the stops if they were to have a chance of breaking the enemies advance. In the meantime, outside the gendarmes' fort, the Omani gunner manning the 25-pounder was hit and severely wounded. Corporal Labalaba took over from the gunner and undertook the entire process of loading, laying and firing drills single-handedly, but soon, under intense fire coming from several different directions, he was hit in the jaw and knocked back against the sandbags surrounding the gun. Despite his injuries, he managed to radio the BATT house for help, and another Fijian trooper sprinted 400m (1312ft) across open ground to give assistance.

After charging across the gap between the BATT house and the gendarmes' fort, Trooper Savesaki applied a dressing to his injured colleague's face, before he too was hit. In an act of incredible bravery, Labalaba picked himself up from the floor and started to fire the field gun again. But then tragedy struck; another hail of bullets hit him, and this was to prove fatal. Nearby, despite suffering many casualties, the gendarmes in the fort were putting up stiff resistance. To the north-west of the BATT house, there was another small fort manned by around 30 Askari tribesmen who were loyal to the Wali of Dhofar, and they too were engaging the rebels with their rifles, acquitting themselves well.

CHRONOLOGY

Date	1970–76
Location	Oman
Operation	SAS is sent to Oman to defeat Communist guerillas attempting to overthrow the government of Oman. This particular operation features a highly successful 'hearts and minds' campaign that persuades other Omanis not to join in the insurgency.

HELP ON ITS WAY

While everybody desperately fought off attack after attack from the determined adoo force, help was on

Above: A small force of the Sultan of Oman's army on board a Skyvan. Rebels were encouraged to switch sides by an amnesty, and those that did so were rearmed and trained to fight the Adoo in groups known as firquats.

its way from Salalah. Even though the conditions for low-level flying were atrocious, a number of pilots from the Sultan's Armed Forces had offered to fly the 23 troopers from G Squadron to Mirbat in three available Omani Huey helicopters. At the same time, over at Mirbat, Captain Kealy had noticed that the 25-pounder had fallen silent and that the adoo were approaching it. He realized that if this gun fell into the hands of the rebels, they could turn it on the BATT house, or on the gendarmes in the fort. Determined not to let this happen, Kealy decided to work his way over towards the 25-pounder with Trooper Tobin, a trained medic, for company.

Despite the oncoming gunfire, they reached the gun pit and began tending to Trooper Savesaki's wounds. But as Tobin administered first aid, he was killed by a single round, leaving only Kealy and one wounded soldier to fight off the approaching horde of rebels.

Above: An Adoo guerrilla fighter with a Soviet-made RPG (rocket-propelled grenade) launcher. The rebels were supplied by South Yemen, at that time a Marxist state and keen to destabilize Oman.

Luckily for the SAS, just as the enemy came within grenade-throwing range, a pair of SOAF Strikemaster attack aircraft appeared out of the mist and strafed the adoo in front of the gun pit. The rebels' attack was broken up, forcing them to withdraw briefly from the gendarmes' fort. The aircraft made numerous passes over the rebels' positions, firing their rockets and guns with deadly effect against the adoo. It was now almost three hours since the attack first began on Mirbat, and yet, against overwhelming odds, the SAS had held on. As the men continued to fire their machine guns at the adoo, the welcome sound of the Hueys could be heard in the distance.

Within minutes of their arrival, G Squadron formed a skirmish line outside the helicopter landing pad and advanced towards the rebels. Their massive firepower was brought to bear on the enemy's flanks, and the enemy broke and fled, leaving over 40 of their dead comrades behind, along with many wounded. G Squadron's arrival could not have been better timed; by now, the machine guns on top of the BATT house had overheated so much that there was steam pouring off them. One of the SAS troopers later admitted that at one stage the adoo were so close and at such short range that he had been forced to pick up the 81mm (3.2in) mortar and hold it to his chest in order to get the right elevation.

For the SAS, its stand at Mirbat will go down in history as a remarkable example of what a small group of highly trained soldiers can achieve with good leadership and motivation. Considering the intensity of the action, it is a remarkable fact that only two members of 8 Troop were killed. The story for the adoo was quite different. They had come to Mirbat with the intention of achieving a great victory over the Sultan, one which would re-establish their credibility with the Omani people. However, after this enormous defeat, they lost face to such an extent that they were unable to mount a similar operation ever again.

This victory over the adoo at Mirbat did not mark the end of the war in southern Oman. But it was a turning point, and it marked the beginning of the end for the adoo. Following the successful action at Mirbat, the Sultan's forces – working alongside special forces from Jordan and Iran – mounted operations against them and these were so effective that the adoo were forced further back towards the Yemeni border. They were also cut off from supplies and reinforcements after defensive lines were established, consisting of mines, barbed wire, ground sensors and local patrols.

This strategy proved highly successful. Before the end of the war in 1976, there was only one major rebel stronghold left, and that was in the coastal town of Rakyut, some 40km (25 miles) from the

Below: SAS troopers prepare to mount a camel patrol from their base in Ibri. Although this was the first operational use of camels in Oman, the patrol was happy with its new mode of transport, which carried its own fuel.

Above: A one-ton truck struggles slowly up the side of a steep wadi in the Yanqul Basin in Oman. As in earlier interventions by the SAS, the difficult terrain in Oman meant that the regiment could not rely on being resupplied by land.

Yemeni border. Just north of Rakyut, the adoo had a major supply dump, which was hidden away in a series of caves above the Wadi Shershitti. The SAS decided to launch an attack against it on 4 January 1975 with the support of the Sultan's Armed Forces and a number of firqat members.

The first phase of the attack began with the SAS spearheading an advance through dense brush while under heavy machine-gun fire from positions near to the caves. The firqats, however, sustained several casualties before a forward operations base could be established. The main SAS attack would come the next morning, but during the previous evening, the adoo mounted an attack. This was beaten back, however, and as dawn broke three Omani companies advanced through thick brush towards the caves to commence their attack.

OMANIS PINNED DOWN

But now there was a problem. The commanding officer of the Omani soldiers had misjudged his position and was advancing from the west flank, instead of the north. This in turn exposed some of his men: moving across open ground, they suddenly found themselves under intense machine-gun fire from adoo

positions overlooking the brush area. Nearby, some SAS troopers had spotted the problem and reacted by sending in small four-man teams in support of the Omanis, while the rest of the troopers laid down heavy suppressive fire to pin down the adoo.

Above: A Squadron, 22 SAS prepare to move out from a temporary base camp in Radfan, Oman. The outline of their truck is just visible under its cover intended to camouflage it from prying eyes.

AIR STRIKES

The attack had now stalled and was in serious trouble. To break the deadlock, an SAS trooper called in air strikes and fire support from mortars that were in place nearby. With the element of surprise gone, there was little chance that the SAS could mount a cave-clearing operation. They decided instead to seal the caves up by shelling them directly with artillery. In order to ensure once and for all that the caves were totally unusable, a Saladin armoured car with a 76mm (3in) gun was brought in to pound the caves with shells. The operation continued for five days until, at last, the SAS was satisfied that the whole supply dump had been rendered totally inoperable.

Although the operation had not gone to plan, the original aims had been achieved, albeit indirectly. The adoo had been compelled to come out of Rakyut in order to reinforce the caves, and this meant leaving the remaining rebels effectively undefended. As a result, Iranian forces were able to mount an attack on the rebel defenders of Rakyut and, after a short battle, capture the town.

For the rest of the year, there was relatively little for the SAS to do in Oman, apart from carrying out liaison duties between the Sultan's forces and the firqats. One operation that had been scheduled for the SAS was cancelled, as the Omani forces had found no remaining rebels in the operational area. The SAS tour in Oman was all but over. The adoo had ceased to be a threat, and the Sultan's forces were now in a much stronger position than they had been at the start of the conflict.

Below: Major Spreull, the commander of A Squadron, 22 SAS Regiment, and his two Arab interpreters interrogate a Bedouin camel driver in Oman, as the latter often had good knowledge of rebel movements.

The campaign in Oman is probably the best example of how a modern counterinsurgency war should be fought, and the SAS can be rightly proud of what it achieved in this six-year period. What is remarkable about this operation is that even at the peak of SAS involvement, only 80 troopers were ever deployed there. Despite the harsh conditions and intense actions, only 12 troopers lost their lives during the campaign.

After the conflict was over, Captain Kealy won a Distinguished Service Order for his outstanding leadership at Mirbat, while two other troopers were awarded medals, one the Military Medal, the other a Distinguished Conduct Medal. There was, however, one area of contention. Corporal Labalaba received

Above: An SAS trooper stands guard at Ibri air strip in Oman as equipment is unloaded from an RAF Beverley transport. By 1975 the adoo had been all but beaten, and SAS involvement in Oman was wound down.

only a mention in despatches, though many insist that his actions that day warranted a Victoria Cross.

Thanks to the SAS, Oman is today a peaceful and prosperous country and still a good friend to the UK. Oman regularly allows British Forces to train and practice warfighting in the desert conditions of its territories – the most welcome force being the Special Air Service Regiment.

MILITARY MEDAL

Right: The Military Medal was introduced in World War I for bravery shown by non-commissioned officers and below. It was awarded to Corporal Bob Bradshaw of B Squadron, 22 SAS, for his part in the defence of the BATT House in Mirbat on 19 July 1972.

CHAPTER SIX

COUNTER-TERRORISM

From the steamy, snake-infested jungles of Malaya to the barren, hot deserts of Oman: what these areas have in common is terrorism, and the fact that Britain's Special Air Service Regiment has fought and beaten terrorists within them. Fighting terrorists is something that the SAS does very well – over the decades it has seen many campaigns in many countries against terrorist organizations.

Up until 1969, the problems of terrorism existed thousands of miles away from Britain's shores. These problems only ever affected members of the armed forces, and not civilians; however, the status quo was about to destroyed, and the catalyst for this radical change came from the streets of a small British territory, Northern Ireland.

Around the late 1960s, there was growing discontent amongst the minority Catholic population in Northern Ireland about the way they were being treated by the Protestant majority. Their grudges were well founded, and eventually they came together as one voice following the formation of a civil rights movement, which campaigned vigorously on the streets of Northern Ireland.

Gradually, due to local police mishandling, the civil rights marches turned violent. Soon they had rapidly escalated into sectarian riots on the streets of Londonderry and later Belfast. By 1969, the police had effectively lost control of the situation and were requesting the help of the British Army to restore law and order. During the first few weeks of their deployment, the soldiers were warmly welcomed within the Catholic areas, being seen as a neutral force that could be trusted. This cosy relationship ended after only a short period of time, following several violent incidents between Scottish soldiers and Catholic civilians.

Left: SAS men carefully frisk a few unlucky members of the Parachute Regiment who were caught during Exercise Sabotage, which was held on the Isle of Wight to hone anti-terrorist skills.

IRISH DUTIES

It was during this initial honeymoon period that D Squadron of 22 SAS deployed to Northern Ireland to carry out patrol duties around the eastern coastal areas of Antrim and Down. From their base in Newtownards, east Belfast, they carried out spot checks on the local ports – and specifically the boats using them – to prevent gun smuggling from Scotland, where the Protestants had strong support. During this period, the SAS wore standard British Army uniforms, along with their regimental berets and 'Winged Dagger' cap badges.

After a short tour they were withdrawn and re-deployed to Oman, where the need for their unique skills was perceived to be greater. This withdrawal, however, was premature. The 'Troubles' in Northern Ireland, as they were called, had deteriorated to such an extent that there were now fears of civil war. As moderate leaders in both communities tried to calm things down, more sinister figures were at work in the background, whipping up public feelings and orchestrating violence against the security forces.

Finally, in 1972, everything came to a head. A civil rights march in Londonderry ended with a confrontation between the Parachute Regiment and the protesters, and 13 people were killed. To this day there is a bitter dispute over who fired the first shots, but the outcome of that tragedy, now known as 'Bloody Sunday', would haunt the British Army for decades and immediately caused the Catholics to turn against the British Army in droves. This bad publicity was the best recruiting sergeant that the IRA (Irish Republican Army) could have wished for.

PIRA

As the 'Troubles' intensified, factions within the terrorist groups began advocating more aggressive action against the British, in particular calling for a campaign of violence on the UK mainland. The most active of these factions was the Provisional Irish Republican Army (PIRA). PIRA had originally been part of the IRA, but broke away in 1970 to pursue a Marxist political agenda, in which they disclosed that one of their aims included the unification of Ireland. This partially served a purpose, portraying the British as an invading force, and made PIRA's task of justifying terrorist action that little bit easier.

Below: British troops patrol the hostile streets of Crossmaglen at the height of the 'Troubles'. Note the whitewashed fronts of the buildings, which gave IRA snipers a clearer target to aim at, and the organization's graffito on the wall on the right.

The Provisional Irish Republican Army dominated the Catholic areas of West Belfast and Londonderry and was particularly strong in South Armagh, or 'bandit country', as the British Army called it. Initially the methods of subversion employed by the PIRA included providing petrol bombs to rioters or sniping at members of the security forces. But this would later extend to extortion, protection rackets, robbery and large-scale bombing operations – in stark contrast to the early days, when they were just content to barricade a road with hooded gunman and to man vehicle checkpoints.

Within the British Army, there was a growing realization that this conflict could not be won by conventional forces. Sooner or later, they would have to take the fight to the terrorists and be more proactive in their methods, rather than reactive. As the Army deliberated over an operational strategy that would subdue the terrorists, a series of tit-for-tat murders took place throughout the province that were shocking even by Northern Ireland's standards.

In one of these incidents, the IRA murdered 10 Protestant passengers in a bus, apparently as an act of reprisal for the murder of five Catholics the previous day. This mass murder was the final straw for the British Government and within days, without going through the normal military chain of command for approval, it had ordered the SAS to deploy to South Armagh for anti-terrorist operations.

Initially, the SAS was able to send only a small force to Northern Ireland because most of its available Sabre Squadrons were still engaged on operations in Oman. Indeed, the decision to deploy came as something of a surprise. Although there were individual members already deployed on intelligence-gathering operations in support of the regular Army,

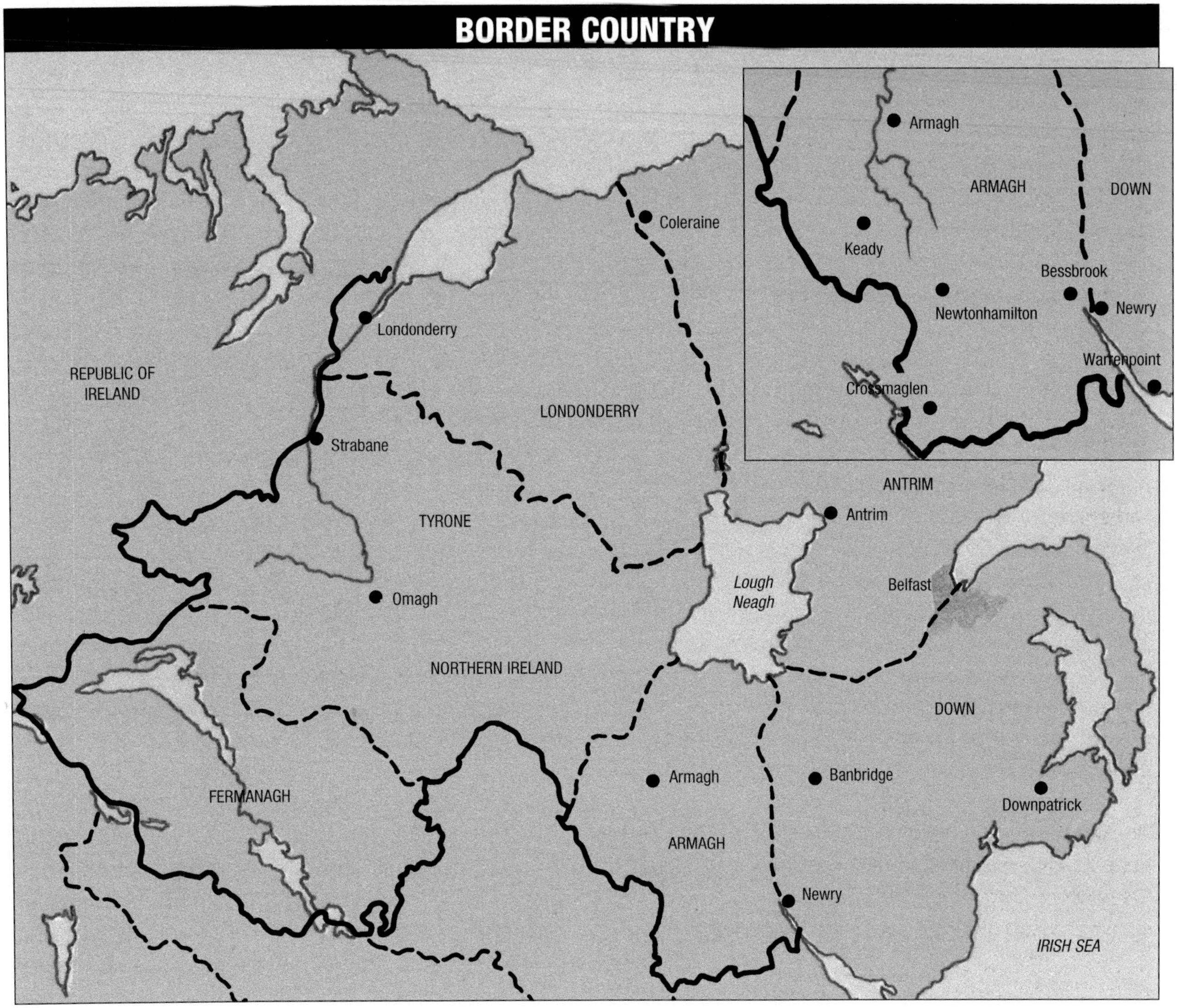

these deployments had been limited in size and scope, and were defensive, rather than offensive.

SAS UNDER PRESSURE

There was a tremendous amount of pressure from the top for a fast result, and upon its arrival the small SAS force immediately set to work planning a strategy for stopping the operations of the assassination squads. Much of the available intelligence had been gleaned from IRA informants and undercover operatives from the highly secret 14 Intelligence company, or '14 Int' as it was known within the British Army. This intelligence was of immense value to the newly deployed SAS team, which had come into the country 'cold', and was anxious to get up to speed as soon as possible. In essence, the roles of 14 Int and the SAS were split: the former was responsible for both overt and covert intelligence-gathering and collation, while the latter had been tasked with close observation and direct action.

After a short time, the SAS was ready to mount the first tentative undercover operations against the IRA in South Armagh. While doing this, the men were extremely mindful of the gruesome consequences of being caught by the IRA. Operating in small four-man teams, they would spend days or even weeks at a time living in cramped, dirty, covert OPs (observation posts), gaining intelligence and tracing the movements of known IRA terrorists and their associates. Known as 'Players' to the SAS, each terrorist cell had its own speciality, be it bomb-making or assassinations. By keeping a constant watch on their movements, the SAS was able to build up a picture of what actions they were planning, and counter-operations could be mounted.

Q CARS

Although the SAS favoured covert OP operations for intelligence-gathering, the men also patrolled around known terrorist areas in unmarked Q cars when a more discreet approach was needed. These operations, however, did have associated risks. On one particular occasion, an SAS Q car strayed over the unmarked border with the Republic of Ireland, and subsequently its occupants were arrested by the Garda (the Irish police). As if this incident wasn't embarrassing enough for the SAS, a second Q car, out searching for the first, also strayed over the border and its occupants arrested. This incident caused a major diplomatic row between the British and Irish governments. Fortunately from a British point of view, the Irish released the men the following day without charge.

Below: Dunloy graveyard, the scene of the tragic shooting of John Boyle. After warning of a hidden IRA arms cache, he wandered into an SAS ambush prepared to trap any terrorists visiting the dump, and was shot in error.

The 'Troubles' were now really causing problems for the SAS. Here was a looking-glass world: while its men were expected to operate within the law, the IRA was free to murder and bomb the innocent, often within the protection of the law. Most SAS soldiers found it highly frustrating that the IRA were doing their utmost to destroy the process of democracy, yet it was that same democracy which protected them from prosecution.

Every now and again the IRA would declare a ceasefire, but there was always a hidden agenda. In most cases, it was simply so that it could re-equip or solve internal quarrels. After all, the group did not hold a monopoly on terrorism in Northern Ireland. Just as active were the Protestant groups, although they attracted much less attention from the SAS because, in general, they did not pursue campaigns against the security forces.

It was around this time that the SAS was accused of operating a 'shoot to kill' policy. There had been a number of incidents in which IRA members had been killed or wounded in unusual circumstances. The first of these allegations related to IRA member Peter Cleary, who died after being captured following a week-long surveillance operation mounted by the SAS against his known safe houses. One day, as Cleary approached his girlfriend's sister's house, the SAS arrested him and immediately radioed for a helicopter extraction, since using the roads was deemed too risky.

As the team waited for the helicopter to arrive, Cleary struggled with one his guards and managed to make a break for the nearby border. Despite being challenged, he failed to stop, and was shot dead by the remaining members of the SAS team who had originally apprehended him. In another separate incident, a prominent PIRA member, Sean

McKenna, was arrested by a four-man SAS team and taken into custody. During his trial, it was claimed that the SAS team had gone over the Irish border and dragged him out of his house, which would have been highly illegal. This was never proved, however, and McKenna was eventually charged with 25 separate terrorist-related offences.

A much-regretted operation came during July 1978, when a young boy called John Boyle discovered a cache of weapons on his father's land and informed the RUC (Royal Ulster Constabulary). The SAS was in turn notified. It decided to mount an operation against the terrorists who had hidden the

Above: British soldiers hastily move into their well protected base on a hillside overlooking South Armagh, or 'Bandit Country' as it was more often called, reflecting the high level of IRA activity and support found there.

M-60

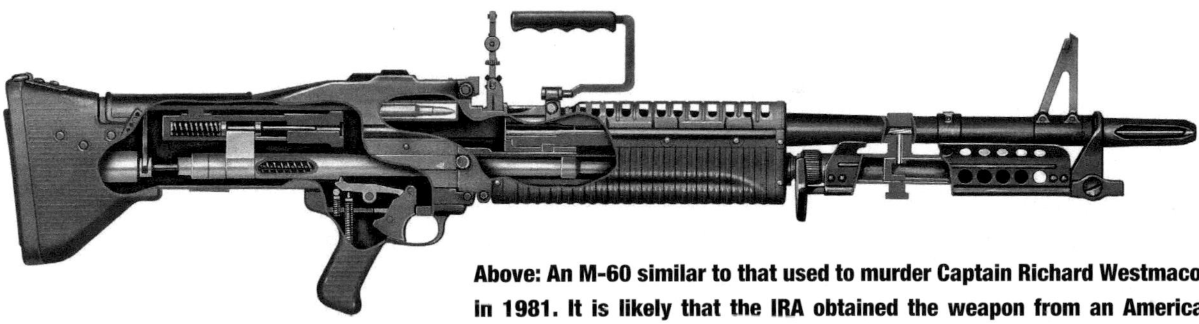

Above: An M-60 similar to that used to murder Captain Richard Westmacott in 1981. It is likely that the IRA obtained the weapon from an American sympathizer. At the time, it was the standard machine gun of the US Army.

weapons there. Before the outset of this operation, they asked the Boyle family to steer clear of this spot. Tragically, the Boyles' youngest son didn't get the message and, after walking straight into an SAS ambush, he was killed.

CAPTAIN WESTMACOTT

The SAS too suffered its own share of tragedy in Northern Ireland, and in one incident – which could have been avoided – one of its members was killed. In May 1981, Captain Richard Westmacott was leading a patrol of seven men against an eight-man IRA cell that was holed up in Belfast's Antrim Road. As the men of the SAS team secured the area around the house, one of the terrorists opened fire on them with an M-60 machine gun, mortally wounding Captain Westmacott. Fearing reprisals from the SAS, the IRA summoned a local priest who negotiated their surrender with the RUC.

Although its involvement in Northern Ireland was a highly sensitive subject, the SAS still had a job to do and on several occasions was spectacularly successful. In one particular operation, an IRA cell had been regularly targeting British Army helicopters as they flew over South Armagh, and the SAS was tasked with taking it out. The SAS devised a very clever sting operation, and sprang it on the unsuspecting terrorists, who were waiting in a wooded area with a 12.7mm (0.5in) heavy machine gun. Acting as bait, a Lynx helicopter flew over the terrorists' ambush site. Predictably they immediately

Below: The ambush at Loughall in May 1987 was a significant blow against the IRA, who had been escalating their campaign against the security forces. Eight terrorists from the East Tyrone Brigade were killed in the attack.

Above: The Toyota van used by the IRA for the attack on Loughall seen after the SAS ambush. The white rods are used to indicate the direction from which the rounds were fired into the van by the SAS.

opened fire. Within minutes of the attack, SAS soldiers arrived in the area in a number of other helicopters and cut off the terrorists' retreat, putting paid to this practice once and for all.

LOUGHALL

If there is one operation that epitomizes the success of the SAS in Northern Ireland, then it must surely be that of the 1987 Loughall ambush, which left eight IRA terrorists dead. Prior to the operation, the IRA had made a bold statement: 'For the security forces to be successful against us they need to be lucky all of the time, whereas for us to be successful against them, we only need to be lucky once.' Although this was basically true, at Loughall it was the SAS who had the luck.

One day, by sheer good fortune, an intelligence operative, who was monitoring IRA communications, picked up on an alarming telephone conversation. In it, known IRA members were openly discussing an attack on the small village police station at Loughall, County Armagh. The IRA deemed this isolated RUC station a soft target, as it was manned only during the day by four lightly armed police

CHRONOLOGY

Date 1969–94
Location Northern Ireland
Operation The SAS supports the British Army and the Royal Ulster Constabulary (RUC) by mounting intelligence-gathering and anti-terrorist operations against the IRA. Numerous operations result in both SAS and IRA fatalities. The most successful is the ambush of IRA terrorists at Loughall, which resulted in the annihilation of their East Tyrone Brigade.

Date 1980
Location London
Operation The SAS wins worldwide recognition, launching a spectacular operation under the gaze of the world's media. The objective of Operation Nimrod is to kill or capture terrorists holding hostages in the Iranian Embassy in London. It is now considered a text-book example of how to execute a hostage rescue mission.

Date 1981
Location Gambia
Operation SAS help to restore President Jawara to power after a coup.

Date 1989
Location Columbia
Operation 22 SAS is deployed to Columbia to take part in the anti-cocaine war after the Britsh Government receives a request for military assistance, This includes training for the Columbian forces and missions against drug barons.

BORDER INCIDENT 1975

3 **An Army Air Corps Scout helicopter lands a four-man covering force on a hill overlooking the IRA escape route. The unit is able to provide covering fire should the main reaction force require it.**

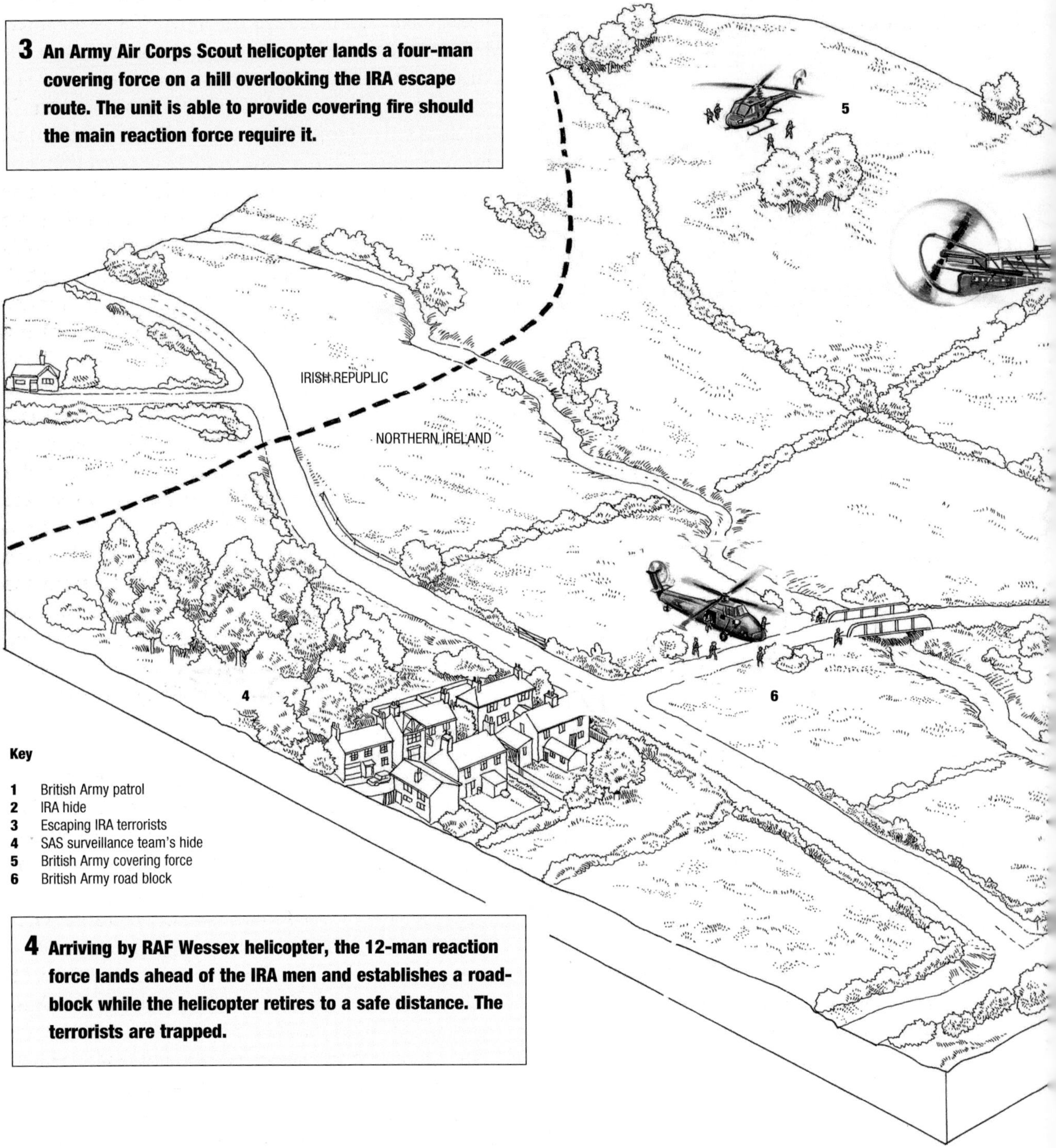

Key

1 British Army patrol
2 IRA hide
3 Escaping IRA terrorists
4 SAS surveillance team's hide
5 British Army covering force
6 British Army road block

4 **Arriving by RAF Wessex helicopter, the 12-man reaction force lands ahead of the IRA men and establishes a road-block while the helicopter retires to a safe distance. The terrorists are trapped.**

2 A two-man reconnaissance team flying a Sioux helicopter mounts a constant watch on the area. As the IRA men attempt to escape across the border, the helicopter calls in a reaction force.

1 A British Army Saracen APC patrols the area near a minor border crossing after SAS reports of suspicious movements. Two IRA members detonate a mine to disable it and escape by motorbike.

officers. A plan was made to attack it with eight heavily armed members of the élite IRA East Tyrone Brigade, nicknamed the 'A-Team'. The IRA plan of attack involved stealing a JCB mechanical digger and driving it through the perimeter fence surrounding the police station. Once inside, they would detonate explosives that they had hidden in the bucket of the JCB; the result would be the total destruction of the station.

This very well-planned operation had just one major drawback: the SAS would be waiting for them. On the evening of Friday 8 May 1987, the JCB digger slowly approached the village of Loughall with its deadly cargo, the 100kg (220lb) of Semtex explosives. On board were three IRA members: Declan Arthurs, Gerald O'Callaghan and Tony Gormley. Ahead of them were five other terrorists: Patrick Kelly, Jim Lynagh, Padraig McKearney, Seamus Donnelly and Eugene Kelly, their job being to recce the police station prior to the JCB's arrival. Once satisfied that the coast was clear, the recce group parked their van across the road from the intended target and summoned the bomb-laden JCB. As it arrived, the men dismounted from the van and proceeded to open fire on the unmanned police station with their heavy weapons. As they did so, SAS soldiers hidden nearby opened fire on them with GPMGs and assault rifles, killing all eight.

EXPLOSION

However, all did not go according to plan. One of the terrorists managed to ignite the bomb fuse just before he died and as a result the bomb exploded, severely damaging the police station and injuring three SAS soldiers in the process.

It was later disclosed that in addition to the eight IRA members shot dead, an innocent civilian was also killed and his friend wounded. One of the SAS cut-off groups opened fire on them after mistaking them for terrorists and it was later revealed that the SAS ambush team had been wrongly informed by intelligence sources that the IRA had a back-up vehicle waiting nearby. It seemed to be just bad luck that this vehicle happened to drive by at the same time.

As for the IRA, Loughall was a major disaster for their cause, as they were never able to mount an operation like this again. Instead they carried out low-risk mortar attacks against the security forces, and stepped up their bombing campaign on the UK mainland and overseas.

The IRA and the SAS were now locked into a bitter, close-quarter war, in which both sides were doing their utmost to come out on top. As the IRA continued to assassinate unarmed civilians and off-duty service personnel, the SAS hit them again, but on this occasion it would be an overseas operation. The IRA hatched a plan to detonate a bomb during a military ceremony on the Rock of Gibraltar; however, the SAS were on their trail, and shot all three terrorists dead before they had even had a chance to trigger the device.

The IRA again complained to the European Court of Human Rights about an SAS 'shoot-to-kill' policy, but it fell on deaf ears. The British Government was still seething over the Brighton bombing of 12 October 1984, and felt it was a bit rich for the IRA to demand its protection: after all, these were the terrorists who had recently attempted to assassinate Prime Minister Margaret Thatcher and her entire cabinet. If anything, most of the world felt that the British were being remarkably restrained, considering the provocation that they were under.

In the early 1990s, the IRA was struggling to find support for its cause. Many of its more moderate members were sick and tired of violence and wanted an end to the perpetual cycle of tit-for-tat killings. However, for those who wanted more and were still determined to pursue a campaign of violence, there was always the risk that they would bump into the SAS, and many of them did.

Left: A trooper from 22 SAS seen in action during the hostage rescue mission at the Iranian Embassy in May 1980. He is wearing black, flame-resistant clothing and is armed with a Heckler & Koch MP5.

In April 1990, Martin Corrigan was killed in Armagh on his way to murder an Army reservist, and Martin McCaughey and Desmond Grew were shot and killed at Loughall while moving weapons. In June 1991, three IRA men were shot dead in Coagh by the SAS while on active service, and a short time later four other IRA men were shot in Clonoe, Coalisland after attacking a police station.

THE TIDE TURNS

The tide was now turning against the PIRA, and it knew it. As it held talks with the British Government to bring about an end to the 'Troubles', another splinter group was waiting in the wings to take centre stage. The so-called 'Real IRA' was determined to continue with the struggle and, in 1998, carried out the worst bombing atrocity in Northern Ireland's history with an attack on the town of Omagh, in which scores of people were either killed or injured.

Although many SAS operations in Northern Ireland still remain shrouded in secrecy, what is known about them is that between 1976 and 1991, around 46 IRA and INLA terrorists were shot dead by the SAS during covert operations, while the SAS lost only four men: Captain Richard Westmacott, Lance-Corporal David Jones, Sergeant Paul Oram and Lance-Corporal Alistair Slater.

Considering the fact that only a small number of its men were deployed at any given time, the SAS was remarkably successful in creating a climate of fear amongst the many terrorists in Northern Ireland. The reason why the SAS deployed so few men in Ulster is simple: if too many men were engaged on anti-terrorist operations, the regiment's other skills would suffer. As a result, in the early 1980s the SAS reduced its strength in Northern Ireland from a full squadron to a troop of just 20 men, which was called 'Ulster Troop'. Its soldiers served in the province for a one-year tour before being rotated, enabling them to become highly proficient in anti-terrorist related operations without losing currency in their other areas of expertise.

Due to the current IRA ceasefire and weapons decommissioning programme, the SAS has had little to do with Northern Ireland in recent years. However, it would be a very brave man who could claim that the 'Troubles' are now at an end, given that the IRA have said, 'We are now no longer at war with the British, but we are not at peace with them either.'

COUNTER-REVOLUTIONARY WARFARE

In the early 1970s, Western democracies suddenly found themselves under threat of attack from a plethora of terrorist organizations, who were hell-bent on voicing their extremist views, forcing everyone to listen. Not content with breeding a

Below: An early photo of a counter-revolutionary warfare (CRW) operator preparing for a hostage rescue exercise. The protective clothing and respirators give the operators a fearsome, inhuman appearance.

Above: Tools of the trade for an SAS CRW team. Weapons shown include a Heckler and Koch MP5 and a MP5SD, a stun grenade and a Browning Hi-power pistol. The respirator is also a key piece of kit, particularly if CS gas is used.

culture of violence and intimidation in their own countries, many of these extremist groups wanted to take their grudges to the West and attack their values also. Many of these terrorist groups had sponsors in the Middle East and Communist Eastern Europe who were doing everything possible to undermine the West, and in September 1972 they showed the world just what they were capable of doing.

The event chosen by the terrorists to achieve maximum publicity for their cause was the Munich Olympic Games. On 5 September 1972, armed members of the Palestinian group 'Black September' took advantage of the low security at the Olympic village in Munich, and seized 11 Israeli athletes. They demanded the release of 234 fellow members of their group and a safe passage to Egypt. If their demands were not met, they said they would start executing the hostages.

The German police had never dealt with a similar situation. They pretended to go along with the terrorists' demands, even taking them to the airport by helicopter. Once the terrorists arrived at the airport, hidden snipers opened fire on them, killing two and wounding several others, including the helicopter pilots. In response, the remaining terrorists took shelter in the helicopters, but came under attack again by German troops with armoured cars. A fierce firelight erupted between them, in which a helicopter exploded, killing several people.

HOSTAGES KILLED

Shortly after, the terrorists executed five other hostages that were being held in another helicopter, before it too was blown up. The rescue operation had been a complete disaster for the German security forces: 5 terrorists and 11 Israeli athletes were dead. But even in death, the terrorists had achieved a victory, as the story dominated the world's headlines for weeks afterwards.

In response, Germany set up a dedicated anti-terrorist organization, giving it the name Grenzschutzgruppe 9, or GSG9 as it is more commonly known. After witnessing the events in Munich, Britain decided to develop a counter-terrorist capability and tasked 22 SAS with forming a Counter-Revolutionary Warfare (CRW) Wing.

Within a short time. the SAS had formed a 20-man CRW team under the command of Lieutenant Colonel Anthony Pearson, which became known as 'Pagoda' Squadron.

Essentially it had three roles to perform: the collection of intelligence on possible terrorist threats; the pre-empting of terrorist activity; and the mounting of direct operations against any terrorist-related threat. It was also tasked with developing specific tactics, techniques and procedures for likely terrorist targets – hostage rescue, in other words, from aircraft, ships, buildings, oil-rigs, nuclear power stations and even public entertainment centres. To enable the SAS to perform these tasks to a high standard, new communication systems and highly sensitive surveillance equipment were procured from sources around the world. Cross training was also carried out with regional police forces throughout the UK, as well as counter-terrorist forces overseas, such as the German GSG9, French GIGN, and US Delta Force.

In 1975, as 'Pagoda' Squadron continued to develop, it received notification of a hijack at London's Stansted airport and was put on standby. However, the incident ended peacefully before the SAS could be deployed. Later that year, a four-man IRA Active Service Unit (ASU) seized an elderly couple and held them hostage in a flat in London's Balcombe Street after being compromised by police during an anti-terrorist operation. With no means of escape, the IRA men were holed up in the flat for almost six days, until they heard a news report on the radio stating that the SAS had been brought in to end the crisis. In part this was true, as 'Pagoda' Squadron had indeed been deployed to London on standby, but it was quite prepared to wait for events to take their course, and the police were themselves slowly bringing the situation to a peaceful conclusion. For the IRA, however, the mere mention of the SAS was enough to convince them that a spell in jail would be preferable to trying to survive an SAS assault. They surrendered.

TRAIN HIJACK

In May 1977, the Dutch authorities requested SAS assistance after a train was hijacked by South Moluccan terrorists. The SAS responded by sending over a small advisory team, whose role was purely passive; although the SAS were present during the rescue mission, they played no part in the actual assault phase of the hostage rescue operation.

This was to be in stark contrast to the next SAS operation, which took place in Mogadishu, Somalia. SAS assistance was requested by the German authorities after one of their country's airliners was hijacked by Palestinian terrorists during a routine flight from Majorca to Frankfurt. Following a refuelling stop in Rome, the Lufthansa Boeing 737 aircraft and its 86 passengers and 5 crew were subjected to a series of stopovers and diversions, before eventually ending up in Mogadishu. Following close behind the hijacked aircraft was another Lufthansa aircraft, which contained German hostage negotiators and 30 members of the GSG9 anti-terrorist unit.

Upon their arrival, they were met by two members of the SAS, Major Alastair Morrison and Sergeant Barry Davies, who had been sent in to assist with the rescue operation. The pace of events suddenly picked up: without any warning, one of the Lufthansa pilots was murdered. The decision was then taken to storm the aircraft. Using 'Stun grenades' provided by the SAS, GSG9 set off a number of them around the aircraft as a diversion before storming it. During the assault phase, three of the four terrorists were killed, and only four passengers injured, making it a very successful operation. The SAS later revealed why the fourth terrorist, a young woman, had survived: a member of the SAS team had taken the decision to shoot to wound, not kill. Some years later, the same SAS soldier and the surviving terrorist met up. She wanted to thank him for sparing her life, now that she was happily married with children.

As for the rest of 'Pagoda' Squadron, they continued to train, knowing that another situation like this could easily develop anywhere in the world with little or no warning. Month in, month out, the SAS practised their hostage-rescue techniques until they were second nature. All they needed now was

Above: A terrorist of the Democratic Revolutionary Front for the Liberation of Arabistan shows his face at the height of the Iranian Embassy siege. The terrorists were demanding the release of 91 Arabs held in Iranian jails.

a chance to show them off, and on 5 May 1980 they got that chance.

IRANIAN EMBASSY

Some days earlier, on the morning of 30 April 1980, six Iraqi-sponsored terrorists, members of the little known Democratic Revolutionary Front for the Liberation of Arabistan, entered the front doorway of the Iranian Embassy in Princes Gate, London. For the lone police officer, PC Trevor Lock, who was standing guard outside the Embassy, the approach of six Arab-looking men seemed to be nothing out of the ordinary. This day, though, was going to be anything but ordinary. Politely, he went to open the door for them, at which point, one of the terrorists pulled a gun and attempted to rush the door. Acting instinctively, the officer pushed him back and slammed the door in his face.

As he did so, the other terrorists pulled out a variety of small pistols and Skorpion submachine guns and opened fire on the Embassy. Some of them then forced the flimsy front door and burst into the Iranian Embassy, firing off their guns. Some Embassy staff attempted to escape, but the terrorists were too quick for most of them. Two female staff did, however, manage to get out through a back door, while a third male member of staff escaped through an adjacent office window. One other member of staff also attempted to escape from an upstairs window, but injured himself during the process and was quickly dragged back into the building by one of the terrorists.

There were 26 hostages within the Embassy, and the terrorists prepared for a long, drawn-out siege. As they took stock of their situation, police began to arrive outside the Embassy in force, having been alerted by PC Lock before he too was captured. Within a very short time, the entire area surrounding the Iranian Embassy was alive with specialist units, including D11 police marksmen, C-13 Anti-terrorist officers, the Special Patrol Group (SPG) and members of Scotland Yard's C7 technical support branch. In addition, SOP (standard operational procedure) meant that the SAS had been notified and were on their way.

At this point, the SAS had around 20 men permanently on standby as part of the Special Projects Team (SPT), their role being anti-terrorist operations. There was also a second SPT, which rotated with the first one to enable 24-7 cover. To ensure that the SAS could deploy at a moment's notice, an RAF C-130 Hercules was on permanent standby, along with a number of Army Air Corps (AAC) Agusta A-109 utility helicopters.

The SAS had now given the Iranian Embassy situation the codename of Operation Nimrod, and a team was based nearby in readiness for further orders. As they waited patiently, the terrorists started issuing their demands to the British Government: the immediate release of 91 Arabs held in Iranian jails – Arabistan is a region of Iran populated by ethnic Arabs rather than Iranians – and the granting to all

Right: SAS 'Pagoda Team' members armed with MP5 submachine-guns leap onto the balcony of the Iranian Embassy to begin storming the building. The cameras of the world's press were watching.

the released prisoners of political asylum in Britain. If these demands were not met, the hostages would start to be killed.

The terrorists also demanded that negotiations be held in London under the supervision of Arab ambassadors, and set a deadline of mid-day on 1 May for full compliance. There was no question of the British Government negotiating with them about anything, as relations with Iran were then very poor following the demise of the pro-western Shah of Iran. Prime Minister Margaret Thatcher was quite determined that Britain should be seen taking a tough stance against terrorism – otherwise situations like this would become commonplace in London.

SITUATION DETERIORATING

By this time, police negotiators had persuaded the terrorists to drop their demands for the release of prisoners, but agreed that they could make a radio broadcast for mediators.

The situation, though, had begun to deteriorate and it was clear that something had to be done before the deadline expired. Prime Minister Margaret Thatcher summoned COBRA, the Cabinet Office Briefing Room, which included members of the SAS, M15, M16, and the Ministry of Defence (MOD). After discussing all the options, they passed on their recommendations to the Joint Operations Centre (JOC) at the Ministry of Defence HQ.

As the COBRA meeting was taking place, SAS planners were discussing methods of entry into the Iranian Embassy with their police colleagues in C7, who had a very sophisticated surveillance operation in place, involving placing microphones, along with miniature cameras capable of providing highly detailed pictures, within Embassy rooms.

At one stage of their operation, they needed extra noise outside the Embassy to drown out the sound of drilling while placing the surveillance devices. When Margaret Thatcher heard of this problem, she immediately ordered the CAA (Civil Aviation Authority) to divert all flights over London so that they flew over the Embassy at a far lower height then normal. In addition, she ordered British Gas to dig the road up outside the rear of the Embassy as cover for C7's operations.

As for the SAS, they were now ready to begin an assault against the Embassy. All they needed now was the word to go in. Their proposed plan was really quite simple: two four-man teams would abseil from the roof top down the rear of the building, and at the same time another team would enter the building via the first floor windows. As the windows were bulletproof, frame charges would be used to blast through them, and once this had been accomplished, stun grenades and CS gas canisters would be tossed into the building to disorientate the terrorists. At this point, the SAS clearance teams would make their entry.

For safety reasons, the SAS team members wore black one-piece overalls, which were very effective

PRINCES GATE

Using surveillance devices lowered down the chimneys and drilled through adjoining walls to locate the exact positions of the terrorists and hostages, the SAS then rapidly abseil down the front and rear of the building to enter by the windows, catching the terrorists by surprise and using stun grenades to disorientate them.

OPERATION NIMROD

1. Operation Nimrod begins. As a diversionary explosion rips through the third-floor skylight, 'Red Team' abseils from the roof (5) while 'Blue Team' gains entry to the library.

2. At the front, a four-man squad from 'Blue Team' blows in the windows and rescues Sim Harris.

3. PC Trevor Lock tackles terrorist leader Awn, who is then killed by the SAS troopers.

4. Another terrorist runs into the Ambassador's office and is killed.

5. On the second floor. 'Red Team' gain entry into the back office, but their grenades set it on fire.

6. A member of 'Red Team' chases a terrorist heading for the telex room.

7. Three terrorists rush into the telex room and begin shooting hostages.

8. A fourth terrorist enters the room, but is shot by a pursuing SAS soldier.

9. The rest of 'Red Team' burst out of the office and head for the telex room.

10. They discover one of the terrorists with a primed grenade and kill him.

11. Those hostages being held in the cypher room are freed.

12. As the hostages are being led away to the first floor, oe of the terrorists is spotted. He pulls a grenade and is riddled with bullets.

13. The hostages are led out to the gardens behind the building. Here the last terrorist is found, wounded but alive.

The building has been cleared. The SAS operation has taken just 17 minutes.

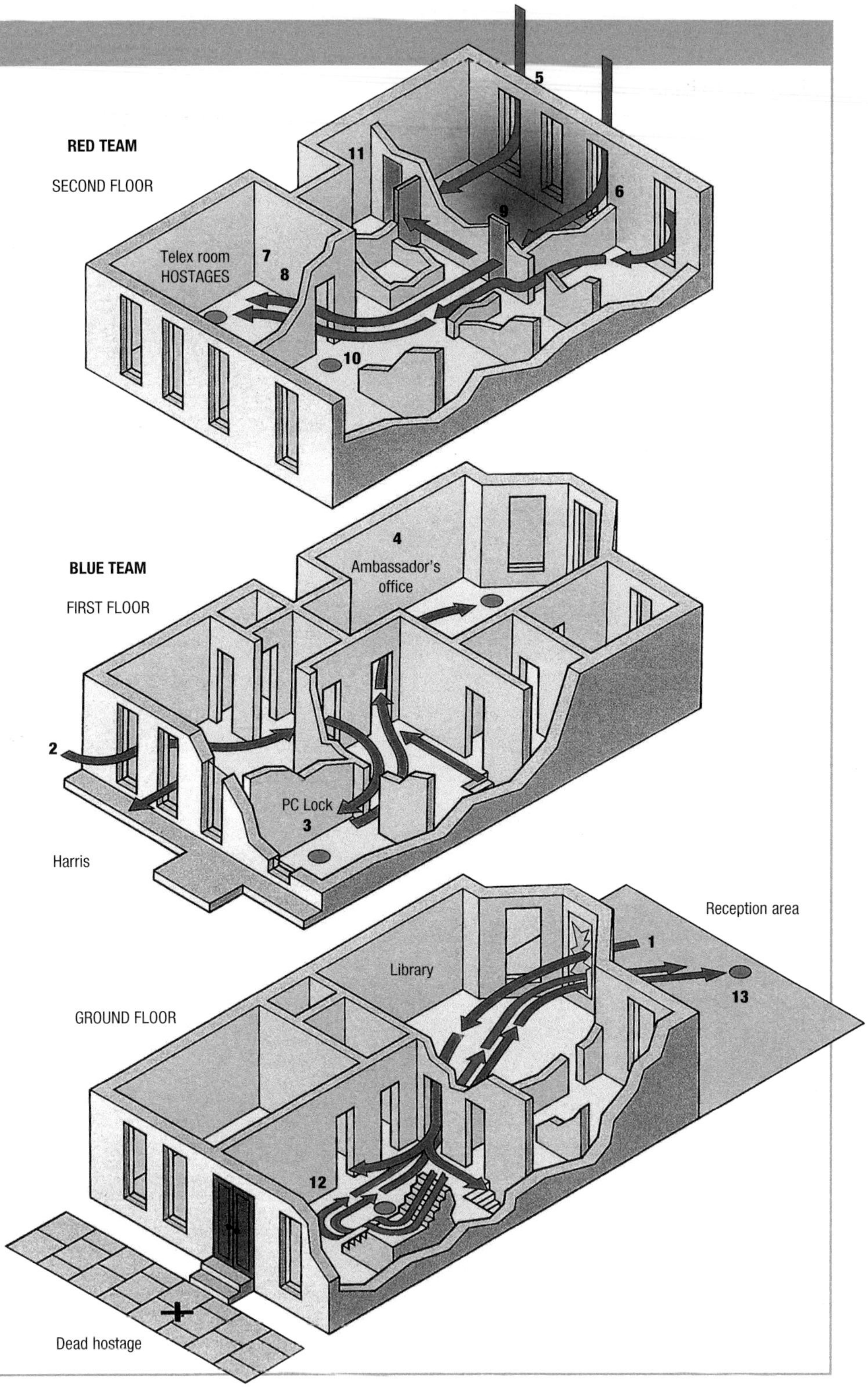

PRINCES GATE 1980

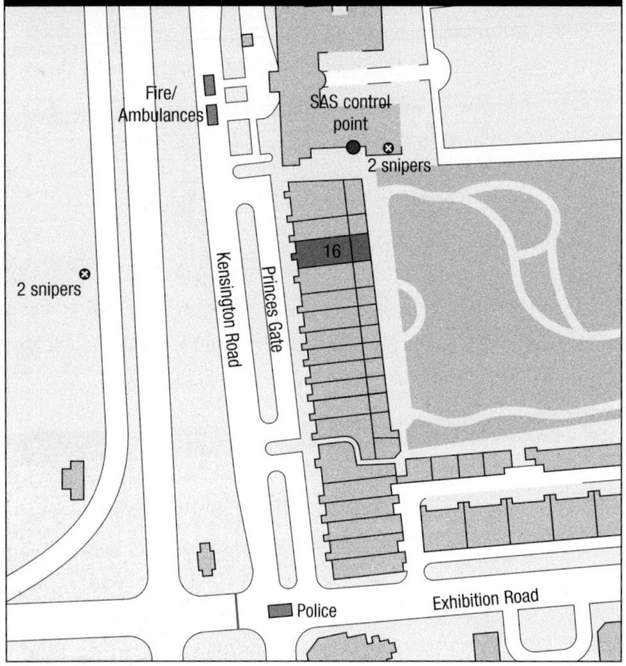

and enabled the soldiers to be seen in smoke-filled rooms. For protection, they wore fragmentation jackets and S6 respirators, which had the additional advantage of creating a powerfully intimidating effect on their enemy. They also carried Heckler & Koch MP5 sub-machine guns, as well as 9mm (0.35in) Browning Hi-Power pistols.

On Monday 5 May, the terrorists' leader, Awn Ali Mohammed, spoke to the police negotiators as normal, but he sounded edgy. At 1850, three shots were heard emanating from within the Embassy. Some time later, the body of the Embassy's chief press officer, Abbas Lavasani, was dumped on the steps outside the building. As the police frantically talked with the terrorists, responsibility for the Embassy operation was now being passed over to the Commanding Officer of the SAS, Lieutenant Colonel Michael Rose.

The SAS had seen enough and decided that it was time to bring this crisis to an end. At 1920, three four-man teams abseiled over the side of the building and began gaining entry via the second- and third-floor windows. At the same time, other SAS members climbed onto the first-floor balcony from an adjacent building and placed framed charges around the windows.

As they did so, another team smashed their way into the embassy through the rear basement windows. Inside the building, there was panic amongst the terrorists as they heard the sound of breaking glass all around them. In one office, there was now a struggle between the terrorist leader and PC Lock, who knew that help was on its way. Within seconds, an SAS soldier burst through the door and opened fire, killing the lead terrorist instantly. As he did so, another terrorist armed with a pistol rushed to the rear of the building and was gunned down by two SAS soldiers before he had a chance to fire.

Meanwhile, on the second floor, SAS members had entered the main office where most of the hostages were held, only to find that the terrorists had moved them into the telex room at the front of the building, which was now locked. As the SAS tried to force the door, one member of the team left the room and climbed out on to the balcony with the idea of entering the locked room from the window. As he did so, he spotted a terrorist attempting to start a fire within the room, but his weapon had jammed and he could not do anything about it.

HOSTAGES BEING SHOT

Within the telex room itself, two of the four remaining terrorists were now shooting the hostages with their hand guns, and the SAS were powerless to stop them. Eventually they burst into the smoke-filled room, only to find that the terrorists had fled and were now posing as hostages. One of them was quickly spotted and pulled away from the genuine hostages, but as he was being dragged away he made a suspicious movement and was instantly shot dead. As his body was turned over, a grenade was seen in his hand, vindicating the SAS decision and preventing a later accusation of murder. A second terrorist armed with a gun was shot dead when he tried to mingle with hostages being evacuated from the burning building.

As for the last living terrorist, he was found hiding amongst the hostages, but as he was unarmed, he was spared. In all, from start to finish it had taken the SAS just 46 minutes to carry out the entire operation, from police handover of responsibility to the return of it. All in all, this was a remarkable achievement for the SAS, made all the more spectacular as it had been captured on live television and beamed across the world.

As for the SAS, once the assault had finished, the men were bundled into waiting vans and driven away at high speed for a well-deserved celebration. In all, around 50 members of the SAS had been involved in the operation, both directly and indirectly. The casualty figures for this day's work were two hostages murdered, two hostages wounded, and one SAS soldier slightly injured by burns caused when his rope became entangled during the initial assault phase. As for the terrorists, six walked into the Embassy, but only one came out alive. That's what happens when you mess with the SAS.

Below: The effect of Operation Nimrod can be clearly seen in this photo of the interior of the Embassy taken after the SAS assault. All but one of the terrorists were killed during the attack: the survivor pretended to be a hostage.

CHAPTER SEVEN

THE FALKLANDS WAR

In 1982, the state of Britain's armed forces was parlous, to say the least. Endless rounds of defence cuts had taken their toll on the military capabilities of the UK, and the only thing that could bring an end to this perpetual rundown would be a war. In April 1982, that's exactly what the British got, when Argentina unexpectedly invaded the Falkland Islands.

The Falkland Islands in the South Atlantic have been under British occupation and administration since 1833. The ownership of the Falklands have always been disputed by its close neighbour, Argentina, who proclaimed the islands as hers, referring to them as Las Malvinas. But even though the islands were over 13,000km (8070 miles) from the UK, the islanders consider themselves to be British rather than Argentinian.

During the 1970s, Argentina started to make noises about taking the Falklands by force, but the dispatch of a small British fleet to the region soon put an end to these minor rumblings. However, in 1982 the subject of the Falklands was on the political agenda in Argentina once again, this time solely as an effective way of diverting public attention from the impending internal crisis that faced the military government, now under the command of General Leopoldo Galtieri.

Left: Argentinian Special Forces (*Buzos Tacticos*) played an important role in the capture of the Falkland Islands and South Georgia. The Royal Marine garrison, taken by surprise, was ordered to surrender to the invaders by the governor.

Meanwhile, back in the UK, the Conservative government under Margaret Thatcher was also going through an unpopular phase with the British public, and a political diversion overseas seemed like a good idea. The scene was set for a showdown in the South Atlantic. At the time, nobody – including the military – really thought that Britain would go to war over a group of islands that, prior to this political crisis, most British people hadn't even known existed, let alone wanted to fight over.

The catalyst for this war came on 19 March 1982, when a group of Argentinians posing as scrap metal dealers landed on the Falklands dependency of South Georgia and, in contravention of diplomatic protocol, raised their national flag. A relatively minor action was, in fact, a major diplomatic incident. At the time, the only inhabitants of South Georgia were a British Antarctic survey team and two documentary film-makers. Amid fears for their safety, a small detachment of Royal Marines from HMS *Endurance*, which was on ice patrol nearby, was ordered to provide an immediate presence on the island.

Although the force consisted of only 22 men, it gave the British survey team a degree of security and allowed intelligence to be gathered on the Argentinian invaders. On East Falkland nearby, the small detachment of Royal Marines permanently based there as part of Naval Party 8901 prepared for possible action. However, as the entire force numbered just 60 men, they could only hope to put up token resistance around key points of the island's capital, Port Stanley.

OPERATION ROSARIO

On Friday 2 April, the feared Argentinian invasion took place under the codename of Operation Rosario. Although heavily outnumbered by the Argentinians, the Royal Marines, under the command of Major Norman, put up stiff resistance until they were ordered to surrender by the islands' governor, Rex Hunt. The shocking news reached Britain, and D Squadron of 22 SAS was immediately put on standby by its commanding officer, Lieutenant Colonel Michael Rose. Within days, D Squadron had been deployed to Ascension Island, which was to become a key staging post for British forces en route to the South Atlantic.

In the meantime, the Royal Marines on South Georgia had been asked to surrender, but they refused. In response, the Argentinians deployed two groups of their Elite Marines by helicopter to Grytviken harbour, which was located close to a Royal Marines defensive position on King Edward Point. On seeing the Argentinians, the Royal Marines opened fire, bringing down a transport helicopter and badly damaging one of the Argentinian observation helicopters.

Realizing that this was going to be no walk-over, the Argentinians summoned a frigate for support. As it entered the bay, the Royal Marines opened fire with an antitank missile and succeeded in holing it below the waterline. The Argentinians attempted to turn around, but were fired on again; this time the effect was a little more serious as their gun turret was put out of action. When this engagement was finally over, the British felt that they had made their point and agreed to negotiate a surrender.

Meanwhile, back in the UK a massive task force was being assembled for the retaking of the Falkland Islands, under the codename of Operation Corporate. It was generally agreed that Britain needed to gain a quick psychological victory over the Argentinians before the main operation began, and so a small force was tasked with the re-capture of South Georgia. Commanded by Royal Marine Major Guy Sheridan, this force consisted of D Squadron, 22 SAS; M Company, 42 Commando; and No 2, Special Boat Squadron (2 SBS). This operation, codenamed Paraquet, would require the services of both the Royal Navy and the Royal Fleet Auxilary, who had the job of getting this force to its objective.

The main enemy now was the weather. The region was prone to severe storms and there were only ever a few hours of daylight. To a point, this factor would work in the favour of the British, as the Argentinians had convinced themselves that nobody would be foolish enough to attack South Georgia at the height of winter. But they had, of course, grossly underestimated the resolve and tenacity of the British. Sheridan had anticipated the Argentinians defending the harbour and inlets near to Grytviken, so instead of ordering a blind amphibious assault, decided to send in members of D Squadron's Mountain Troop as a close target recce team (CTR).

RECONNAISSANCE MISSION

Mountain Troop's task was to analyze enemy strengths and positions, and to identify a suitable place for a landing. It would be flown in by helicopter to the west of Leith, and from there make its own way on foot to the various objectives. At the same time as D Squadron was being inserted by air, 2 SBS would go ashore south-west of Grytviken, using Gemini inflatable boats. Once both teams had completed their missions, they were to launch diversion raids as the main Royal Marine force landed.

Right: The SAS were present on the Falkland Islands before the main landings took place at San Carlos, observing the Argentine positions and scouting out potential landing areas for the task force.

OPERATION CORPORATE

The opening phase of the South Atlantic campaign of 1982, the retaking of South Georgia, saw two SAS landings in the vicinity of suspected enemy positions. Despite near disaster when two Wessex helicopters crashed in a blizzard, the SAS took part in the recapture of the island along with a mixed force of Marines. During the battle for the Falklands, SAS patrols carried out forward observation duties to identify Argentine targets. On 14 May, D Squadron attacked Pebble Island. As British forces closed on Stanley, SAS detachments roamed behind the enemy lines.

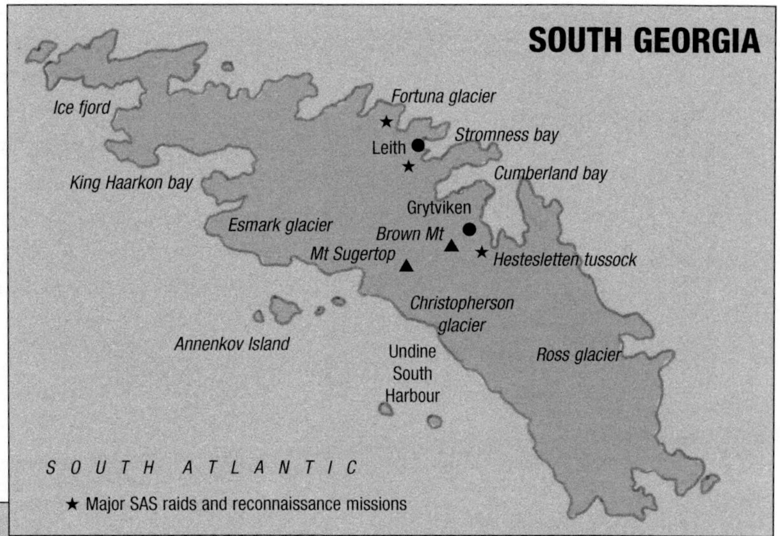

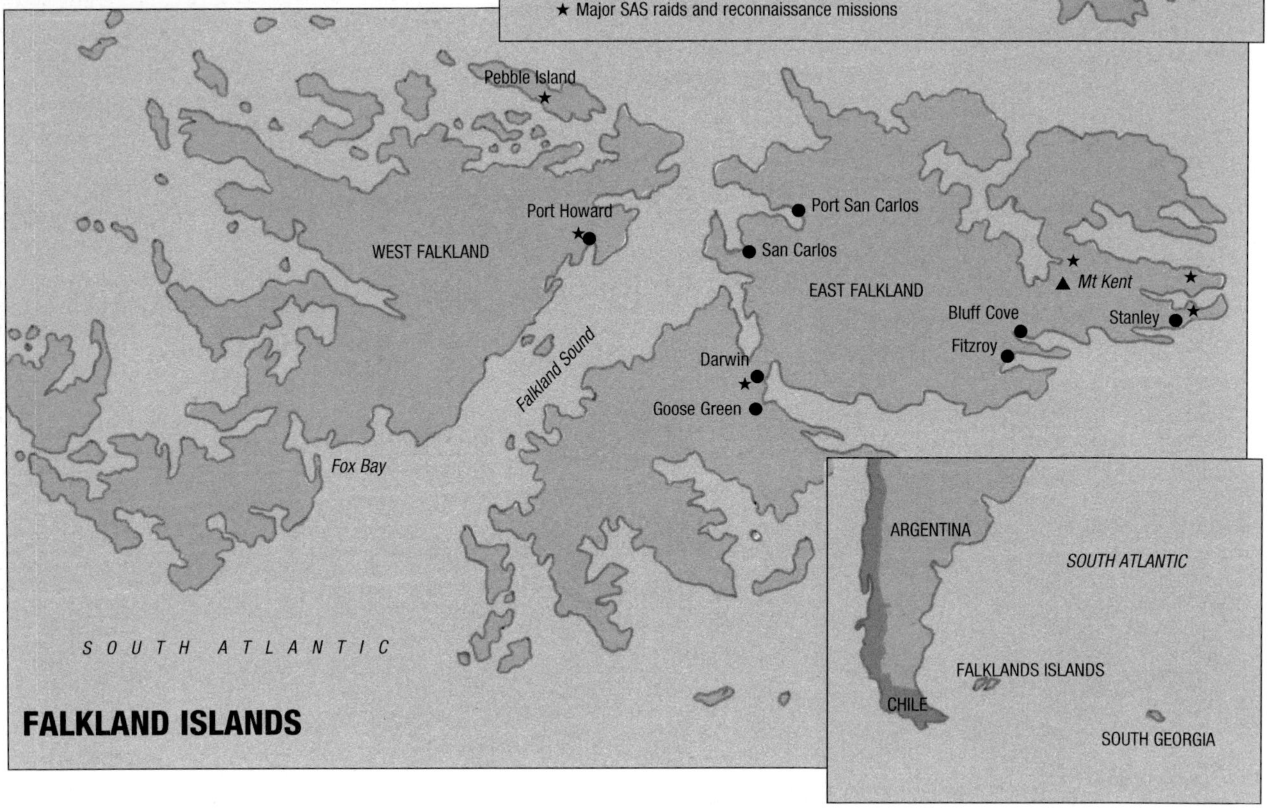

Prior to this phase of the operation, the British Ministry Of Defence agreed to the full deployment of D Squadron on Operation Paraquet, bringing the total strength of the assault force to just over 300 men; obviously this was good news for the force. On 21 April, Operation Paraquet began with the insertion of 16 SAS mountain warfare specialists on the Fortuna Glacier. As they arrived, the weather conditions were absolutely atrocious, with barely enough visibility for the helicopter pilots to operate safely. In fact, the flying conditions were virtually whiteout; it was almost impossible to tell where the ground was in relation to the helicopters' positions.

Once the helicopters had left, the SAS attempted to move off Fortuna Glacier but could not make any headway because of the gale-force wind conditions. With each man carrying almost 35kg (77lb) of equipment in their Bergens and pulling heavy sledges, it was clear that they would not make any progress fast. In fact, after five hours, they had barely covered 1km (0.6 miles). With the light now fading, they decided to take shelter from the driving blizzard, but even this was impossible: the winds were just too strong.

THE DECISION TO EVACUATE

It was now clear that they were in serious trouble and would have to abandon the mission. Another day of weather along these lines would prove fatal. Having carefully considered their options, they requested an extraction, but there was a problem: the blizzard still prevailed over Fortuna Glacier. At this point, the Royal Navy decided to go in with two troop-carrying Wessex helicopters plus a radar-equipped anti-submarine Wessex, which would act as a leader for the others to follow.

During a lull in the storm, the Wessex helicopters managed to fly in and successfully pick up the SAS team without incident. As they left the glacier, however, one of the helicopters entered a whiteout and crashed, and one trooper was injured. The two remaining helicopters returned to the crash-site to pick up the survivors, but as they climbed away, one hit a ridge and also crashed. The remaining helicopter landed nearby to ensure everyone was all right before returning to HMS *Antrim* with its passengers. Despite the ordeal he had just been through, the pilot, Lieutenant Commander Ian Stanley, volunteered to pick up the survivors from the glacier.

With the Fortuna operation now officially postponed, the SAS decided on an alternative plan. With five inflatable boats, each carrying three troopers, the SAS set off for an island just offshore of Leith. As the boats approached the island, three developed engine problems and had to be towed in by the remaining two. However, their problems were not yet over.

As they neared the shore, two boats broke free and could not be retrieved. One of the teams plunged into the water and swam ashore, but the other boat was whipped out to sea by the strong winds. Fortunately for the troopers on board, a helicopter discovered them and took them to safety, just before the arrival of a fresh storm. Despite these setbacks, the other three teams managed to get ashore and were now observing their assigned targets from covert hides at various points around the island.

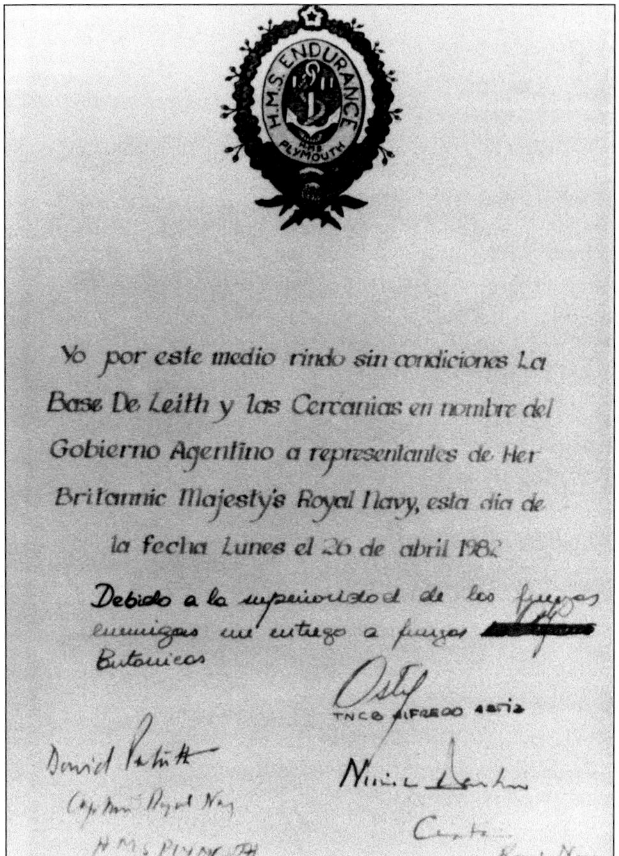
H.M.S. ENDURANCE

PLYMOUTH

Yo por este medio rindo sin condiciones La Base De Leith y las Cercanias en nombre del Gobierno Agentino a representantes de Her Britannic Majesty's Royal Navy, esta dia de la fecha Lunes el 26 de abril 1982

Debido a la superioridad de las fuerzas enemigas me entrego a fuerzas [redacted] Britanicas

TNCB ALFREDO ASTIZ

Captain Royal Navy
H.M.S. PLYMOUTH

Captain
Royal Navy

Right: The document signed by representatives of both sides agreeing the Argentine surrender of South Georgia, dated 26 April 1982. However, the fight for the Falkland Islands would be a much tougher prospect.

Above: This dramatic picture shows the wreckage of one of two helicopters lost during the attempt to extract D Squadron's Mountain Troop from Fortuna Glacier on South Georgia. A Wessex helicopter waits in the background.

The SAS was not alone in experiencing problems with boats that day. Further down the coast, SBS colleagues were forced to abandon their plans after ice punctured their inflatables. However, they were re-inserted by helicopter a short time later and completed their mission.

As if they did not have enough problems to contend with, there was now the very real threat of a submarine attack. Obviously the assault on South Georgia would have to be delayed. However, as the British tactical commanders took stock of their situation, they had an unexpected piece of good luck.

After dropping off the SBS team, the Royal Navy Wessex was returning to its ship when its crew spotted the Argentinian submarine, the *Santa Fe*, on the surface. Wasting no time, the crew dropped depth-charges near it, causing just enough damage to prevent it from submerging. Within minutes, a number of other Wasp and Lynx helicopters joined in the attack and began strafing the *Santa Fe* with machine guns and rockets. Although they failed to sink it, the damage inflicted was so severe that the captain was forced to beach her in Grytviken harbour.

ARGENTINIAN SURRENDER

Now that the British had the initiative, they naturally wanted to exploit it as soon as possible. The element of surprise now gone, and with most of the original assault team too far offshore to provide support, an ad hoc group had to be assembled using the company on board HMS *Antrim*. A small assault force was cobbled together: two SAS Troops, a small SBS team, and a small number of Royal Marines made up from

Antrim's company. As an initial gambit, *Antrim* started to drop shells near to, but not on, the Argentinian positions, in the hopes of eliciting a surrender before the assault force landed. It was a well-judged decision, as the Argentinian forces surrendered as soon as the first British helicopters appeared.

The following day, two SAS Troops and one SBS team flew into Leith by helicopter to accept the surrender of the Argentinian 16-man detachment based at this remote location. The retaking of South Georgia was a major boost for British morale and set the pace for the battles yet to come. As for D Squadron, it had no time for celebration; it was needed in the Falkland Islands as soon as possible.

As the British task force began to gather near the Falkland Islands, the demand for intelligence intensified. Without it, any large-scale landing would be doomed. As the Falkland Islands were so remote from any other country, it was virtually impossible for the British to gain any first-hand information other than by using ground forces. Using aircraft was limited not only by their range, but also by the fact that they would have to operate from aircraft carriers, which were far too precious to be risked for such a role.

Originally there were hopes that Britain's allies, the Americans, would assist by providing satellite

Below: D Squadron 22 SAS leaves its calling card with the destruction of the Argentinian Pucara fleet on Pebble Island. These aircraft posed a significant threat to the British Task Force and were a high priority target.

imagery of the islands and the occupying forces, but these were soon dashed when the Central Intelligence Agency (CIA) refused to cooperate – it needed to keep on good terms with General Galtieri, who figured in US plans for South America. When it came to supplying advanced military hardware for the British task force, however, the Americans were extremely helpful.

From 1 May onwards, the priority for both the SAS and SBS was intelligence-gathering on the Falklands. The most important information for the task force related to those sites most suitable for a large-scale landing. The Commander of the Carrier Battle Group, Rear-Admiral Woodward, was also desperate for intelligence on the exact locations of the Argentinians' trailer-mounted Exocet anti-shipping missiles, as they posed a considerable threat to the British Task Force. Also of importance was the location of Argentinian troop positions and their supporting assets – in other words, aircraft, helicopters, artillery and armour.

Below: The remains of an Argentinian Pucara ground attack aircraft are examined by a couple of curious locals. They were the only Argentinian fixed-wing aircraft capable of flying from Pebble Island airstrip.

PUCARA

Below: The Argentine Pucara aircraft were the only fixed-wing ground attack assets available to the Argentinian commander once the airstrip at Port Stanley was out of action. It was essential that the SAS destroy them.

The British needed answers to these questions fast, so from the beginning of May onwards, members of G Squadron's Air, Mountain and Mobility Troop were inserted by helicopter all over the Falklands. As the demands for more information grew, patrols from D Squadron were sent in to either replace or supplement their fellow troopers.

At this time, the SAS had around 10 four-man patrols on the islands. Their typical routine involved laying up during the day in hides dug out of the damp, peaty soil or, if they were lucky, a sheltered rock outcrop. Once darkness fell, they would move around the Argentinian positions, plotting their lines of defence, locating machine-gun positions, identifying command and control centres, and picking up daily routines.

BURST RADIOS

As the patrols gathered information, they relayed it back to the operational command centre onboard the aircraft carrier HMS *Hermes*. This was done by sending encoded messages via highly sophisticated radio transmitters, known as 'Burst' radios, as they translated information into alpha-numeric codes before sending it out in a short, high-frequency burst. These transmissions generally lasted less than one second, making it impossible for the Argentinians to monitor the message or trace the location of the source by electronic direction-finding equipment.

For the covertly operating SAS patrols, life was tough. They were expected to remain undercover for weeks at a time, eating mainly cold food and living in damp, cold conditions. A typical routine would involve two men on duty, one resting, while the other carried out personal admin, such as cleaning weapons, checking equipment, preparing food or sending radio transmissions. Where possible, the SAS would create two hides close together, one used as an OP (observation post) and the other as an LUP (lying-up position).

The main intelligence-gathering operations concentrated around Stanley, Bluff Cove, Fox Bay, Berkeley Sound, Port Salvador, San Carlos Water, Cow Bay, Port Howard, Goose Green and Pebble Island. What is remarkable about these patrols is that throughout the entire operation, only one hide was ever discovered by the Argentinians, and this occurred on 10 June.

The Argentinians later revealed what had happened. As they approached the hide, Captain John Hamilton of D Squadron opened fire on them, while his signaller escaped. Sadly, after putting up stiff resistance for a considerable period of time, he

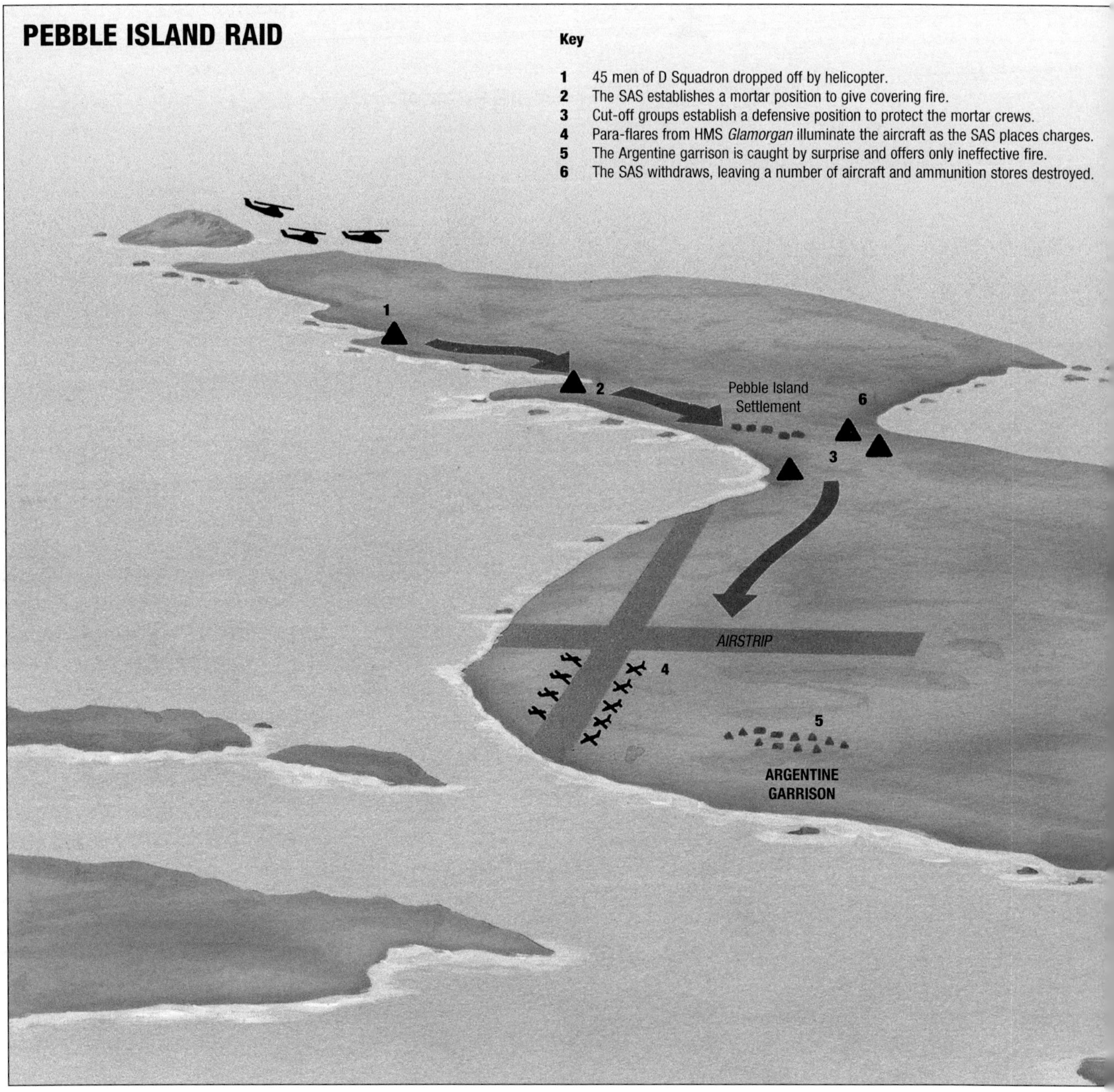

was eventually killed and his signaller captured. The Argentinian officer who led the attack against him later stated that Hamilton deserved a Victoria Cross. Indeed, after the war ended, Hamilton was awarded a posthumous Military Cross for his actions.

CHILEAN ADVENTURE

One of the most secretive SAS patrols during the Falklands War involved an illegal trip to Chile. In early May 1982, the Chilean Government demanded that the British explain why the burned-out carcass

CHRONOLOGY

Date 1982

Location Falkland Islands

Operation The SAS is deployed to the Falkland Islands to carry out intelligence and raiding operations against Argentinian forces that are occupying the island illegally. Although many significant missions are undertaken, the key operations during this conflict are the retaking of Grytviken, South Georgia and the Pebble Island raid. The SAS are highly successful during this war, but regrettably lose 18 men in a non-combat related helicopter crash.

of a Sea King helicopter had been discovered on farmland in Chile. In response, the British Government stated that the helicopter had been forced to make a diversion to Chile due to engine trouble. Although the Chileans refused to accept this explanation, they chose to do no more than complain: after all, Britain had always been a good friend to them.

It later transpired, of course, that this story was a cover and that the Sea King had been stripped out to increase its range for a one-way flight, as the SAS urgently needed to put a team into Argentina to observe a key Argentinian Air Force base that was plaguing the British Task Force. It is believed that the team sent back highly detailed intelligence concerning the movements of aircraft, and that in effect they were acting as an early-warning system for the vulnerable British Fleet. Around this time, another audacious operation was being planned along these lines, but the SAS was far from enthusiastic about it.

Deemed as a 'Stake in the Heart' operation, the plan was that two RAF C-130 Hercules transport aircraft would make a steep 'Khe Sanh' approach towards the main runway at Port Stanley. Once lined up, Sea Harriers from the nearby Fleet would strafe the Argentinian defensive positions in and around the airfield. At this point, the Hercules would land and disgorge their cargo of SAS troopers. Once on the ground, the squadron-strength force was to assault

the main command-and-control centre on the airfield and seize the senior officers. Upon hearing the news of their capture, the theory ran, the remainder of the Argentinian forces would surrender.

It was an interesting plan, but its critics compared it to Market Garden, the operation that had led to the disaster at Arnhem, during World War II. Not surprisingly, the idea fell flat on its face, especially when it was announced that for most of the men involved, it would be a one-way mission. Now firmly ruled out for Port Stanley, this type of assault was, however, still very much on the agenda for another area. The commander of the SAS Group, Brigadier Peter de la Billière, backed the concept of such a daring plan, deciding instead that it should be used on mainland Argentina.

This time, however, the plan involved absolutely no air support. The target was the Argentinian airbase from where the Etendard strike aircraft, carrying the deadly French Exocet anti-shipping missiles, were causing severe operational problems for the British. The essential difference in this enterprising plan was the objective: the SAS was required to destroy all of the ground-attack aircraft found at the base, plus their stock of Exocet missiles. In addition, the SAS men were to kill all the Argentinian Etendard pilots before making their withdrawal.

To say the very least, this operation was highly controversial and pushed the loyalties of the SAS troopers to the limit. They knew that for many of them, it would be a one-way ticket; their transport aircraft would probably be destroyed in the initial assault phase, leaving them with the prospect of escaping and evading the Argentinian special forces

Left: An SAS trooper in the Falklands armed with an American M16 rifle. He wears civilian mountaineering boots and waterproof gaiters, with a windproof smock and trousers for protection against the cold.

Above: An SAS patrol dismounts from a Scout helicopter at Bluff Cove, crouching to avoid the rotor blades. Light helicopters such as the Scout were ideally suited for inserting the small SAS patrols behind enemy lines.

over miles of open area. Obviously any Argentinian pursuers would be less than sympathetic to the SAS, especially if they had just killed their unarmed pilots in cold blood.

The briefing almost prompted a mutiny within the SAS ranks, but in the end a compromise was reached with the senior officers: there would be no attack on the Argentinian mainland. Instead an operation would be mounted against the Argentinian airstrip on Pebble Island, which is located to the north of West Falkland.

PEBBLE ISLAND RAID

The Argentinian airstrip at Pebble Island contained mainly Pucara ground-attack aircraft, which were highly effective against ground forces and were well within the flight range of the proposed Task Force landing site at San Carlos. On the night of 9 May, two four-man patrols from D Squadron's Boat Troop were due to be sent on a detailed recce of the airstrip, but the operation was cancelled due to bad weather. The following night, the patrols were inserted by helicopter to West Falkland and, from there, made the crossing to Pebble Island in collapsible canoes.

Upon landing, they split into two groups, one staying put with the canoes while the second carried out a detailed recce of the airstrip. After a few hours, the men of the second group withdrew to their canoes and transmitted a report to the Task Force. Admiral Woodward was pleased with the intelligence collected by the SAS recce team and immediately sanctioned a raid.

As word reached D Squadron, its men set about making preparations for the raid, now scheduled for 14 May. The attack force comprised around 60

Above: Anticipating an air attack from the Argentinian Air Force, British forces take cover in the barren landscape of the Falkland Islands. In the background can be seen numerous foxholes dug by the British troops.

men, and included a forward observation officer from 148th Commando Battery, Royal Artillery. The main attack force was made up of Mountain Troop, with Mobility and Air Troop acting in support, while the remaining members of the D Squadron's Boat Troop were assigned to the mortar team, which would lay down covering fire during the withdrawal phase.

For additional fire support, the SAS could call in naval gunfire from HMS *Glamorgan*, stationed 10km (6 miles) offshore. Each man carried an M-16 assault rifle, along with extra ammunition for the General Purpose Machine Gun (GPMG) and mortar. In addition, a number of them carried light antitank weapons, which were ideal for knocking out aircraft.

APPROACH TO THE AIRFIELD

The helicopter lift to the island was tasked to 846 Naval Air Squadron, which dropped the assault force within a few miles of the airstrip. Once on the ground, D Squadron met up with the recce team from Boat Troop and made their way towards the objective. At 0700, Mountain Troop began its attack on the airstrip, while HMS *Glamorgan* opened fire on the nearby Argentinian troop positions.

As the men of the SAS made their way around the parked aircraft, they planted explosive charges on the same spot of each airframe. The reason for this was simple: the Argentinians would be unable to repair any of the aircraft by swapping parts. The Argentinians put up little resistance during the raid, and the SAS troopers went about their business with almost no intervention. Within 15 minutes of the start of the attack, 11 aircraft had been either destroyed or severely damaged, with no SAS losses. As the troopers withdrew to the pick-up point, the helicopters arrived and extracted them back to the Task Force, giving the Argentinians no chance to counterattack.

FATAL ACCIDENT

The Pebble Island raid had been a great success, leaving the Argentinians in no doubt that the SAS meant business and that they could expect more of the same. However, on 19 May, disaster struck the SAS when a Sea King helicopter carrying members of D Squadron plunged into the sea following an engine failure, the result of a bird-strike, during a routine cross-decking transfer from the aircraft carrier HMS *Hermes* to the assault ship HMS *Intrepid*.

Although there were survivors, very few were from the SAS. Once a final head count had been established with D Squadron, they discovered to their horror that 18 men were dead. This was the Regiment's worse single loss of life since World War II. After Pebble Island, the SAS carried out a diversionary raid on Darwin, while the main Task force landed at San Carlos Water. Returning from the raid, they spotted a Pucara ground-attack aircraft heading for San Carlos and shot it down with a Stinger SAM.

Following the landings, both the SAS and SBS carried out deep penetration patrols around the

Below: British foxholes come under heavy Argentinian artillery bombardment from a battery in Port Stanley. They were unable to return fire because the Argentinians had sited their guns next to houses containing civilians.

surrounding area of East Falkland, and on 30 May the SAS joined up with 42 Commando and assisted them in the capture of Mount Kent. During one of these patrols, an SAS team came across an Argentinian helicopter FOB (forward operations base) and called in an air strike. Highly successful for the British, it left most of the helicopters either damaged or destroyed. On 13 June a combined force of SAS, SBS and Royal Marines carried out a final raid on Stanley Harbour as part of a diversion for 2 Para, which was at that time assaulting Wireless Ridge. Although the raid served its purpose, the force came under heavy Argentinian fire and had to withdraw.

As these raids were taking place, the commanding officer of 22 SAS, Lieutenant Colonel Mike Rose, had been directing a psychological warfare operation against the Argentinian forces on the Falklands. Broadcasting a message to the Argentinians on a daily basis over the open radio net, he provided them with an appraisal of their ever-declining military

Below: The face of defeat as seen in these Argentinian soldiers parading in Port Stanley after surrendering to the British. The SAS had played a key role in locating enemy defences and weak points for the main British forces.

Left: An SAS trooper on West Falkland armed with an American Stinger anti-aircraft missile, which was lighter than the British Blowpipe and, being infrared-guided, was a 'fire-and-forget' system.

successes, urging them to surrender. Eventually, Rose was invited to negotiate terms of surrender with the Argentinian Commander-in-Chief, General Menendez. Also present was Captain Bell, a Royal Marine officer who spoke Spanish, and General Jeremy Moore, commander of British land forces. At first, Menendez would agree to a partial surrender only, but Rose refused to accept this and demanded a full surrender, or the deal was off.

However, unbeknown to Menendez, the British Government was willing to accept a partial surrender. Its military situation was also very difficult after the loss of the supply ship *Atlantic Conveyor*, which contained valuable equipment for the British forces. Rose, though, would have made a great poker player, and played his cards so perfectly that eventually Menendez accepted defeat, agreeing to surrender on Britain's generous terms, which allowed the Argentinian forces to leave the Falkland islands without losing face. Lt Col Mike Rose had made his point very well, and fully lived up to the SAS motto of 'Who Dares Wins'.

Right: A Fijian SAS trooper on the Falklands in 1982. He wears a civilian weatherproof jacket with standard British camouflage trousers. He is armed with an SLR rifle.

CHAPTER EIGHT

DESERT STORM 1990–91

On 2 August 1990, Kuwait was invaded by its neighbour, Iraq, thus giving Iraq's leader, Saddam Hussein, control over a significant proportion of the world's oil resources. The weak armed forces of Kuwait were no match for the Iraqis. Around the world, the fear was the same: if the West failed to react, Saudi Arabia, the key Middle Eastern oil-producer, would be likely to suffer the same fate.

The US President, George Bush Snr, realized that this situation was potentially extremely dangerous, and he initiated Operation Desert Shield to prevent an invasion of Saudi Arabia. Under the flag of the UN, an international coalition force was put together with a mandate to retake Kuwait, and it saw the largest concentration of special forces ever assembled for a single conflict.

Under the aegis of Special Operations Command (SOCOM), based in Tampa, Florida, the United States provided the main contribution of special forces personnel, closely followed by the UK. The French also sent over a significant contingent of their Foreign Legion and 6th Parachute Division, while Australia and New Zealand provided a combined ANZAC SAS Squadron.

Recognizing the key role that special forces had played during the 1982 Falklands War, the UK sent almost the entire regular SAS Regiment to the region, a force that amounted to some 700 men. It was made up from A, B and D squadrons, plus 15 reservist volunteers from R Squadron. G Squadron was committed to other operations – including counter-terrorist duties back in the UK – and was not deployed to the Gulf. In support of the SAS, members of the Royal Marines, Special Boat Service (SBS) were deployed to the region, along with RAF special operations aircrew. Clearly, for the UK this was a major operation, and the Coalition would later express how greatly it valued the participation of the SAS in support of its mission.

Left: SAS soldiers pose for a photo prior to their operational deployment in Desert Storm. General Schwarzkopf was initially reluctant to give a major role to special forces in the operation, but was quickly persuaded otherwise.

HUMAN SHIELDS

As the Coalition Forces gathered together in Saudi Arabia for the forthcoming operation, there was a serious and troubling development. Having anticipated a response from the West, Saddam Hussein had been busy placing hostages, who had been captured at the outbreak of the conflict, around likely military targets. In effect, he had turned these people into 'human shields'.

The American forces, led by General Schwarzkopf, and the British, led by General de la Billière, wasted

Above: British troops go into an all-round defence formation after exiting an RAF Puma during work-up training in the Gulf. In the meantime, the SAS was planning how to extract British hostages from Iraq.

no time in planning a rescue mission for their respective national hostages. There was, however, a major obstacle in their way: the hostages had been positioned around numerous sites, meaning that to coordinate simultaneous attacks on all of them would have been impossible. The Coalition leaders were quick to realize that even if some of the hostages could be rescued by the SAS and Delta, it was fair to assume that the others would be executed in reprisal. The risks were just too great to contemplate such a mission.

As the SAS tentatively considered their options, the hostage crisis suddenly came to an end. Saddam Hussein decided to release the hostages as a gesture of goodwill, following intense international political pressure. This was to be just the first of many mind games that he would play during the conflict, but for now the SAS was relieved to be able to get on with planning other missions that would, it hoped, bring about a swift conclusion to the Gulf crisis.

SAS VETERAN

General Sir Peter de la Billière, the joint British Commander-in-Chief in the Gulf, was a veteran of the SAS and knew the value of the force. This was to be of key importance in convincing General Norman Schwarzkopf, the commander of the Coalition ground forces, that the SAS could play a major part in this operation if given permission to operate behind Iraqi front lines. General Schwarzkopf was initially sceptical of the SAS's potential to operate behind enemy lines in the way first proposed, but he was impressed with the regiment's track record and gave permission for two squadrons to be deployed on 20 January 1991.

The SAS wasted no time in infiltrating Iraqi territory. Within hours of their deployment, men were driving around deep behind enemy lines searching for targets of opportunity. In many ways, they were performing like the forefathers of the SAS, the Long Range Desert Group (LRDG) of World War II.

A and D Squadrons had been divided into mobile fighting columns, each with eight Land Rover 110s armed with Browning 12.7mm (0.5in) heavy machine guns. In addition to the primary armament, they carried other weapons such as 7.62mm (0.3in) GPMGs, 40mm (1.57in) Mk 19 grenade-launchers, and Milan antitank missiles. The SAS were in particular impressed with the Milan, as its thermal-imaging sight gave them the ability to operate in total darkness. It could generate imagery out to a range of 8km (5 miles); the missile itself, however, being wire-guided, was limited to a range of 2000m (2187yd).

COLUMN EQUIPMENT

Each column also had a Unimog utility vehicle, which carried the bulk of the extra stores needed for long-range operations. Typically this consisted of fuel, rations, ammunition, vehicle spares, and Nuclear, Biological and Chemical (NBC) equipment. Several motorbikes also accompanied each column, providing a scout capability to the front and side flanks. Before embarking on the journey to Iraq, the SAS had been training in the United Arab Emirates, honing their skills for what was to come. During this training, they decided not to take their Light Strike Vehicles (LSV) into Iraq. These Dune Buggy-like vehicles could carry massive firepower over rough terrain very quickly; however, they were not as reliable as the Land Rover 110s and, when loaded up with equipment, suffered from problems with their centre of gravity.

On average, each mobility column had 30 SAS troops assigned to it, each with their own personal weapons. Most carried an M16 assault rifle fitted with a 40mm (1.57in) M203 grenade-launcher, along with a small pistol for personal protection. The firepower each mobility column possessed was truly awesome, and this would give the SAS a major advantage over the enemy during each contact. For navigation, the SAS had Global Positioning Systems (GPS), compasses and, in some cases, sextants. They also carried secure state-of-the-art communication systems to enable them to receive orders and to relay information back to their command centre.

Each column was tasked with a different area of responsibility within a region, and some of these

Below: The biggest threat to the Allied Coalition came from this weapon, the Scud surface-to-surface missile, which had the range to reach Israel. When Iraq began to attack Tel Aviv, the destruction of the Scuds became top priority for the SAS.

ATTACKING A SCUD SITE

Key

1 SAS Land Rovers launch Milan missiles at the site.
2 Mobile Scud launchers and command and control vehicles are the priority targets.
3 Iraqi BMP and BRDM armoured vehicles attempt to respond to the SAS attack.
4 After launching their missiles, the SAS evades any pursuers.
5 Any remaining targets of worth are destroyed by air attack.

extended almost 400km (250 miles) behind enemy lines. The SAS generally operated at night, taking full advantage of the hours of darkness, as the Iraqi forces had very little night-vision capability at troop level. During the hours of daylight, the SAS would lay-up in what ever cover was available, be it a wadi or a sunken feature in what was generally a flat landscape. The terrain in western Iraq was mainly lava bed mixed with wadis, which proved to be hard going for the mobility columns, but which also hampered Iraqi movements.

The SAS spaced their vehicles out as much as possible when on the move in order to prevent enemy ambushes. Sometimes the spread of these vehicles could be as much as 1km (0.6 miles), making it very difficult for an Iraqi force to hit them all during an attack. One major advantage that the SAS enjoyed over the Iraqi forces was that it was setting the agenda. The Iraqi soldiers simply never knew when, or where, the SAS would strike, and their morale plummeted.

MISTAKEN IDENTITY

On one occasion, a recce unit for an Iraqi artillery brigade stumbled onto an SAS position. Thinking these were friendly forces, the men stopped their Russian-built Gaz-69 truck close by the SAS unit. An Iraqi officer carrying a map case got out of the vehicle and walked towards the SAS soldiers. As he came nearer, however, he realized his mistake. When he pulled out a pistol, the SAS patrol had no choice but to open fire, and in the subsequent firefight all of the Iraqi soldiers were killed, bar one. The surviving Iraqi soldier was taken prisoner and flown back to Saudi Arabia for interrogation, along with maps and plans that the SAS had discovered in the Gaz-69.

After gaining good intelligence from this patrol, the SAS was able to identify further high-value targets that had not previously been detected by air assets.

The biggest problem these men faced was the weather, rather than the enemy. Intelligence had failed to brief them on the severity of the cold in the region and so the SAS soldiers carried only lightweight smocks that were totally unsuitable for these conditions. As an interim solution, Arab blanket coats were procured in the region, along with gloves and local head-dress. These items were then issued during routine re-supply drops made by the RAF using Chinook helicopters.

As the SAS continued operations behind Iraqi lines, they were tasked with several priority missions. Military planners in Riyadh needed to know if the ground in Iraq could support the weight of tanks and heavy vehicles, so samples were required before any major ground war could begin. The SAS carried out this mission with great success, and the results proved to be invaluable to the Coalition.

COMMUNICATION WEAKNESS

The missions intensified, and the SAS realized that the Achilles' heel of the Iraqis' war machine was their communications network. This consisted of fibre-optic cables buried underground. These were difficult to find from the air, but could easily be destroyed by small teams on the ground. The SAS used two tactics against them: first, the men would blow up some of the cables with hand-placed charges, then they would leave booby traps for the Iraqi repair teams in or around the cables, forcing the Iraqis to spend precious time finding these hidden devices. This time factor was critical to the Coalition forces. The longer the SAS kept the Iraqi forces in the dark about what was going on around the battlefield, the easier it would be for conventional military forces to operate.

Right: A trooper from 22 SAS in the Gulf in 1991. He wears a thick ribbed sweater for warmth, combat trousers and lightweight desert boots. He is armed with the L1A1 SLR, an old rifle but accurate up to 600m (1970ft).

Above: An SAS Land Rover equipped with a Milan anti-tank missile post makes a deadly combination. The SAS found the Milan's imaging system of great value during desert operations, as it enabled the men to pick out distant targets.

On one particular operation, the SAS was tasked with destroying a communications tower deep behind Iraqi lines. Attacking at night using heavy vehicle-mounted weapons, the men succeeded in destroying the tower and all of its support equipment. The SAS men who carried out the attack were somewhat surprised at just how little resistance they met during the firefight. They later found out that the Iraqi soldiers had been under the impression that they were being attacked from the air and had taken shelter in their underground bunkers. Indeed, this was to be a common occurrence because at this time the Iraqis had no idea that the SAS were operating in such a mobile way so deep within their lines.

In fact, the SAS were causing absolute chaos behind the Iraqi lines, and this forced the Iraqi commanders to withdraw troops from their front-line duties and re-deploy them in defensive roles around their rear echelon areas. The SAS tactics of cutting roads and creating diversions was clearly paying off and, combined with coordinated air operations, the effect was devastating.

On 24 January 1991, the role of the SAS was abruptly changed to that of anti-Scud missile operations, and this would be the case for the remainder of the war. The sudden reason for this change came on the night of 18 January 1991, when Iraq attacked Israel with Scud missiles. It suddenly became apparent to the Coalition that if these attacks continued against Israel, there was a real danger that Israel would enter the conflict in retaliation, which would have resulted in most of the Arab contingents leaving the Coalition.

SCUD ATTACKS

General Schwarzkopf quickly realized the implications of these Scud attacks and ordered a maximum effort against both the Scuds and their launch sites. Western intelligence was well aware that Iraq had a great number of these surface-to-surface missiles and had launched over 200 against Iran in 1988 alone. It was also known that Iraq had received over 800 Scuds from the Soviets in the early 1980s, and that a number of them had been modified to carry chemical warheads. This capability was of huge concern to the Coalition. Its members had seen Saddam Hussein use chemical weapons against his own people without any hesitation, and knew that he had both the method and the means of delivering them into Israel or any other country that fell within range of his launch sites.

It was estimated that Iraq had 28 static launch sites and around 36 mobile launchers, which were mounted on large eight-wheeled vehicles and required a number of support units in order to operate. At first, the Coalition felt that this threat could be eliminated by air power alone; however, it found the Scuds extremely difficult to locate from the air, and even when it was successful in finding them, the time taken to assemble an air strike was too long. Indeed, in many cases, they arrived after the Scuds had left.

The SAS knew that the Scuds were the key issue of the war for the Coalition, and that their destruction was imperative to ensure victory over the Iraqis. Never a unit to do anything half-heartedly, it decided to attack the Scud threat in three ways. First, it would deploy road-watch patrols to report on Scud movements. Second, mobility columns (which had proved so successful at the start of the conflict) would be used to attack the Scud convoys at every opportunity. Third, SAS units would intensify their operations against the Iraqis' underground communications network, which was the principal means of issuing orders from Baghdad to the Scud units. The road-watch patrols were supplied by B Squadron and were made up of three eight-man teams, which were tasked with observing the Iraqis' three main supply routes (MSRs), running from the Euphrates valley to the Jordanian border. The teams were called the North, Central and South road-watch teams and were inserted into western Iraq by RAF Chinooks on 22 January.

Up until this point, things had been going rather well for the SAS. However, everything was about to change for the worse. Before the three road-watch teams were inserted, there had been problems with

CHRONOLOGY

Date	1990–91
Location	The Gulf
Operation	The SAS is deployed to the Gulf in support of the UN-led campaign to remove Iraq from Kuwait. The Regiment undertakes missions in Iraq, mainly against the Iraqis' Scud missiles and their support infrastructure. Highly successful, it operates in ways that are very similar to the original SAS in North Africa.
Date	1998
Location	The Gulf
Operation	In February 1998, the SAS deploy a squadron to the Gulf when Saddam Hussein threatens to start another war. It is tasked with reconnaissance missions and also the rescue of downed Allied pilots.

the supply of various items of kit for the mission, since the other squadrons had taken the majority of the stores with them on their anti-Scud patrols. As a result, B Squadron was short of several essential items, such as grenades for their M203 grenade-launchers. There was also a problem with the maps. Intelligence had pilots' charts, but these showed only basic land features in a very small scale and were of little use to a soldier planning a mission.

ROAD WATCH MISSIONS

Their very character means that SAS soldiers are not quitters, so they decided to go ahead with the road-watch missions and just tough it out, despite these setbacks. On the way to their respective drop-off points (DOPs), the men of B Squadron landed at a US forward operating base (FOB) to take on extra fuel for their RAF Chinook helicopters. While on the ground, scrounged extra ammunition and rations for their mission from the American ground personnel who were refuelling their helicopters. Although they were allies, nothing was discussed regarding their final destination. In fact, each SAS team operated separately from the other, with no details being exchanged about where they were being dropped off, or at what time; it was a strictly need-to-know operation and as standard operating procedure (SOP), only the mission planners would know where each team was to operate.

Within hours of being inserted into Iraq, there were more problems. There simply was no practical cover for the teams to lay-up during the day, and the proposed operating areas were crawling with Iraqi soldiers and, in some cases, civilians. The nature of the territory also caused setbacks for the US special forces, and in one case an A-Team had to

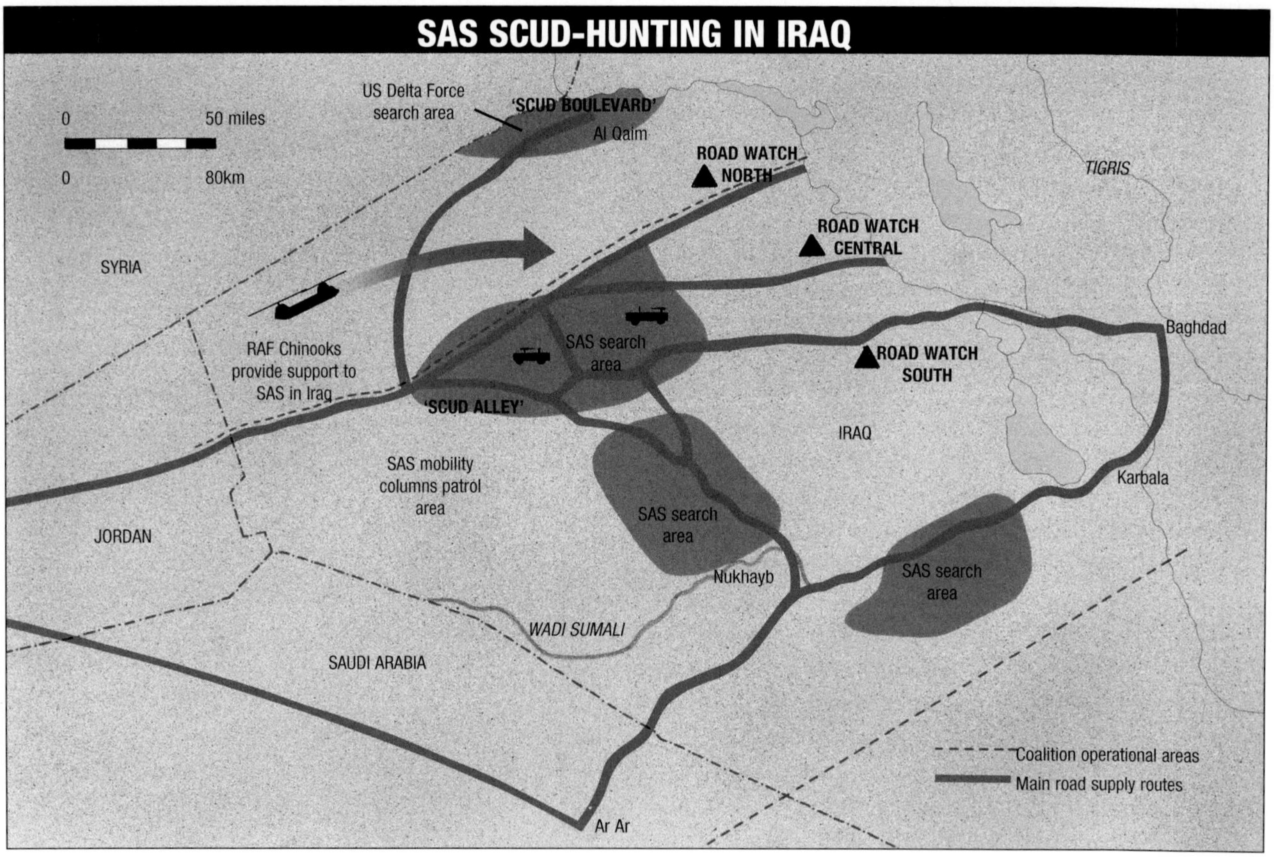

be extracted in a spectacular manner while receiving heavy enemy fire.

For two SAS teams, South and Central, the ground situation was totally unsuitable for them to operate within in a covert manner for any length of time. The risk of being compromised was just too great. After carefully considering their options, they decided to abort their missions and return to base. One team returned in the Chinook that had brought them in, while the other walked all the way back to Saudi Arabia, a distance of some 200km (124 miles).

ABORTED MISSIONS

Naturally there were a few raised eyebrows regarding the two aborted missions. The section commander of one was virtually accused of being a coward, while the other was given a pat on the back for calling in an air strike on two mobile Iraqi radar systems located near to them. As the fate of the other team became known, the section commanders' decisions were considered to have been correct; their first duty is to the men under their command, not the mission.

The story of the team that remained behind was to become a legend in modern warfare. Northern road-watch team – or 'Bravo Two Zero' as it was codenamed – decided to stay in Iraq and perform its mission as best as it could under the circumstances. Only hours into the mission, serious issues arose. The men discovered that they were laying up near an Iraqi encampment and, to make matters worse, they were suddenly plunged into every soldier's worst nightmare. A civilian, a young Iraqi boy, had spotted the SAS team. They now faced a dreadful decision: either to kill the boy and give themselves the chance to get away; or let him live and face the consequences of the Iraqi Army being alerted to their presence. SAS soldiers are men of great honour and do not wage war against civilians. The choice had been made: they were going to take a chance and make a run for it, remembering the motto that he 'Who fights and runs away, lives to fight another day.'

With the alarm now raised, the Iraqis were immediately on the trail of the SAS. The men had little choice but to escape and evade capture as best they possibly could by putting some distance between them and the Iraqi patrols. They decided to make for Syria, which offered them the best chance of survival since there was little hope of their being extracted by helicopter. Under the command of Sergeant Andy McNab, the men 'tabbed' at a frantic pace to keep ahead of the Iraqis. They could take some comfort in knowing that the Coalition had total air supremacy and there was little chance of Iraqi helicopters being sent in to search for them. But as the SAS soldiers crossed the Arabian desert, fate played a dreadful card. The weather conditions were appalling and the soldiers found themselves battling through a lethal cocktail of rain, sleet, driving wind and snow. Even with warm clothing, this would have been a challenge, but as they had been forced to ditch their spare kit in an effort to make better progress, these men were wearing only lightweight smocks.

In an effort to increase their overall chances of survival, the team split up into two groups. As they pushed themselves to the edge of exhaustion, one soldier, Sergeant Vince Phillips, got separated from his group and died of hypothermia. The other team members tried in vain to find him; however, due to the hard, driving sleet they were caught up in, this proved impossible. What remained of their luck now ran out: they found themselves surrounded by Iraqi soldiers. One was forced to surrender, but the other made a spectacular escape. Walking day and night, he covered over 200km (124 miles) on foot and made it to the Syrian border. If ever there was an example of what gives a man the right to wear the SAS beret, this surely was it. For the last two days of this soldier's journey, he had no water, and yet nonetheless he pushed on. At no time did he ever consider giving up.

TWO ZERO CAPTURED

Meanwhile, the other five members of the team made it to a town called Al Qaim, near the Jordanian border, and here their luck also ran out. Having fought their way through many firefights, they bumped into a large group of Iraqi soldiers, and all hell broke loose. Although heavily outnumbered, they fought a series of running battles and inflicted heavy casualties on the Iraqis as they tried to shake them off. One of the SAS soldiers, Trooper Robert Consiglio, was killed as he covered his team's withdrawal, and soon after this, a further two were captured after running out of ammunition. Amazingly, the remaining two team members managed to avoid capture and found shelter in a small cabin. Then tragedy struck. One of the soldiers, Lance-Corporal Lane, collapsed and later died of hypothermia. The soldier who had been with him tried to escape, but was captured as he fled towards the border. This final capture marked the end of the SAS team 'Bravo Two Zero'.

Although technically this mission failed to carry out its objectives, it caused absolute chaos to the Iraqi forces, leaving over 250 of their soldiers dead and several hundred injured. The after-effects of the mission rippled across Iraq,resulting in more Iraqi units being withdrawn from the front line to search for any remaining SAS teams operating behind their lines.

The road-watch teams had been unable to gain intelligence on the Scuds' movements, as they had

SAS GULF WAR LAND ROVER

A typical Land Rover converted by the SAS for use in the Gulf War. A Milan anti-tank launcher is mounted on top of the vehicle for knocking out SCUD missiles. A grenade launcher and machine gun are also fitted.

Above: Although this photo was taken in 1991 at the height of the Gulf War, the principles of desert warfare were the same as in North Africa during World War II. Just surviving in the desert can be as demanding as fighting the enemy.

originally been tasked, but the destruction of the Scuds remained a top priority for the SAS. For the other squadrons, it was business as usual as they went about looking for mobile Scud units to attack in their designated operational areas. The SAS's operational area was based around the Iraqi H-2 airfield – an area 32km (20 miles) long by 26km (17 miles) wide – and was designated the 'Southern Scud Box'. The SAS, however, called it 'Scud Alley'. American special forces worked very closely with the SAS, and were responsible for the 'Northern Scud Box', based around Al Qaim. Like the SAS, they created their own nickname for their operational area: to them, it was 'Scud Boulevard'.

Within days of crossing the border into Iraq, one of the SAS mobility columns discovered a camouflaged Scud site on the verge of launching a salvo of missiles against Israel. Knowing they had to act quickly, they called in an air strike, and within minutes of their request USAAF strike aircraft pummelled the site and completely destroyed it. The SAS wasted no time in leaving the scene: there were very real concerns that some of the Scud missiles might have chemical warheads imbued with nerve agents such as Sarin, which Iraq had formerly used against Iran.

CIRCLE THE WAGONS

Mindful that Iraqi patrols were out looking for them, the SAS men had to be constantly vigilant. Whenever they stopped to refuel or re-arm, they formed a defensive circle using their vehicles for protection against an attack. On one occasion, this tactic paid off when an SAS mobility column found itself under attack from a larger Iraqi force, and a fierce firefight ensued. Eventually the Iraqis withdrew after taking a number of casualties and losing three of their vehicles from heavy machine-gun fire.

PROMISORY NOTE

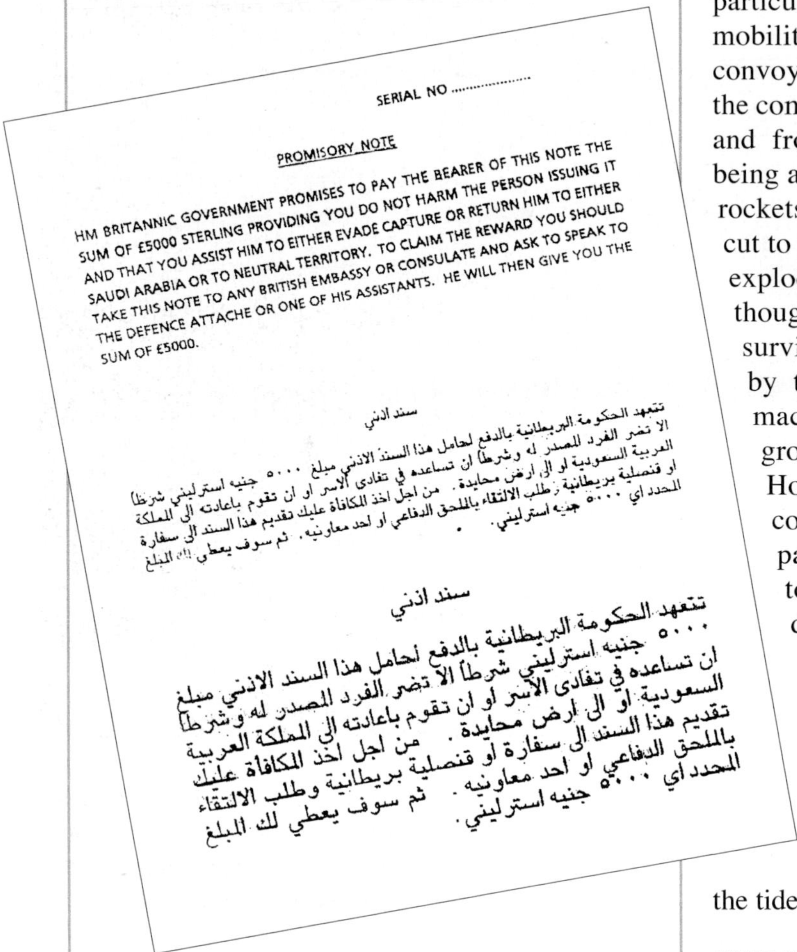

SERIAL NO ....

PROMISORY NOTE

HM BRITANNIC GOVERNMENT PROMISES TO PAY THE BEARER OF THIS NOTE THE SUM OF £5000 STERLING PROVIDING YOU DO NOT HARM THE PERSON ISSUING IT AND THAT YOU ASSIST HIM TO EITHER EVADE CAPTURE OR RETURN HIM TO EITHER SAUDI ARABIA OR TO NEUTRAL TERRITORY. TO CLAIM THE REWARD YOU SHOULD TAKE THIS NOTE TO ANY BRITISH EMBASSY OR CONSULATE AND ASK TO SPEAK TO THE DEFENCE ATTACHE OR ONE OF HIS ASSISTANTS. HE WILL THEN GIVE YOU THE SUM OF £5000.

سند اذني

تتعهد الحكومة البريطانية بالدفع لحامل هذا السند الاذني مبلغ ٥٠٠٠ جنيه استرليني شرطا
الا تضر الفرد المصدر له وشرطا ان تساعده في تفادى الاسر او ان تقوم باعادته الى المملكة
العربية السعودية او الى ارض محايدة . من اجل اخذ المكافاة عليك تقديم هذا السند الى سفارة
او قنصلية بريطانية وطلب الالتقاء بالملحق الدفاعي او احد معاونيه . ثم سوف يعطي لك المبلغ
المحدد اي ٥٠٠٠ جنيه استرليني .

سند اذني

تتعهد الحكومة البريطانية بالدفع لحامل هذا السند الاذني مبلغ
٥٠٠٠ جنيه استرليني شرطاً الا تضر الفرد المصدر له وشرطاً
ان تساعده في تفادى الاسر او ان تقوم باعادته الى المملكة العربية
السعودية او الى ارض محايدة . من اجل اخذ المكافاة عليك
تقديم هذا السند الى سفارة او قنصلية بريطانية وطلب الالتقاء
بالملحق الدفاعي او احد معاونيه . ثم سوف يعطي لك المبلغ
المحدد اي ٥٠٠٠ جنيه استرليني .

Every SAS soldier carried a note like this one, which promised £5000 to any person who helped the bearer evade capture and return to friendly lines – a significant sum of money for any Iraqi villager. A translation of the text was provided in Arabic and the local dialect, as most Iraqis had only a limited command of English. The SAS were also issued with gold sovereigns as 'blood money', which could be used to bribe any captor to help their escape. Blood money is notorious for being 'lost in action' – one SAS trooper reputedly used some of his gold to have a winged dagger made for him by a goldsmith, who charged a fee of two sovereigns for the work.

The SAS concentrated their patrols around Wadi Amij, near the town of Ar Rutbah, an area that was particularly good for trade. On 3 February 1991, a mobility column from D Squadron spotted an Iraqi convoy with 14 vehicles in the area. Immediately the commander of the column called in an air strike, and from a vantage point, watched the convoy being attacked by American F-15s and A-10s using rockets, bombs and cannon fire. The Iraqis were cut to pieces by the ordnance, and several vehicles exploded in a spectacular manner. Amazingly, though, a number of vehicles and their crews survived the attack and later had to be engaged by the SAS ground force. Using their heavy machine guns and Milan antitank missiles, the ground force picked off the remaining vehicles. However, the Iraqi soldiers had now got into cover and were returning heavy fire. The SAS patrol was forced to call in another air strike to finish off the convoy before withdrawing during its execution.

For the Iraqis, life was becoming increasingly difficult. They were being forced to use more and more troops to protect their Scud convoys, but this served only to make them larger targets. The continuous combination of air strikes and ground attacks was beginning to take its toll and the tide was now turning in the Coalition's favour.

HUNTING THE SCUDS

Although 'Scud Alley' was the SAS's prime hunting ground for Scuds, not all encounters occurred there. On one particular mission, an SAS mobility column was having problems in locating a suspected Scud launching site. Unable to contact its HQ for verification of the details, the column commander decided, after three days of searching the suspected area, to return his men to their base over the Allied border. As the SAS vehicles sped through the barren, flat desert, they suddenly spotted a convoy ahead of them. Closing to within 600m (656yd), they discovered that it was a mobile Scud launcher, complete with support vehicles. The Iraqi convoy had stopped and

Above: Making good use of a dip in the groud as cover, these SAS troopers in a mobility column sort out their kit in preparation for forthcoming operations agains mobile SCUDs. Rations, fuel, ammunition and spare tyres are all visible.

its soldiers were in the process of camouflaging their vehicles; however, they had neglected to post any sentries. For them, of course, this would prove to be a fatal mistake. The SAS soldiers rapidly assumed an attack formation and opened fire on the Iraqis with their Milans, hitting and destroying all of the Scud vehicles. Because of the thick acrid smoke now pouring out of the burning vehicles, the Iraqis could see nothing and were unable to return fire.

On another occasion, an SAS column spotted a large Scud site, which was heavily protected by Iraqi troops in good defensive positions. Feeling it would be a difficult target to attack without sustaining heavy losses, the SAS commander called in an air strike. As the SAS column withdrew, a number of USAAF F-15s flew over them and attacked the Scud site with cluster bombs and laser-guided munitions. Under normal circumstances, the SAS would have observed the strike and reported back on its effectiveness, but the large amount of Iraqi forces in the area made this impossible.

Some hours later, the SAS commander was informed that the USAAF had carried out a recce of the Scud site and found that some of the launchers and their missiles had survived the air strike and were still operable. To be sure of their destruction, further attacks were necessary, but this time it was down to the SAS. The commander of the SAS mobility column agreed to attack the Scud site, but said he needed more men. HQ Squadron deployed a small team of SAS soldiers by helicopter to reinforce the mobility column, and a hastily drawn-up plan was put together.

Above: The SAS fighting columns made great use of motor bikes as small reconnaissance platforms, which let them scout ahead of the columns and provide valuable intelligence on the terrain ahead.

The column commander decided to attack at dawn, but would first draw the Iraqi soldiers out of their heavily defended encampment in order to have a better chance of success against the remaining targets. With typical SAS ingenuity, he ordered his men to place small charges about 1km (0.6 miles) from the Iraqi positions, the theory being that when they were detonated, the Iraqi troops would be lured out of their positions. The SAS would then take advantage of the confusion and begin the attack.

As dawn broke the next morning, the charges exploded, but to their credit, the Iraqis stayed put. Now they were on their guard and well prepared for an attack. Out of the blue they started firing, shooting wildly at any place where a vehicle or soldier could hide, but hitting nothing. Nor did they have to wait long for an SAS response. On a nearby ridge, the British force had formed up their vehicles in a crescent-shaped formation, allowing the maximum concentration of firepower to be brought to bear. They placed their Milan posts on the outside flanks, along with the newly arrived reinforcements, while the machine-gun equipped vehicles were positioned in the centre of the formation. As they opened fire, chaos descended on the Iraqis. The machine guns concentrated on the Iraqi soldiers, leaving the Milans to pick off the Scud launchers. One by one they exploded, sending massive fireballs into the air that could be seen for miles. Completely overwhelmed by the lethal concentration of firepower, the Iraqi forces sustained heavy casualties. Once the SAS commander was satisfied that every target of value had been destroyed, he ordered his men to withdraw.

Although the destruction of the Scud launchers remained of paramount importance, the SAS nonetheless had to find and destroy any Iraqi facility that supported their operation. Both the SAS and SBS had mounted operations against the Iraqis' communication network in an attempt to starve them of information, and this in part had been successful. However, a number of facilities were still supporting the Scuds, and these too had to be taken out. On 21 February 1991, A Squadron was involved in an attack on a communications facility that supported the Scuds operations and, on withdrawing from the attack, came under intense enemy fire. An SAS motorcyclist, Lance Corporal David Denbury, was hit and fatally wounded. The SAS went on to fight further running battles with the Iraqis over the next few days, but it was becoming clear that the Iraqis could now no longer operate in 'Scud Alley' without the threat of attack.

As a result of the intensive anti-Scud operations, the Iraqis started to withdraw their remaining mobile launchers deeper into Iraq for greater protection. The withdrawal meant that Iraq could now no longer target the Israelis: they were out of Scud range. But that didn't stop them from firing at Saudi Arabia, which they continued to do right up until the end of the war.

For the SAS, the Gulf War showed off the Regiment's unique capabilities in a spectacular

SECRET

United States Central Command
Office of the Commander-in-Chief
Operation Desert Storm
APO New York 09852-0006

9 March 1991

To: Sir Patrick Hine
Air Chief Marshal
Joint Headquarters
Royal Air Force Wycombe
Buckinghamshire
HP14 4UE

Thru: Sir Peter de la Billière
KCB, CBE, DSO, MC
Lieutenant-General
British Forces Commander
Middle East
Riyadh, Saudi Arabia

Subject: Letter of Commendation for the 22 Special Air Service (SAS) Regiment

1. I wish to officially commend the 22 Special Air Service (SAS) Regiment for their totally outstanding performance of military operations during Operation Desert Storm.

2. Shortly after the initiation of the strategic air campaign, it became apparent that the Coalition forces would be unable to eliminate Iraq's firing of Scud missiles from western Iraq into Israel. The continued firing of Scuds on Israel carried with it enormous unfavourable political ramifications and could, in fact, have resulted in the dismantling of the carefully crafted Coalition. Such a dismantling would have adversely affected in ways difficult to measure the ultimate outcome of the military campaign. It became apparent that the only way that the Coalition could succeed in reducing these Scud launches was by physically placing military forces on the ground in the vicinity of the western launch sites. At that time, the majority of available Coalition forces were committed to the forthcoming military campaign in the eastern portion of the theatre of operations. Further, none of these forces possessed the requisite skills and abilities required to conduct such a dangerous operation. The only force deemed qualified for this critical mission was the 22 Special Air Service (SAS) Regiment.

3. From the first day they were assigned their mission until the last day of the conflict, the performance of the 22 Special Air Service (SAS) Regiment was courageous and highly professional. The area in which they were committed proved to contain far more numerous enemy forces than had been predicted by every intelligence estimate, the terrain was much more difficult than expected and the weather conditions were unseasonably brutal. Despite these hazards, in a very short period of time the 22 Special Air Service (SAS) Regiment was successful in totally denying the central corridor of western Iraq Scud units.

cont.

cont.

The result was that the principal areas used by the Iraqis to fire Scuds on Tel Aviv were no longer available to them. They were required to move their Scud missile firing forces to the north-west portion of Iraq and from that location the firing of Scud missiles was essentially militarily ineffective.

4. When it became necessary to introduce United States Special Operations Forces into the area to attempt to close down the north-west Scud areas, the 22 Special Air Service (SAS) Regiment provided invaluable assistance to the US forces. They took every possible measure to ensure the US forces were thoroughly briefed and were able to profit from the valuable lessons that had been learned by earlier SAS deployments into western Iraq. I am completely convinced that had the US forces not received these thorough indoctrinations by SAS personnel, US forces would have suffered a much higher rate of casualties than was ultimately the case. Further, the SAS and US joint forces immediately merged into a combined fighting force where the synergetic effect of these fine units ultimately caused the enemy to be convinced that they were facing forces in western Iraq that were more than tenfold the size of those they were actually facing. As a result, large numbers of enemy forces that might otherwise have been deployed in the eastern theatre were tied down in Western Iraq.

5. The performance of the 22 Special Air Service (SAS) Regiment during Operation Desert Storm was in the highest traditions of the professional military service and in keeping with the proud history and tradition that had been established by that regiment. Please ensure that this commendation receives appropriate attention and is passed on to the unit and its members.

H. Norman Schwarzkopf
General, US Army
Commander-in-Chief

Above: An SAS fighting column moves across the barren, featureless desert of North West Iraq in search of mobile SCUD missile launchers. Thanks to Allied air superiority, the SAS had little fear of air attack.

manner, and in many cases it demonstrated just how little had changed since the original hit-and-run tactics used in North Africa during World War II. One piece of equipment that proved highly effective for the SAS in the desert was the Global Positioning System (GPS). These small hand-held devices received information from orbiting satellites regarding their relative position and, accurate to within a few metres, enabled SAS teams to know exactly where they were at any given time. The benefits of such a system were enormous. They allowed SAS teams to call in air strikes with absolute precision and avoided any risk of collateral damage.

The Gulf War gave the SAS the chance to prove how a small team could cause chaos and destruction to a large army in a way that was out of all proportion to the size of the force used. However, although the SAS inflicted significant losses on the Iraqi Army, it paid a price for this victory. In all, four members of the SAS Regiment lost their lives, two from actual combat, and two from the severe weather conditions that prevailed in the region.

Many people will recall the visible side of the Gulf War – the air strikes, the ground invasion – but few really appreciate the unseen war that took place in 1991. It is no exaggeration to say that the SAS played a key role in this war. Had the men failed in their Scud-busting missions, the result of the war could have been very different.

After the war was over, it was revealed that the USAAF, Special Operations Group (SOG), had launched a major operation to rescue the 'Bravo Two Zero' team. However, they failed to find the team because their radios were set to a different frequency to the SAS, and they had no way of knowing where they were heading.

LETTER OF COMMENDATION

It is ironic that General Schwarzkopf – at first reluctant to deploy the SAS as he felt that it could do nothing that could not be achieved by air power and ground forces alone – went on after the conflict had ended to write a letter of commendation to the regiment, openly and frankly stating how important the SAS role had been in bringing about victory over the Iraqis in what was a complicated and difficult operation.

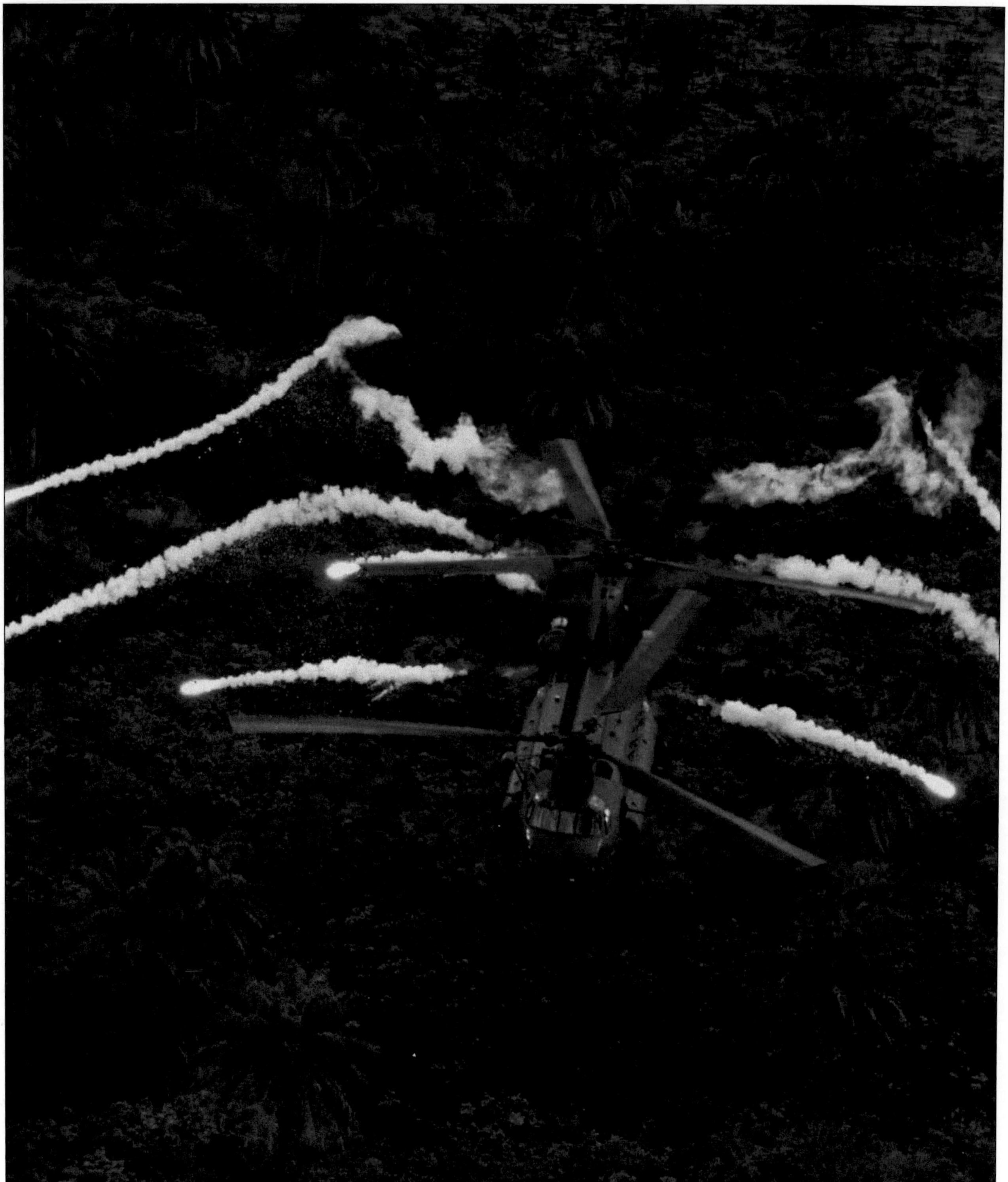

CHAPTER NINE

THE BALKANS AND SIERRA LEONE

As somebody once said, 'The Balkans, the Balkans, never ever get involved in the Balkans' – advice that the British wished they had taken. World War I began there, and World War II saw several German divisions tied down there for the best part of the war; for the British, however, the Balkans was a vacuum into which they were sucked to carry out a humanitarian operation that would eventually cause immense frustration for the Army.

In the Balkans, the British Army saw a conflict that knew little compassion but had enough ethnic hatred to fuel some of the world's worst war criminals in an orgy of unprecedented violence. The outbreak of violence can be traced back to the summer of 1992, when the former Yugoslav republic of Bosnia Herzegovina found itself embroiled in a civil war involving Serbs, Croats and Muslims. Fearing that events in the area could have a domino effect impacting beyond the region, the UN authorized UNPROFOR (UN Protection Force) to escort aid convoys and their workers, who were being attacked and murdered as they tried to help those in need. The first British troops to arrive as part of UNPROFOR were members of the Cheshire Regiment, who set up bases in Vitez, Gornji Vakuf and Tuzla.

Attached to the Cheshires were members of the SAS, who helped them with liaison officers and interpreters for the difficult and frustrating task of negotiating with the warring parties for permission to move aid through their territory. The situation was highly volatile, and in the UK there were genuine fears that British soldiers might be taken hostage by the warlords. Should this happen, the SAS were ready and willing to go into Bosnia and perform a rescue mission at a moment's notice with a troop based in Split, Croatia that was assigned to both HRT (hostage-rescue tasks) and general forces support duties.

Left: An RAF Chinook seen launching anti-missile flares over Sierra Leone. The SAS and regular British forces were heavily dependent on helicopters in both the Balkans and Sierra Leone, as they could not rely on travelling safely by road.

ANOTHER SAS VETERAN

Around this time, former SAS commander Lieutenant General Sir Michael Rose was appointed commander of UN forces, Bosnia. Rose belonged to a new generation of British Army officers who knew the job inside out and he was well liked and respected by his men. Although he was reluctant to say anything in public about his UN colleagues, Rose was frustrated at the sheer lack of knowledge and purpose that seemed to dog this well-intentioned, yet naive, UN mission. To enable him to operate with more confidence in Bosnia, Rose wanted eyes and ears on the ground that he could trust to provide him with well-informed, reliable intelligence, and the only unit qualified was the SAS.

The first task he set the SAS men was to monitor the newly formed Bosnia-Croat alliance and its leader. In addition, they were to ensure that everything ran smoothly and that any difficulties between them and the Bosnian-Croats were quickly ironed out. To soften its true purpose in Bosnia, the force was called Joint Commission Observers (JCOs), and had permission to drive around the various warring factions in highly conspicuous, white Land Rovers. Their first major success came in March 1994, when they negotiated the withdrawal of Croat HVO forces from the Muslim town of Maglai.

Rose was pleased with the results and decided to send the SAS to the Muslim town of Gorazde, now surrounded by the Serbs. When the SAS arrived, they were shocked at what they saw: the place had been decimated by constant shelling from nearby Serbian artillery emplaced in the surrounding hills. As if this wasn't enough, the Serbians were regularly sniping at the Muslim civilians as they went about their daily business.

Below: Regular British forces also played a key role in the Balkans. Here British paratroopers with their famous red berets stand guard at a political rally, watchful for any potential hostile threat.

SERBIAN CHECKPOINTS

On their way into Gorazde, the SAS team had sensed hostility from the Serbs as they passed through their check-points. At the time, however, the Serbs were unaware that they had just waved though a British special forces team, believing them to be casual UK liaison officers, and nothing more. To help with their cover, the seven men were armed only with standard British Army SA-80 assault rifles and wore normal issue combats. Once settled in Gorazde, they set up an OP on top of the wrecked Hotel Gradina, which offered a good view of the surrounding hills and local roads. They chose for their HQ an old bank, the most secure building in the town, and its strength would later prove to be something of a lifesaver for them. As standard operational procedure (SOP), the SAS began local patrols around the Serb positions in a bid to monitor their build-up and to report back to Rose on any significant activity.

The Serbs did not take kindly to the British snooping around their lines, and opened fire on them on several occasions. In response, the SAS called in air strikes, and a confrontational mentality started to develop between the two sides. The situation finally came to a head on 15 April 1994, when an SAS patrol came under effective enemy fire and two SAS troopers were seriously wounded.

The SAS negotiated a ceasefire with the Serbs to allow a casevac helicopter time to safely land and extract the wounded soldiers. Not wanting to appear difficult, the Serbs agreed to a short pause in their shelling and one of the soldiers, Corporal Fergus Rennie, was evacuated but sadly later died of his injuries. As for the other wounded soldier, he refused to be evacuated and insisted on staying with his colleagues. The SAS decided to teach the Serbs a lesson and called in further air strikes against their tanks and artillery, but on this occasion the air attack backfired, with disastrous consequences for both the pilot and the SAS.

In modern air warfare, there is a simple rule: if you fail to hit a target on the first pass, you leave it; otherwise it is very likely that you will become a target yourself. Easy words to say, but hard to follow when you have an SAS Forward Air Controller (FAC) calling for your support as he and his fellow troopers are being shelled from all sides. The unlucky pilot was Lieutenant Nick Richardson of the Royal Navy, who was flying a Sea Harrier on a practice air-support mission when he received a request for air support from the SAS in Gorazde. As he lined up for an attack on a number of Serbian tanks on a hillside, his HUD (head-up display) failed to lock-on when he tried to release his bombs. Forced to break away from the attack, he tried again, but when he lined up, his HUD failed again and he was forced to abort the attack run.

HARRIER DOWN

By now, the FAC was frustrated with the whole situation and asked the pilot to go around again. Richardson was, he realized, caught between a rock and a hard place – if he went around again, he really would be pushing his luck, but at the same time, he was not prepared to let his fellow countrymen down. As he rolled in for a third attempt, disaster struck: he was hit by a Serbian SAM (surface-to-air missile) and forced to eject from his stricken aircraft.

Fortunately for him, he landed near some friendly Muslim forces, who took him to the SAS in Gorazde. On arrival at the bank HQ, he was greeted by an SAS officer who explained that he had just jumped out of the frying pan and into the fire. Richardson at first did not understood what this meant, but he was soon to find out. It transpired that the SAS were in serious trouble as the local Muslims had turned against the men because of NATO's failure to protect them from the Serbs.

As the SAS officer appraised the situation, a lynch mob gathered at the front door of the bank and began smashing it down. The situation was clearly untenable. Contacting his superiors, the SAS officer asked for permission to withdraw, reluctant to let his men get into a firefight with the very people that they were supposed to be helping. But permission to withdraw was refused, and the SAS were told to just tough it out for the next four days until a relief convoy could get through to Gorazde.

The SAS would have been lucky to survive four hours, let alone four days. With this in mind, the officer went direct to General Rose and again asked for permission to withdraw. Thankfully, this time it was granted. It was impossible for a helicopter to land in Gorazde – the risks were just too great – so the men would have to make their way to an extraction site located for them in a valley. This site, however, was some distance away.

The main problem now was getting the team out of Gorazde with an injured trooper, downed pilot, and a local guide called Ahmed, all without being spotted by either the Muslims or the Serbs. It was decided that the best time to leave would be just after dark, as the SAS had good night-vision sights and the Muslims had none. With typical SAS stealth, the team and their guests slowly made their way out of the town without being seen.

VERTICAL CLIMB

After going through a forest and making good time, they suddenly found themselves facing a climb up a hill that was practically vertical in places. Even for the experienced men of the SAS, this climb was tough enough, but they also had a pilot and an injured trooper to think about. As for Ahmed, he was having difficulty getting his bearings and at one stage he got the patrol lost. As the men were on a tight schedule, there was no choice but to climb the hill, and that was the end of the matter.

One person who impressed every member of the team was the injured trooper. Despite having lost a lot of blood from his injured arm – which was held together only by a few bolts and a couple of steel rods – he bravely carried on. He was in agony.

Time was now running out for the SAS patrol, Alpha Two-One, and they knew it. As they struggled to make up the minutes, there was a further setback. All around the valley, the distant sound of artillery could be heard as the Serbs threw shell upon shell on Gorazde, and burning fires could be seen ahead of the SAS team. This meant only one thing: the area was crawling with Serb soldiers and there was no way that a rescue helicopter would be able to land. As they pondered their fate, a Serb patrol passed close by. In a firefight, the SAS could easily beat them, but once the shooting started, other Serbs would reinforce the patrol and they would effectively be cut off. After a few tense minutes, however, the Serbs moved on, much to the relief of the SAS.

With this delay, there was no way that they could reach the original RV point, so they used their radios to try and make contact with the pilots, but there was nothing. They then worked out that they were roughly on the probable flight-path, so even without radio contact, they could place landing markers down for the helicopters. As they waited, however, it suddenly dawned on them that there was not going to be a helicopter, as nobody in Sarajevo would believe

Below: An SAS radio operator in the Balkans, wearing a peaked cap to make it easier to use headphones. The SAS used radios that transmitted in a rapid 'burst', reducing the ability of the Serbs to track the unit's position from its transmissions.

BOMBING CAMPAIGN

Above: The bombing campaign against the Serbs was directed in part by SAS teams on the ground, who identified Serb targets and, if necessary, laser-designated them for bombs dropped by UN aircraft.

they had made it this far. Infuriated by this thought, the team set up their sat-net communications system and called General Rose in person. There was now only 30 minutes until dawn, and they knew that no rescue crew would fly in broad daylight over enemy territory. This time, their luck was in. General Rose personally arranged for a French rescue helicopter to come in and get them.

PUMA RESCUE

With only minutes to go until first light, they heard the welcome sound of a Puma helicopter as it made its way up the valley towards their position. Within minutes, they were safely on board and speeding back towards Sarajevo. After landing, the SAS team walked around to the front of the helicopter to thank the crew for their bravery in risking their lives for them. They commented that it had been an uneventful flight back. At this point, the pilot showed them the bullet holes in his Puma: the men had been laughing and joking so much on board the Puma that they had failed to hear the bullets hitting the airframe.

Thankfully for the rest of the Bosnia tour, nothing like this ever happened again. Eventually 400 British UN troops moved into Gorazde and some semblance of normality returned to the Muslim population. However, on another occasion, a JCO team was in the Bihac area and found itself under fear of attack from Serbian forces. Eventually the Serbians backed off after being threatened with NATO air strikes. General Rose favoured an aggressive line against the Serbs, but the UN wanted a softly, softly approach.

In May 1995, the UN paid heavily for its inconsistent policy in Bosnia when the Serbs seized hundreds of UN soldiers, including 40 British troops. To counter this, the United Nations' Rapid Reaction Force was formed, including two SAS Squadrons who were tasked with breaking through Serb lines and relieving the UN garrison in Sarajevo. Despite their best efforts, the United Nations failed to prevent the massacre of Muslim prisoners at Srebrenica, where over 8000 local citizens were murdered in cold blood by the Serbs after Dutch troops had surrendered to them. Prior to this massacre, a JCO team had been with the Dutch forces, directing air strikes in support of the Srebrenican people, but the attacks failed to stop the Serbs' advance.

In August 1995, the UN retaliated against the Serbs by launching constant air attacks against their positions throughout Bosnia, causing considerable damage to their war effort. These attacks were supported with artillery barrages from both British and French guns on Mount Igman, the guns acting in response to SAS teams that were identifying targets for them. In addition, the SAS infiltrated deep behind Serb lines to act as Forward Air Controllers in support of NATO airstrikes, the primary task being to find and designate targets for the attacking aircraft, and act as a rescue force should a pilot be downed.

Eventually, the Serbs gave in to NATO and began a supervised withdrawal from Sarajevo. By now, there was no-one who doubted just how devious the Serbs could be, and the SAS was given the task of supervising this. Building on this success, the SAS helped the new NATO Peace Implementation Force (IFOR) by providing detailed information on the known troop lines and their levels of equipment, as required by the Dayton Accord. The SAS also played a key role in keeping the various factions under observation until conventional forces were deployed to police the peace. On one occasion, an SAS team attached to US forces helped to diffuse a potentially dangerous situation after Muslim refugees attempted to re-occupy their village, now in Serb territory. Thanks to the team's tact and diplomacy, a potential crisis was averted.

With the ink barely dry on the Dayton Accord, it was only a matter of time before trouble flared up again in the Balkans. In March 1999, the storm clouds of war were gathering over Kosovo, a small country barely the size of Wales that borders Albania, Macedonia, Montenegro and Serbia. Under the orders of Serbian President Slobodan Milosevic, Kosovo was invaded by both Serbian military

Below: The SAS team from Gorazde with the downed Harrier pilot and their local guide, awaiting pick-up outside the town by a French helicopter. This photograph was taken with the aid of night vision equipment.

THE SAS IN KOSOVO

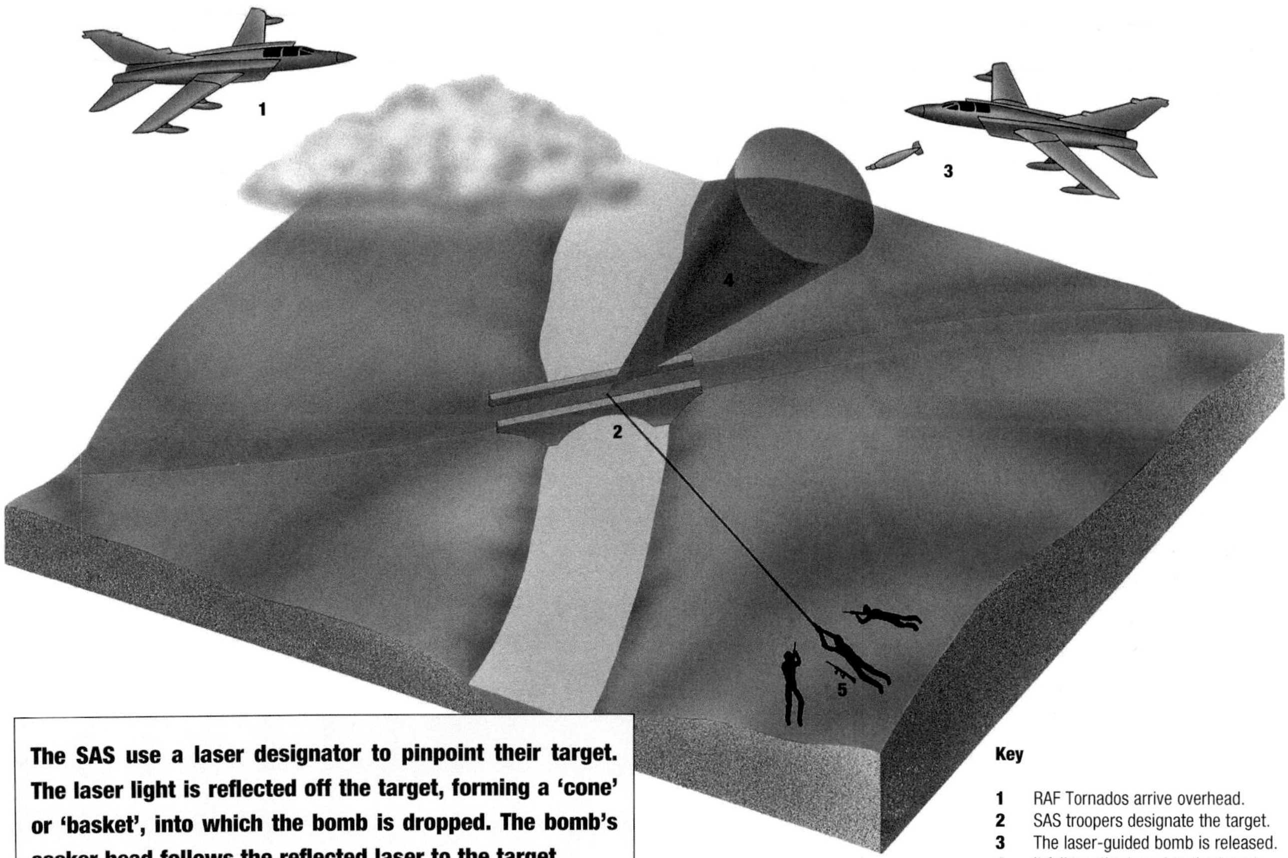

The SAS use a laser designator to pinpoint their target. The laser light is reflected off the target, forming a 'cone' or 'basket', into which the bomb is dropped. The bomb's seeker head follows the reflected laser to the target.

Key

1 RAF Tornados arrive overhead.
2 SAS troopers designate the target.
3 The laser-guided bomb is released.
4 It follows the 'cone' to the target.
5 The SAS troopers withdraw.

and para-military police forces. In appalling acts of almost medieval barbarity, the Serbs began systematically to 'ethnically cleanse' Kosovo. As a huge refugee crisis developed, NATO warned Serbia that it faced military action if it failed to rein in its military forces, who were carrying out human rights abuses on an unprecedented scale. A deadline was set for compliance – and was ignored by Milosevic and his henchmen. NATO now had no choice but to embark on an intensive bombing campaign against both Serbia and its fielded forces in Kosovo.

WEATHER PROBLEMS

As the air operations gathered pace, an unexpected factor began to hinder the safety and accuracy of the air strikes – as before, it was weather conditions. These were now causing NATO very severe operational problems, with many sorties being either cancelled prior to take-off, or aborted over their intended targets, as there was just too much risk of causing collateral damage.

Obviously this situation could not be allowed to continue, so it was decided that special forces should be deployed to identify targets by using laser designators. Since the SAS had performed so well in Bosnia, it was considered to be the best placed to carry out this mission.

In response to the NATO request for SAS support, a number of squadrons were deployed for immediate action, their key role being target designation for air strikes. Several four-man teams were sent into both Serbia and Kosovo to find, identify and destroy targets of value. In addition, NATO was desperate for reliable and accurate information on Serbian troop movements within Kosovo. The reason for this was simple: air-based intelligence-gathering was failing NATO, not because it was providing too little data on the Serbs, but because it was providing way too much. Their analysts were getting so much information from aircraft, UAVs (unmanned air vehicles), satellites and ground sensors that they were simply unable to cope with the volume. In some cases, they were taking three days to evaluate the information. By the time strike aircraft were tasked with acting on it, the intended target had moved.

Below: Thanks to the SAS's reconnaissance, NATO learnt that there were very few bridges in Kosovo capable of bearing the weight of a modern tank, so the decision was made to airlift forces in instead using helicopters like this RAF Chinook.

TRAINING THE KLA

The SAS was also tasked with training and supporting the KLA (Kosovo Liberation Army) in its operations against the Serbian fielded forces in Kosovo. At first, the KLA struggled to make any headway against the Serbs, but with SAS direction and guidance, its men became a potent and highly effective force. Indeed, the SAS often used them as intelligence-gatherers; obviously they had intimate knowledge of their own country and its geography. One invaluable piece of intelligence the SAS discovered for NATO concerned the bridges in Kosovo.

It was found that very few of these bridges could take the weight of modern tanks, a serious issue if

a land invasion was launched. As a result, NATO decided to invade Kosovo by mounting a helicopter assault using British Paras from the 5th Airborne Brigade. After SAS recce missions near to the border with Macedonia, a number of invasion routes were identified as being suitable for both troops and vehicles. Small teams were also deployed to the ridges overlooking the roads to ensure that the Serbs were not able to ambush NATO ground forces as they entered Kosovo on 12 June 1999.

The invasion went smoothly and no resistance was encountered until British forces entered the city of Pristina, and even then it was very light. There was, however, one incident that caused NATO immense concern, and that related to the Russians and their seizure of Pristina airfield.

As NATO dithered over Russia's role in Kosovo's future, the Russians decided their own fate and first occupied Pristina airfield, then took responsibility for it. This led to a temporary stand-off between the Russians and NATO, which caused serious concerns internationally. Before the Russian intervention, the Americans, under General Wesley Clark, had asked the British to block the airfield's runways and use force if necessary to prevent their occupation. However, the British, under General Mike Jackson, recognized the risk involved and fused to comply with the demand. Ultimately diplomatic efforts were used to resolve the crisis – just as well, because the SAS would have found itself in the thick of what could have been a very serious confrontation.

Shortly after the crisis ended, details emerged of an SAS mission that had been planned for 11 June 1999, against the Russian airborne forces occupying Pristina Airport. the plan was that two SAS teams were to be inserted into Kosovo ahead of the Russians advancing on Pristina. Their mission was to stop the Russian advance. However, as the RAF Hercules carrying the SAS team neared the airport, its cargo of SAS Landrovers and motorcycles shifted, causing the pilot to have severe control difficulties. An emergency landing was attempted, but the aircraft clipped a building on its approach and crash landed. Fortunately most of the SAS escaped with only light

CHRONOLOGY

Date	1994–95
Location	Bosnia
Operation	Small SAS teams gather intelligence on the Serbian forces and provide target designation for air strikes.
Date	1998
Location	Albania
Operation	In March, a four-man team is deployed to Albania to rescue a British aidworker. The team locate him and drive to the coast using Land Rovers. They are met by two helicopters. One provides a security force, while the other extracts the rescue team and their vehicles.
Date	1999
Location	Kosovo
Operation	Following the invasion of Kosovo by Serbian forces, the SAS is deployed to assist in finding targets for NATO aircraft and to rescue downed aircrew. It also helps train the Kosovo Liberation Army and apprehends Serbian war criminals.
Date	2000
Location	Sierra Leone
Operation	The SAS is initially called in to provide an overt presence in Sierra Leone in support of UN peacekeepers. However, a number of British soldiers are captured and held hostage by the 'West Side Boys'. In response, the SAS launches a joint rescue operation with 1 Para and secures the release of the hostages – for the loss of only one soldier.

injuries, but one soldier was trapped in the wreckage and badly burned.

Eventually the Serbs agreed to leave Kosovo, and were supervised by the SAS to ensure that they complied with the withdrawal procedures as laid down by NATO. After the conflict ended, the SAS was involved in tracking down and apprehending known Serbian war criminals and their cronies. On one occasion, as they went to arrest a known suspect, a firefight broke out between the SAS and the Serbs, in which a war criminal was killed and one SAS soldier slightly injured. Kosovo will not go down in history as being NATO's finest hour, but the SAS did its bit, and did it well.

SIERRA LEONE 2000

On 6 May 2000, Britain launched Operation Palliser in response to the advance on Freetown, the capital of Sierra Leone, of rebel forces who were endangering the lives of British, Commonwealth and European citizens. For the British Armed Forces, this was their largest solo operation since the Falklands War of 1982, involving just over 4500 military personnel from all three services.

Their potential enemy was the Revolutionary United Front (RUF), a group of cold-blooded murderers who took great pleasure in raping women and butchering young children by hacking their limbs off. Although the RUF was large in number, there were also other maverick militias for the British to contend with, the most renowned being the 'West Side Boys' (WSB), a bizarre group who paraded around in odd clothing and frequently wore women's wigs during public parades. A motley crew made up of ex-RUF members and deserters from the Sierra Leone Army (SLA), they were almost perpetually drunk or high on drugs. Although at first treated as something of a joke, the WSBs were however good fighters, and a real menace, being totally unpredictable.

CHINOOK

Above: The Chinook helicopter was used by the British in the operation to rescue the hostages in Sierra Leone. Some RAF Chinooks have now been upgraded with new equipment for use by the SAS on covert missions.

HOSTAGE RESCUE IN SIERRA LEONE

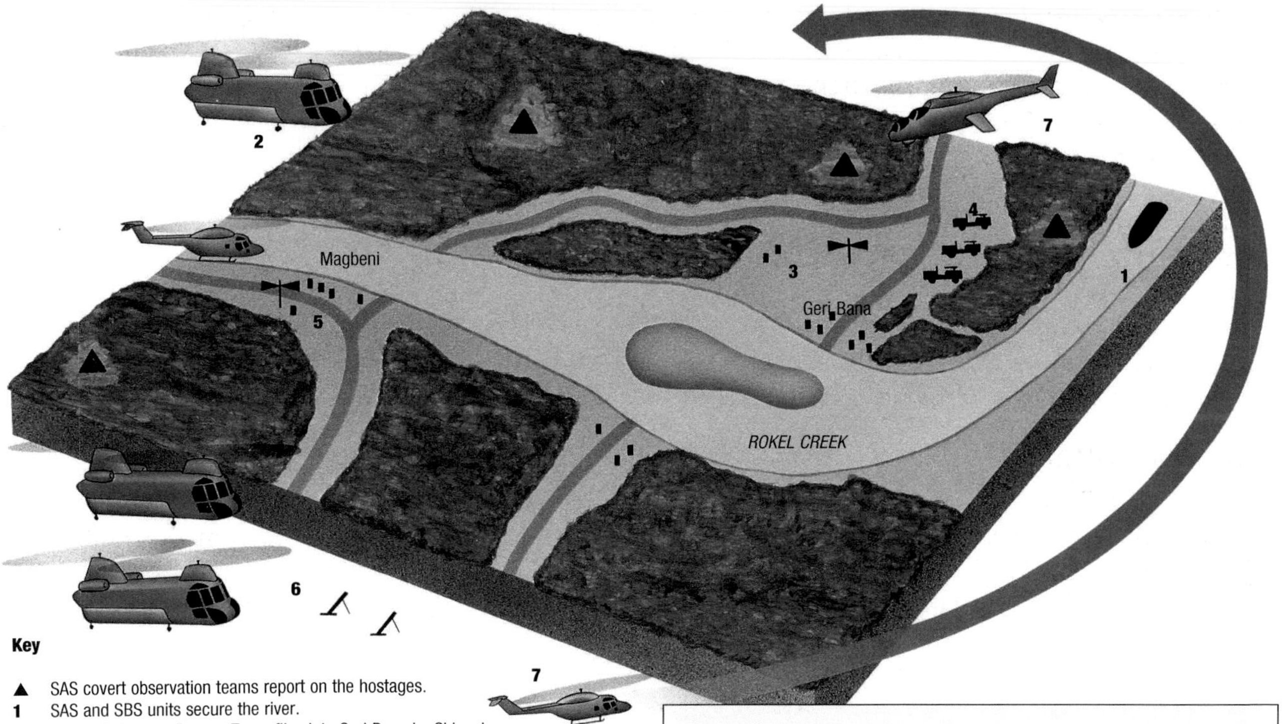

Key

- ▲ SAS covert observation teams report on the hostages.
- 1 SAS and SBS units secure the river.
- 2 The SAS Hostage Rescue Team flies into Geri Bana by Chinook.
- 3 The hostages are rescued and evacuated.
- 4 SAS Landrovers provide fire support for the rescue.
- 5 1 Para is inserted in Magbeni to take on the main West Side Boys force.
- 6 1 Para Support Company provide mortar fire support.
- 7 A Sierra Leonean Hind and British Lynx provide top cover for the operation.

While the SAS successfully rescued the British hostages held in a camp at Geri Bana, 1 Para attacked the main force of the West Side Boys at Magbeni.

Within Sierra Leone there was a UN presence, but this was virtually ineffective. Its troops rarely ventured out of the main urban areas for fear of being attacked, and with nobody to challenge them, the rebels were having a field day. However, with the arrival of the British, it would be a different story, and the rebels knew it.

THE PARAS ARRIVE

The first official British forces to arrive in Sierra Leone were members of the élite Pathfinders and two companies from the 1st Battalion of the Parachute Regiment. After flying into Lungi airport on 7 May, they had secured the airport within hours and were mounting patrols in the local area to reassure Freetown's citizens that they were safe from rebel attacks.

Prior to the arrival of 1 Para, Sierra Leone had, of course, received other unofficial visitors. These were members of the SAS; their job, to gather intelligence on the rebel forces and to recce good defensive positions for 1 Para. For mobility, the SAS initially used a number of locally commandeered Toyota pickup trucks for liaison and utility duties. As soon as their role became more overt, however, they began driving around in Land Rover 110 Desert Patrol Vehicles (DPVs), which were heavily armed with a mixture of 7.62mm (0.3in) General Purpose Machine Guns (GPMGs) and 12.7mm (0.5in) heavy machine guns, or occasionally a 40mm (1.57in) grenade-launcher.

In a highly unusual procedure for the SAS, they openly patrolled during daylight hours, making no

Above: At the height of operations against the 'West Side Boys', British forces mount a river patrol in Sierra Leone in a bid to cut off rebel supply routes. The rebels lacked the air support of the British and Sierra Leone forces.

attempt to disguise who they were or their intentions. It soon became clear that their tactics were designed to intimidate the rebels and provoke them to make a move, and this would eventually pay off. One aspect of SAS operations, the 'hearts and minds' campaign which was often used to win over local people, was made easy for the British. In Sierra Leone, the locals despised the rebels and welcomed the British forces with open arms. Soon, SAS intelligence-gathering amongst the local population revealed that the WSBs were bragging publicly about attacking on British forces, but they never made their exact target clear.

In a bid to set a trap for the WSBs, the SAS started to patrol aggressively near the rebels' favourite haunts, especially around the area of Massiaka, where they had set up road blocks to loot passing trucks and cars. In some cases, the WSBs' victims were able to pay them off with money or alcohol, but on many occasions they were robbed and then murdered for the sheer pleasure of it.

To increase the pressure on the rebels, both the Paras and Pathfinders mounted extra patrols in set areas, and deliberately ignored others. The idea was that the WSBs would be encouraged to enter a designated trap area without realizing it. One particular area had been cleared of brush and vegetation, so that its road check-point could easily be seen from the distance, giving the impression that it was a soft target. However, out of sight were a number of machine gun nests and mortar pits, and these were manned by the awesome 1 Para.

Although the original plan was aimed at the WSBs, it was the RUF that took the bait and launched an attack against a patrol of Pathfinders at Lungi Lo, 16km (10 miles) east of Freetown airport. A fierce firefight developed and many rebels were killed in the first stage of the attack, but for the RUF, the situation was about to get much worse. As the Pathfinders sprung their trap, reinforcements were flown in by Chinook helicopters, and these engaged the rebels with machine guns and mortars.

The overwhelming firepower broke the rebels' attack and they fled into the bush. However, the British had more surprises in store. Above the fleeing rebels were a number of heavily armed Chinooks, which opened fire with both their mini-guns and machine guns. The effect was devastating for the RUF, and their attack force was decimated. To add further insult to injury, the RUF leader, Foday Sankoh, was captured by the SAS in Freetown and taken into protective custody. However, as the news of the British victory spread, it was tempered by the tragic loss of one Nigerian soldier serving with the UN and six members of the SLA, who had been killed by the RUF in an unrelated attack.

For a time, everything settled down in Sierra Leone. Occasional rebel attacks were mounted against the UN peacekeepers, but these were generally ineffective. After a couple of weeks, the Paras were withdrawn and replaced by Royal Marines, who kept up the good work and enjoyed a relatively quiet deployment. For the SAS, however, it was business as usual, and the men continued to patrol the coastal areas in an effort to force the rebels back further into the bush, where they would be of little threat to the locals.

Just as everything seemed to be going so well for the British, disaster struck. On 25 August 2000, an 11-man patrol from the Royal Irish Regiment (RIR), along with a Sierra Leonean colleague, strayed into an area that was positively crawling with members of the 'West Side Boys', and were taken prisoner. This was a nightmare scenario for the British, and 22 SAS were rapidly tasked with locating the rebels base and mounting an OP (Observation Post). The British Government decided to play the patience game first and see what transpired, while at the same time formulating a rescue plan.

Once contact had been established with the WSB, a dialogue developed, which was deliberately non-confrontational. Knowing how temperamental the rebels could be, the British did nothing to antagonize them. At first the rebels' demands were quite modest – they wanted food and drink for both themselves and the hostages – but once these demands were met, the rebels' confidence inevitably grew.

HOSTAGES RELEASED

Deciding to be compliant, the British gave in, asking only that their soldiers be treated decently and humanely. As trust developed between the WSBs and the British negotiators, the British requested the release of some of their soldiers as an act of goodwill. Much to their surprise, on 30 August 2000 five members of the RIR were released unharmed and in remarkably good health considering what they had been through.

Negotiations continued with the rebels, while the SAS moved more troopers into the vicinity of the rebels' base in the hamlet of Geri Bana. Continuing with their observations, the SAS discovered that the rebels had another camp about 300m (328yd) away from where the hostages were being held. This was a hamlet called Magbeni, just south of Geri Bana, and it was well placed to provide mutual fire support to the other camp. To further complicate matters for the SAS, the camps were divided by the Rokel Creek, which the WSBs made good use of for transporting their supplies and ill-gotten gains.

As the SAS planners worked out a rescue strategy, the West Side Boys' leader, 24-year-old Foday Kallay – a self-styled Brigadier and former NCO in the Sierra Leone Army – started to make political demands for the release of one his men, known locally as Brigadier Bomb Blast, or Brigadier Papa. In addition to this demand, Kallay wanted a safe passage out of Sierra Leone, an education abroad – and an outboard motor for one of his dinghies.

Up till now, the British had tolerated the West Side Boys. Now they understood that matters were coming to a head. Fears for the safety of the hostages were growing; the WSBs were now quite openly flaunting their power by carrying out mock executions on the British soldiers. The SAS had seen enough, and requested permission to mount a rescue attempt as soon as possible.

As the British Government deliberated over what action to take, a serious new development made the decision for them. A UN helicopter strayed over the West Side Boys' base by accident and the rebels, believing that they were about to be attacked, had dragged the prisoners out into the open as if to shoot them, but thought better of it. Fortunately for the hostages, the British negotiator managed to convince the rebels that this was a genuine mistake, and nothing more. Realizing that something like this could easily happen again – and next time they might not be so lucky – the British Government sanctioned a rescue mission, codenamed Operation Barras.

Time was now of the essence. The media in the UK was openly speculating about an imminent rescue attempt, further reinforced by the announcement that 1 Para was to return to Sierra Leone immediately. Well aware that the WSBs regularly listened to the BBC World Service, and would execute the hostages if they suspected something was in the air, the planners of Operation Barras took the decision to mount a tri-service operation on 10 September 2000.

At 0616 local time, elements of the SAS boat

Below: A Landrover similar to those used in the attack on the West Side Boys' camp at Geri Bana. The hostage rescue was a perfect example of a small SAS operation that enhanced the unit's reputation yet further.

troop and members of the Royal Marines' Special Boat Service (SBS) sealed off the river leading to Rokel Creek. At the same time, members of the Jordanian UN battalion secured the main Massiaka highway to prevent the WSBs from escaping during the rescue. Once all security elements were in place, the operation's main thrust began with an assault on Magbeni and Geri Bana by three troop-carrying Chinook helicopters, supported by two smaller Lynx helicopters in the fire support role.

The timing of the operation was crucial. There had to be just enough light for the helicopters to see their target, but not enough for them to be seen by the rebels. Speed was also essential: the hostages were all in one place, meaning that their captors could execute them very quickly. From the rescuers' point of view, though, this also made them easier to find.

As the helicopters swooped in at low level, the West Side Boys opened fire with every weapon available, including captured heavy machine guns from the Royal Irish Regiment's vehicles. In a highly coordinated movement, the SAS opened fire on the rebels guarding the hostages, while the Paras, after being inserted by the Chinooks, made their assault.

Although initially taken by surprise, the WSBs lost no time in assuming their defensive positions surrounding both camps. To make matters worse, as the Paras moved forward, their assault temporarily stalled due to the terrain. They were moving through an area near Rokel Creek, which had looked from the air like a flat field covered in long grass. In reality, it was more of a paddy field, and the Paras were now laboriously wading through water up to chest level. Spotting their predicament, the West Side Boys opened fire with all their heavy weapons. The Paras sustained many casualties, but thankfully none that were fatal.

Seeing that the Paras were in serious trouble, the SAS directed their firepower at the WSBs, while the RAF Chinook pilots, risking their own lives, flew in front of the rebel positions to recover the injured soldiers. As they performed this brave act, the other helicopters involved in the operation directed their weapons at the rebels' main defensive positions in order to suppress their fire.

Within a few minutes, the officers and NCOs of 1 Para had rallied their men and were now assaulting the WSBs' main positions at Magbeni. As they did so, the SAS launched their assault on Geri Bana and secured the building where the hostages were being held. Despite a short firefight, during which a number of rebels were either killed or injured, all of the hostages were rescued unharmed.

HEAVY RESISTANCE

At Magbeni, the WSB were still putting up heavy resistance, although a number of them had fled when the shooting started. To their credit, the WSBs were still fighting two hours later, and it was only when the Paras brought in mortars and extra firepower from vehicle-based weapons that they finally surrendered. Amongst those taken prisoner was the West Side Boys' leader, Foday Kallay, who later expressed regret for what he had done.

The WSBs were to pay a heavy price for crossing the British. The number of confirmed dead was put at 25, but later investigations showed that it was considerably higher. The WSBs were now a spent force in Sierra Leone and never recovered from the devastating British operation. But the British also paid a price for their victory. During the initial assault at Geri Bana, Bombardier Brad Tinnion, serving with 22 SAS, was fatally wounded. Despite desperate efforts to save him, he died before reaching RFA Sir Percival, which was berthed in Freetown. The Paras also suffered 12 casualties; all went on to make full recoveries from their injuries.

Operation Barras will go down as a textbook example of how to perform a hostage rescue in difficult and demanding conditions. It was a well-planned and well-executed operation, owing much to the bravery and professionalism of the British Armed Forces, in particular the SAS, who spent weeks gathering intelligence on the WSBs while living and operating covertly in what was an extremely hostile environment.

CHAPTER TEN

AFGHANISTAN AND AL-QAEDA

The date 11 September 2001 will be etched in the minds of people around the world for decades to come. It marks the day that terrorism perpetrated its biggest and most spectacular attack on the world's most powerful nation, the United States of America. As a result, the SAS would once more be called to work alongside US special forces, this time in Afghanistan.

The attack began at 0845, US Eastern Standard Time, when a Boeing 767 of American Airlines crashed into the giant North Tower of the World Trade Center in New York. At first, it was generally assumed that this had been a dreadful accident; 11 minutes later, however, when another Boeing 767 from United Airlines hit the South Tower, it was clear that something extremely sinister was going on. As millions of people around the world watched the events unfold on live television, the first of the two towers began a horrific and violent collapse. Barely 20 minutes later, the second tower imploded in the same way.

Giant clouds of grey dust filled New York's skyline, and a cold reality dawned on people around the world: they had just witnessed the worst terrorist atrocity in history. Thousands of innocent people from all walks of life and from many nations had been murdered in cold blood before their very eyes.

Left: The impact of the second hijacked airliner on the World Trade Center on 11 September 2001. Within months, the SAS would be in Afghanistan, helping to evict the Taliban from power and hunting for Osama Bin Laden.

It was a sickening scene, but there was more still to come. News began to come in of a further two incidents involving airliners, and it was soon confirmed that a Boeing 757 of American Airlines had crashed at 0938 into the symbol of America's military power, the Pentagon. All 58 passengers and 6 crewmembers were killed, along with 190 people on the ground. Later it was announced that a fourth aircraft had also crashed near Pittsburgh in suspicious circumstances. Fearing that more attacks were still to come, President George W. Bush was advised to take to the air in his personal aircraft, Airforce One, the theory being that while he was airborne, he was safe from attack.

OSAMA BIN LADEN

During the days and weeks after the attack, it was revealed that the aircraft had all been hijacked by Arab terrorists under the alleged leadership of America's arch enemy, Osama bin Laden. The attacks had been meticulously planned and executed by a very sophisticated and well-connected terrorist network. Naturally, this caused great embarrassment to the American Intelligence Agencies. They had

Above: The American AC-130 Specter Gunship, which carries mini-guns, 40mm (1.57in) cannon and even a 105mm (4.1in) howitzer. Both British and American special forces made great use of them in Afghanistan.

failed to stop them, despite the growing evidence of an intended attack on the American mainland.

BUSH'S REACTION

As the political and emotional fallout began over who was to blame for the events of 11 September 2001 – now being referred to as nine-one-one, or nine-eleven – there was just one question: what was America and her allies going to do about it? In this highly charged and emotional period in America's history, there were fears of a rash reaction from America's President George W. Bush, but he remained remarkably composed and rational.

As America considered its response to the attack, the world's media insisted that this atrocity had been suffered by America, giving little thought and sympathy to other countries who had also lost their nationals. Certainly, this was America's worst terrorist outrage, but it was Britain's, too, despite more than 30 years of terrorism emanating from the 'Troubles' in Northern Ireland.

On 4 October 2001, the British Prime Minister, Tony Blair, announced in the House of Commons that evidence had come to light linking Osama bin Laden and his Al-Qaeda (The Base) terrorist network to the attacks on the Pentagon and the World Trade Center on 11 September. Meanwhile, as military operations were being considered in response to the attacks, it was confirmed that Osama bin Laden was in Afghanistan under the protection of the Taliban regime.

OMANI EXERCISE

There was now no doubt that military action was on the cards, but what form it would take had yet to be decided. By sheer coincidence and good fortune, the British already had a massive force of air, sea and ground assets in the Gulf of Oman as part of Exercise Saif Sareea II (Swift Sword II), and the British Government put this entire force at the United States' disposal, literally inviting them to help themselves. Although appreciating this kind and generous offer, there were only two assets that the US decided it needed from Britain's armed forces: her RAF tanker aircraft and the Special Air Service Regiment.

In late September 2001, George W. Bush issued an ultimatum to the Taliban: either turn Osama bin Laden and his Al-Qaeda supporters in, or face the consequences. As the days ticked by, it was becoming clear that the Taliban had no intention of complying with the Americans' request; instead, they defiantly threatened a Jihad (Holy War). Although there was no deadline for the commencement of military action, the planners in the Pentagon were aware that they had only a short window of opportunity until the onset of the Afghanistan winter, when the weather conditions would became a serious factor impeding the execution of air strikes.

HUNTING AL-QAEDA

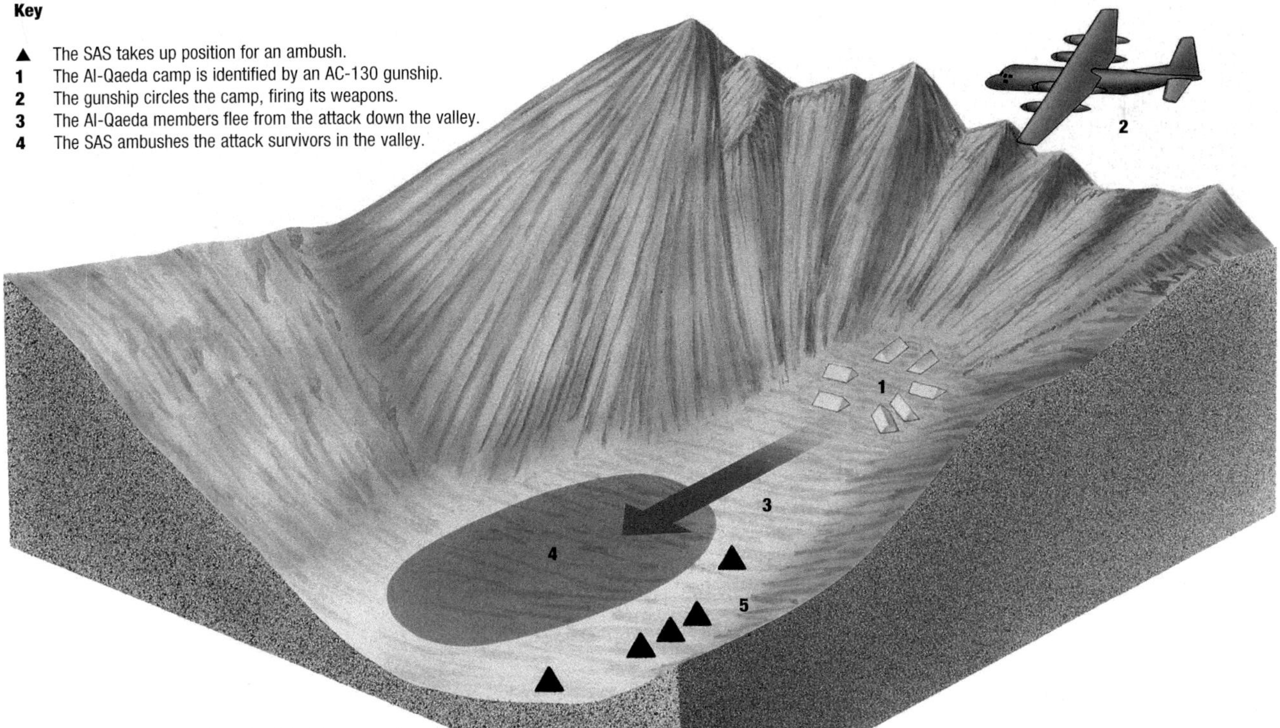

American AC-130 gunships were used to 'flush out' Al-Qaeda members from their base camps. As they retreated, they were ambushed by the SAS. Any survivors were taken to Camp X-Ray in Guantanamo Bay, Cuba.

As the tension mounted, reports started to circulate that SAS units had been involved in firefights with the Taliban in Northern Afghanistan, but these were denied by the UK Ministry of Defence. Also around this time, the Taliban claimed that it had shot down an American spy aircraft flying over its territory. It was, in fact, a UAV (Unmanned Air Vehicle) lost due to control failure rather than enemy action, but it did, confirm that US forces were operating very close to Afghanistan. Obviously it would be only a matter of time before the shooting started.

THE AIR WAR BEGINS

On 7 October, the air war finally began with multiple attacks on Taliban air-defence systems, command-and-control centres, and fighter aircraft parked on airfields throughout Afghanistan. Although much of the intelligence for these initial air strikes came from air-based assets, some had clearly been obtained by covert ground forces operating from a base in Uzbekistan. Both British and American special forces were now operating in large numbers within Afghanistan, their main roles being recce, target designation, and 'shoot-and-scoot' operations.

For the SAS, Afghanistan was an old hunting ground. They had seen action there during the 1980s performing covert operations in support of the Mujahedeen against the Russians; in fact, at one point they were even training Afghanis in Scotland

Below: The old, but highly effective B-52 executed most of the carpet bombing missions in Afghanistan and played a great part in bringing about the collapse of the Taliban regime, who were the main sponsors of the Al-Qaeda terrorist network.

Above: The results of a B-52 raid near Khost – a huge dust cloud rises from a suspected Taliban/Al Qaeda position. With such firepower at its disposal, the SAS could quickly eliminate any major opposition it came across in Afghanistan.

until locals assumed they were illegal immigrants and called the police. Although this put paid to the their training programme in the UK, the Afghanis now had access to western weapons and military intelligence, which proved invaluable in support of their cause. This experience would be an advantage when it came to training the anti-Taliban Northern Alliance, because the SAS already had a good rapport with many of their leaders.

The Northern Alliance forces were based primarily in North-Western Afghanistan and numbered around 15,000 men, while their enemy, the Taliban, dominated the Eastern part of the country and fielded around 50,000 soldiers and several hundred Al-Qaeda terrorists.

Although enthusiastic and well intentioned, prior to the involvement of western special forces, the Northern Alliance had had very little military success for some years in their struggle against the Taliban after being ousted from power. However, within weeks of the western special forces' arrival, the Northern Alliance had made substantial gains in territory and gained more recruits.

On one particular training exercise, an SAS team were instructing the Northern Alliance in standard British Army tactics for assaulting an objective while under effective enemy fire. However, as the Northern Alliance men moved towards the real target, a Taliban-held village, they suddenly and without warning abandoned the British tactics and advice and, in a scene out of a Rambo movie, proceeded to attack using dozens of horsemen as cavalry. As they charged, the rest of the force sat down on rocks nearby and watched the spectacle without firing any of their weapons at the defending Taliban forces. Fortunately for the Northern Alliance, the Taliban fled on this occasion, but the SAS was now concerned about the reliability of its new friends.

The SAS quickly learned that getting the best from the Northern Alliance required patience and understanding, and that you never told them what to do, but merely advised them. The operations in Afghanistan meant the deployment of almost every available SAS Squadron, as their mission tasking was growing by the day. The lack of roads hampered the speed at which SAS mobility columns could move; even by SAS standards, the going was tough.

In one operation near Mazar-e-Sharif, a number of vehicles got bogged down while operating off road, and as they tried to extract themselves a group of Taliban soldiers opened fire from a distant ridge with heavy machine guns and RPGs (Rocket-Propelled Grenades). The SAS responded with their vehicle-mounted GPMGs and 40mm grenade-launchers and after a fierce firefight, in which many Taliban were killed or injured, they withdrew.

For the SAS, the key task was to identify Taliban troop positions for the American bombers. Wherever possible, the SAS men were also to provide intelligence on tank and artillery assets, which could then be hit by US Navy strike aircraft flying local support sorties – or 'blat and splat' missions, as the SAS teams called them.

In addition to their original assignments, a further role was tasked to the SAS, one of a humanitarian nature. This was vitally important, as it was virtually impossible to get enough aid in by truck. America

Below: American special forces soldiers return from a mission on horseback with friendly Afghan forces. It is likely that the SAS were also using such methods of transport in a country that lacks any kind of road network.

had promised to drop food aid packages from USAAF transport aircraft to the starving Afghan people. There was, however, a serious problem with the aid drops. Afghanistan is littered with millions of anti-personnel mines, and these were killing dozens of people every day as they tried to reach the food packages. To reduce these risks, the SAS carried out surveys on suitable sites that were free of mines and marked these for the transport aircraft. It was a very successful mission, and saved many innocent lives. SAS Squadrons were now extremely active on several different fronts within Afghanistan, especially near the lower slopes of the southern Hindu Kush Mountains and around Bagram airfield near Mazar-e-Sharif.

As the combined air- and ground operations gathered pace throughout Afghanistan during late 2001 – part of a combined allied operation involving both British and American ground forces as well as the Northern Alliance – the SAS began direct attacks against Al-Qaeda and Taliban training camps. The camps were generally very well hidden, often featuring cave complexes that were virtually impossible to attack from the air.

Above: British, American and Australian special forces worked as military advisors to the Northern Alliance, whose use as a proxy force against the Taliban and Al-Qaeda was politically more acceptable to the Afghan people.

GUNSHIP ROUNDUPS

One tactic the SAS used to great effect in the mountain regions of Afghanistan involved a combination of Sabre Squadrons and US AC-130 Spectre Gunships. After identifying a training camp and keeping it under surveillance for a few days until satisfied that it was an important target, the SAS would summon a strike to deliver deep penetration bombs straight into the mouths of the cave entrances. Once this mission was completed, a Spectre Gunship would be called in to hit the dazed survivors of the first attack by strafing the ground with its deadly armament of mini-guns, 40mm (1.57in) cannon and howitzer.

The SAS recce team then plotted the predicted escape route of the enemy forces after the end of this attack, and arranged for the rest of their squadron to mount an ambush against them. If planned well, an enemy force could be decimated before they even realized what was happening to them. This highly effective tactic was based on the Russian 'Hammer and Anvil' concept, developed during the Soviet occupation of Afghanistan and used to good effect against the Mujahedeen.

The SAS was also able to draw on operational experiences in Aden and Oman for tactics, techniques and procedures in this conflict. This was to be of great importance. During the first few weeks of deployment in Afghanistan, the US special forces found operations difficult, as they had little comparable combat experience in such an environment, and so a small number of four-man SAS teams were assigned to them as advisors.

It was during one of these combined operations that America suffered its first combat casualty

Above: An FBI wanted poster shows the faces of two of the world's most dangerous men. Yet, despite the massive cash reward for information leading to their capture, very little intelligence has been gained from this campaign.

while operating near Mazar-e-Sharif. After weeks of fighting between the Northern Alliance and the Taliban over the strategically important airfield of Bagram, it finally fell and many Taliban soldiers were taken prisoner. These prisoners soon found themselves in the stronghold of the Qala-e-Jhangi fortress, an impressive collection of mud-walled compounds just outside Mazar-e-Sharif.

TALIBAN REVOLT

One day, as the prisoners were being interrogated by the CIA, a revolt broke out, and a CIA operative was killed, along with many Northern Alliance and Taliban soldiers. It took several days of heavy fighting – including the calling in of air strikes – before order could be restored by the SAS and US special forces, who were acting as advisors to the Northern Alliance. At the height of the revolt, a number of SAS soldiers were seen on live television arriving at the fortress in white Land Rovers, bristling with machine guns. The soldiers quickly put on masks to protect their identities and wore a mixture of camouflaged combats and local Afghan dress. After the rebellion had been subdued, the SAS troopers withdrew to resume other tasks in the local area. They were lucky to escape without taking casualties, as it had been a ferocious and bloody action in which hundreds had died.

By now, the Taliban were in retreat and had very few strongholds left in which to take sanctuary. All the towns they had once occupied had fallen and were in the hands of the Northern Alliance. With the Taliban now out of the way, the priority was to find Osama bin Laden and the remaining Al-Qaeda terrorists who were still putting up resistance, despite intensive American bombing on their known positions. One report suggested that bin Laden was holed up in an Al-Qaeda training camp near to

Right: Masked SAS men arrive at the Qala-e-Jhangi fortress near Mazar-e-Sharif to help suppress a revolt by Taliban and Al-Qaeda prisoners, which left hundreds dead, including one CIA operative.

Kandahar in southern Afghanistan; unfortunately, this could not be confirmed.

Nonetheless, the SAS were given the task of attacking the camp. After observing it for a few days, the higher powers deemed a ground assault to be more appropriate than an air strike, as part of the camp was underground and would be difficult to target from the air. Even by SAS standards, this would be a tough mission. The terrorists had sworn to fight to the death and previous experience suggested that they were not bluffing.

SURPRISE FLANK ATTACK

The SAS attacked with two full squadrons, comprising about 100 men who were well armed and highly experienced in this type of warfare. As they fought their way through Al-Qaeda's defensive positions, they were met by fierce resistance from a number of well-placed machine guns positioned on a ridge set into the side of a deep gully. As the SAS tried to work their way around the position, they were attacked by a large number of Taliban and Al-Qaeda fighters, who emerged suddenly from an underground bunker via a cave entrance. This attack caught the SAS completely by surprise, and they were now in serious danger of being outflanked by a much larger enemy force that was hell-bent on their destruction.

With the threat of being overrun, the SAS advanced forward in a classic charge, which involved them coming face-to-face with their enemy at very close range, and included hand-to-hand combat. As the fighting continued, a number of SAS soldiers who had been manning the communications base saw what was happening and raced to the aid of their fellow troopers, who were now fighting for their lives.

After several minutes of intense fighting, the SAS turned the Al-Qaeda and Taliban fighters back and the action ended. Although they had been heavily outnumbered, the SAS suffered only 4 casualties but left 27 enemy dead and 35 wounded.

After this, SAS involvement in Afghanistan was limited to supporting the Northern Alliance rather than leading them in further operations. This was deliberate, as the SAS did not want to upstage the Northern Alliance in front of the Afghan people, or cause a lack of confidence in their ability to defend the country from further insurrection. The SAS was also asked to help in the destruction of the terrorists' opium fields, as this was their main source of income in Afghanistan. The SAS was well qualified to perform this task effectively, since it had experience of anti-drug operations in Columbia during 1989.

TORA BORA CAVE COMPLEXES

The last operation of any significance for the SAS in Afghanistan involved helping the Northern Alliance to clear the cave complexes of Tora Bora, located just south of Jalalabad and on the border with Pakistan. These caves were the last known hiding place of Osama bin Laden, and even though they had been continuously bombed for weeks, survivors remained inside them who posed a considerable threat. With experience in this type of warfare, the SAS showed the Northern Alliance how to clear caves and bunker complexes, and their expertise was greatly appreciated by all who took part in this extremely dangerous work.

Despite extensive searches for Osama bin Laden throughout Afghanistan, no trace was found of him. Many assumed that he had been killed during the bombing campaign, but as there was no positive proof, America and its allies vowed to continue searching for him and the remains of his Al-Qaeda network. Indeed, these men still pose a considerable threat to the West.

During one of these search operations, an SAS team identified a fortified Al-Qaeda position in the mountain ranges of eastern Afghanistan. Under normal circumstances they would have called in an air-strike, but having observed the position for several days, they believed that Osama bin Laden was in hiding

Left: A masked member of the British special forces departing on a patrol in Afghanistan. He wears a mixture of civilian and military clothing, along with a traditional form of Afghan headgear. His firearm has been heavily customized.

Above: The SAS continue to experiment with new technology. The Avpro Aerospace EXINT Pod is a personnel- or equipment-carrying capsule designed for special operations and can be attached to a helicopter's underwing pylon.

there, as there were hundreds of Al-Qaeda terrorists guarding the site. By this time, the SAS had teams at both ends of the valley leading up to the position, but not enough men to launch an attack. As they called for reinforcements, they were ordered to withdraw, as the credit for capturing bin Laden was to be given to US forces for political reasons. The SAS withdrew to a nearby valley and awaited the Americans' arrival. Finally, three days later, on 2 March 2002, the US launched Operation Anaconda, which lasted for 16 days. It hit problems from the word go, as most of the US forces were dropped in the middle of the target valley instead of outside it. As a result, the US forces were ambushed by a massive Al-Qaeda force and suffered many casualties, including eight fatalities and 73 wounded. The firefight was of such intensity that every helicopter involved in supporting the ground forces was hit by effective enemy fire, resulting in the loss of two Chinooks and several others severely damaged. Despite these setbacks, the US forces fought back with great determination and killed hundreds of Al-Qaeda before withdrawing. Although they failed to capture bin Laden or indeed any of his lieutenants, the operation was deemed successful as it forced the remaining Al-Qaeda out of Afghanistan.

America takes the view that until Osama bin Laden is found, be it dead or alive, nobody is safe; he is an extremely dangerous man and cannot be allowed to remain free. Afghanistan itself is now a relatively peaceful country compared to the utter chaos that reigned before the Taliban's downfall.

The Special Air Service Regiment can be proud of the part they played in the war against terrorism; it was able to achieve so much with so little. As US Defense Secretary Donald Rumsfeld said of the SAS, 'They are amongst the best soldiers in the world, and are truly exceptional men.'

SAS OPERATIONS 1941–2002

1941–2 North Africa
SAS is formed and carries out hit-and-run attacks on German and Italian airfields, with great success; however, other raids on Axis shipping in ports end in failure, or are aborted.

1943 Mediterranean
In Italy, Sardinia and Sicily, the SAS attacks railway lines, communications and airfields, and rescues POWs.

1944 Europe
In France and Italy, the SAS gathers intelligence, attacks road and rail, and harasses Axis forces.

1945 Europe
The SAS carries out attacks and support missions in various countries including Italy, Germany, Holland and Norway.

1950–1960 Malaya
The SAS is re-formed to fight Communist Terrorists after the murder of British citizens and their employees. During this period, the SAS becomes highly skilled in jungle warfare.

1958–59 Jebel Akhdar, Oman
Two squadrons are deployed to Oman to put down a rebellion on the formidable natural fortress of Jebel Akhdar.

1963–66 Borneo
The SAS is back in the jungle, fighting Indonesian forces and rebel guerillas who are opposed to the formation of the Federation of Malaysia.

1964–67 Aden
'Keeni-Meeni' operations are mounted in the Radfan area against tribesmen and guerrillas.

1969–94 Northern Ireland
The SAS supports the British Army and the Royal Ulster Constabulary (RUC) by mounting intelligence-gathering and anti-terrorist operations against the IRA and its supporters. Numerous operations result in both SAS and IRA fatalities. The most successful is the ambush of the IRA East Tyrone Brigade at Loughall.

1970–76 Oman
SAS is sent to defeat Communist guerrillas attempting to overthrow the government. The operation features a 'hearts and minds' campaign, which persuades other Omanis not to join the insurgency.

1980 London
The SAS wins worldwide recognition, launching an operation in full view of the world's media. The objective of Operation Nimrod is to kill or capture terrorists holding hostages in the Iranian Embassy in London. It is a textbook example of a hostage rescue mission.

1981 Gambia
SAS helps to restore President Jawara to power in The Gambia after a coup.

1982 Falkland Islands
The SAS is deployed for intelligence and raiding operations against Argentinian forces occupying the island. Key operations are the retaking of Grytviken, South Georgia and the Pebble Island raid. The SAS is very successful, but loses 18 men in a non-combat related helicopter crash.

1989 Columbia
22 SAS takes part in the anti-cocaine war after the Britsh Government receive a request for military assistance. This includes training for the Columbian forces and missions against drug barons.

1990–91 The Gulf
The SAS is deployed in support of the UN-led campaign to remove Iraq from Kuwait. It undertakes missions in Iraq, mainly against the Iraqis' Scud missiles and their support infrastructure. Highly successful, it operates in ways similar to the original SAS in North Africa.

1994–95 Bosnia
Small SAS teams gather intelligence on the Serbian forces and provide target designation for RAF strike aircraft.

1997 Peru
Six-man SAS team sent to Lima, along with US Delta Force operators, following the takeover of the Japanese Ambassador's residence in January.

1998 The Gulf
In February, the SAS deploy a squadron when Saddam Hussein threatens war. Its role is reconnaissance and rescuing downed pilots.

1998 Albania
In March, a four-man team rescues a British aidworker, Robert Welch. The team locate him and secure his rescue by driving to the coast in Land Rovers. There, two helicopters are waiting, one to provide a security force while the other extracts the team and its vehicles.

1999 Kosovo
After Serbian forces invade, the SAS helps find targets for NATO aircraft and rescues downed aircrew. It also supports the Kosovo Liberation Army (KLA) and helps apprehend Serbian war criminals.

2000 Sierra Leone
The SAS is initially called in to provide overt support for UN peacekeepers. Then British soldiers are captured by a ruthless militia, known as the 'West Side Boys'. In response, the SAS launches a joint rescue operation with 1 Para and secures the hostages for the loss of one soldier.

2001 Afghanistan
After the terrorists attacks on the US of 11 September 2001, the SAS supports operations against terrorism. It carries out recce and targeting missions for US forces against Taliban and Al-Qaeda soldiers and their equipment. It also supports the Northern Alliance and helps to find safe areas for delivering humanitarian aid. It plays a key role in this war and is extremely successful, though operating in difficult and demanding conditions.

2002 Somalia
SAS teams sent to Mogadishu following an intelligence tip-off that Al-Qaeda are setting up a base with Somali warlords.

2002 Zimbabwe
SAS teams are deployed in Zimbabwe on covert reconnaissance missions following death threats to British nationals living there.

2002 Iraq
SAS teams deploy on the Iraqi border during August following the threat of a new war with Iraq.

SAS ORGANIZATION (2002)

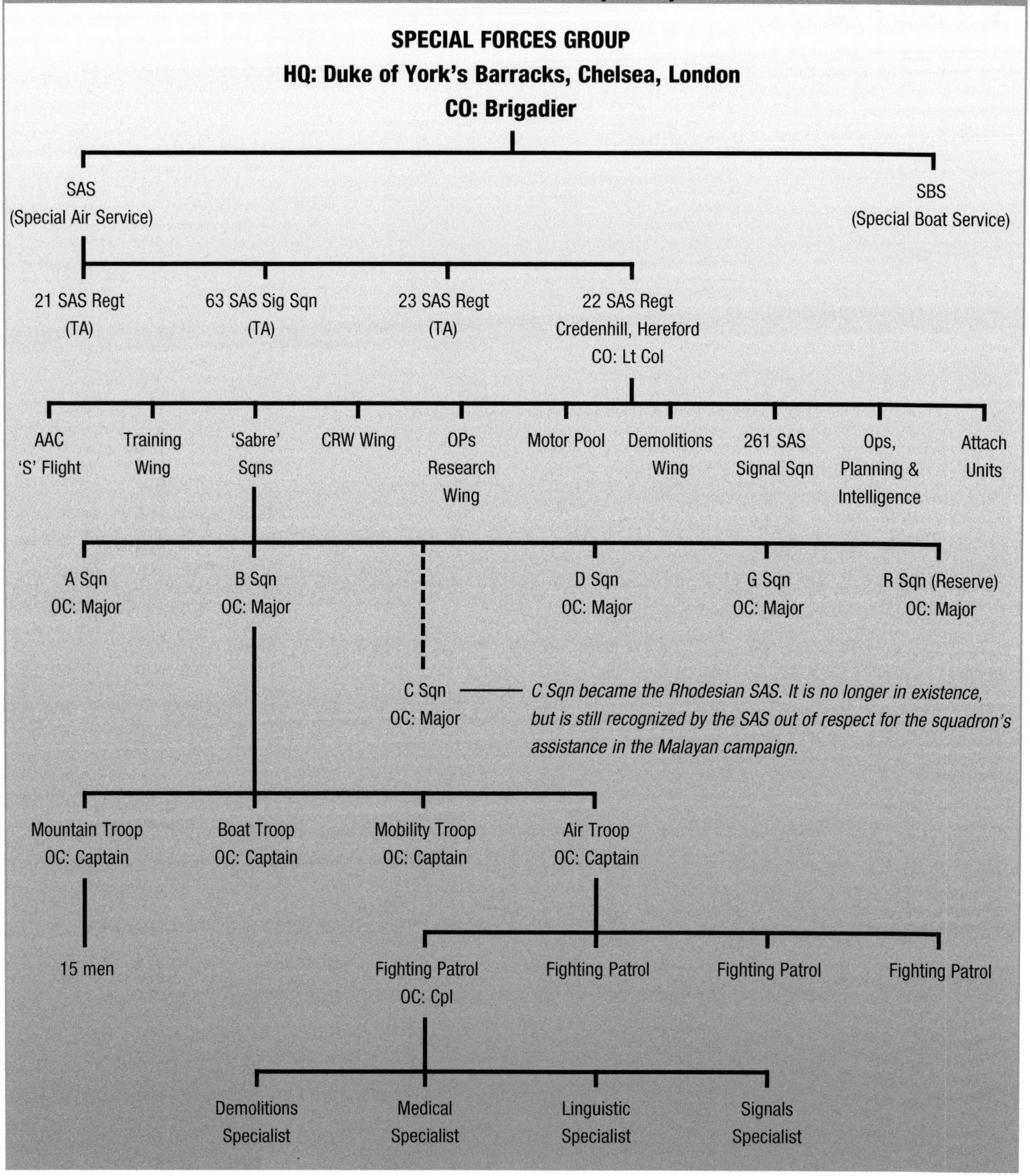

INDEX

Page numbers in **bold** indicate captions